The U-Turn

'*The U-Turn* is a book which will have wide appeal. It is not just those who have significant emotional or interpersonal problems who will welcome its wisdom but the person on the street who has to deal with the day-to-day travails of life. Conor Farren has produced a volume that is both sensitive and practical, that does not minimise the difficulties we face dealing with the rawness of life, but yet offers a path through the forest of worry, anxiety and fear that confronts us all from time to time. He explores the hidden underpinnings of our reactions to life stressors and then provides us with help in tapping into the resources around us that can guide us through these. As in his other works, Conor writes in a style that engages the reader at a human and personal level, and assists in the journey to contentment and happiness.'

Professor Patricia Casey, University College Dublin

Disclaimer

While every care has been taken in the production of this book, no legal responsibility is accepted, warranted or implied by the author, editor or publisher in respect of any errors, omissions or mis-statements. You should always seek professional advice from a suitably qualified person when appropriate.

The U-Turn

A Guide To Happiness

Conor Farren

ORPEN PRESS

Published by
Orpen Press
Lonsdale House
Avoca Avenue
Blackrock
Co. Dublin
Ireland

e-mail: info@orpenpress.com
www.orpenpress.com

Paperback ISBN: 978-1-871305-88-3
ePub ISBN: 978-1-909518-08-7
Kindle ISBN: 978-1-909518-09-4

Printed in Ireland by Colorman Ltd

This book is dedicated to my wife, Anne, and to my children,
Ciara, Annemarie and Lucas.

About the Author

Dr Conor Farren, Consultant Psychiatrist, St Patrick's University Hospital, and Clinical Senior Lecturer, Trinity College Dublin.

Conor Farren graduated in medicine from University College Dublin in 1985. He went on to train in psychiatry at St Patrick's University Hospital, Dublin. He taught and conducted research in psychiatry at Yale University, New Haven, Connecticut, where he began work on the ideas contained in this book. He went on to take charge of the addiction and mental health section of Mount Sinai School of Medicine and the Bronx Veterans Hospital, New York for a number of years, before returning to Ireland. He is a consultant psychiatrist based in Dublin, and also lectures in and conducts research at Trinity College Dublin. He has written numerous scientific articles on the subject of mental health, and has also written extensively for newspapers and popular journals and participated in media discussions on radio and television on the same topic. He is the author of *Overcoming Alcohol Misuse: A 28-Day Guide* (Orpen Press, 2011). He is married and lives in Dublin.

Further information is available at www.conorfarren.com.

Contents

Introduction

What Is the U-Turn?

We all think we are good at understanding other people, but many of us are not so good at understanding ourselves. Even those of us – such as psychiatrists and mental health professionals – who try to help people understand and help themselves for a living are not so hot when it comes to understanding and helping ourselves when it is our turn to go through an emotional rough patch.

The U-Turn will take you on a journey of understanding – of your emotions, of your personal make-up and of your relationships – with the aim of guiding you to a life of joy and self-fulfilment. That concept of the U-turn signifies a journey of transformation; a journey in which a person with a lot of self-hatred at one end of the scale can be transformed into a person with self-appreciation at the other. The 'U' in the U-turn denotes understanding. The journey out of negative emotions, unhappiness and low self-esteem is through understanding – understanding yourself, understanding the emotional forces that govern you, and understanding how to complete a personal U-turn.

As we all know, emotional logic is not 'logical' logic; the emotional world is governed by different and unclear laws. This book aims to clarify those laws and reveal your underlying emotional logic, ultimately guiding you to a better place.

1

This book is divided into five sections. The first section is a general introduction to the book and an overview of just what the book is about. The second section is an exploration of the traumatic and negative emotions that can take over a sufferer's mentality and leave little room for anything else. This section contains an explanation of the reasons and forces behind negative emotions and includes exercises on how to overcome them. The third section deals with the basic underlying mental structures revealed by an analysis of negative emotions. It explores the different aspects of self-esteem, self-presentation and character, explaining how these structures underlie our emotions and how understanding them leads to self-development. The fourth section deals with relationships, how underlying forces influence them, and how we can use knowledge of these forces to take action and correct the bad way we run them. The last section is a synthesis of different ideas in the book, discussing how the rules we have learned, the structures we have understood and the emotions we have controlled can be used to help us gain direction and purpose in our lives.

Throughout this book the journey through self-understanding to self-fulfilment is mapped out by the U-turn principles. These principles are very simple. They are *feel*, *think* and *act*. These principles will guide you through the different stages of the journey and let you plan a route for yourself. And although each section of the book deals with very different emotions – and the very different structures behind these emotions – these principles will guide you on your U-turn at every stage.

Each section of this book takes a different aspect of the U-turn, and brings you to a greater understanding of what causes hurt and unhappiness and what makes you fulfilled and content. The journey is personal and the route to be followed is also personal. There can be only one author – you. If you are not content with what you are at the moment and if you are suffering because of this discontent, you need to dig inside yourself before you make your move outside. This book maps out the pathway to self-understanding through the very emotions that make you unhappy. It explores the underlying principles that govern those emotions and shows you why you feel the way you do. It then moves through the most fundamental aspects of your relationships to show you how to make them a positive and happy force in your life. Finally, it explores the journey you have to make to reach your ultimate goals, and helps you find out just what those goals are.

The main method advocated in this book is one of action. The purpose of the journey of understanding is to make possible a journey of action and change. The purpose of self-understanding is to use that understanding to transform your life from suffering to contentment, and you need both things – understanding *and* action – to do this. You can't have one without the other. Understanding without action leads to greater self-hatred and lower self-esteem. Action without understanding leads to frustration and unhappiness, because it is purposeless. The other important point about action is that it must be worked out personally in order to have the desired effect on your life and happiness. By understanding what oppresses us, we can learn what we truly want from life. By taking action against our oppression, we can fundamentally change what we think of ourselves. We can decide to take back control of our lives, armed with self-understanding in one hand and a plan of action in the other.

Using this book, and the principles of *feel*, *think* and *act*, you can turn your life around. And as you will see, these principles and the journey they will set out for you are very easy to say but much more difficult to carry out. No matter what any other book may tell you, the U-turn in your life is not a painless process and it is not going to happen without effort and action. Is this going to be just an interesting read?

Or is it going to be a fulfilling journey? The only person who can answer this is you. You can take a U-turn in your life and make it like your wildest dream, or you can let it go and leave it simply a dream. The choice is yours.

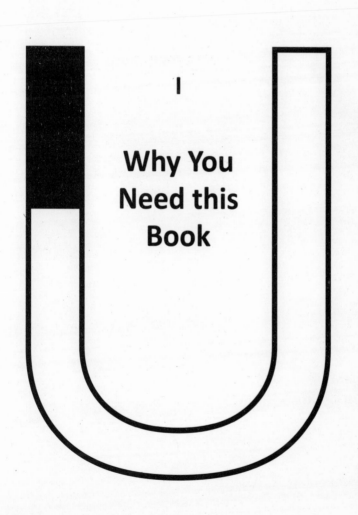

1

Why You Need this Book

1

Self-Understanding

> **Our emotions are a guide to what lies beneath**

Life, the Universe and Everything is the title of a book in a comic series about a space traveller who jumps spaceships, meets aliens, has strange adventures and generally potters about in a surreal and disorganised world. He travels to different planets; he deals with various peculiar and disturbed personalities; and he can't find his own way back to the safe existence he once knew. Does that sound familiar? Don't we all potter about, or occasionally rush around, our own little universe, busy with our own little lives? Don't we have our own little adventures, our own strange encounters, and amuse ourselves with everyday events and trivia? Don't we all just meander along the riverbanks of life, looking at the great surging flood of world happenings and life events, wondering what it's all about in a vague, confused and slightly uninterested way?

We can get away with it, too. We can tick over, immersed in everyday trivia, 'wallowing in the habitual, the banal', as the poet Patrick Kavanagh said, unfocused and undirected but not exactly miserable, until 'It' happens. What is 'It'? 'It' can be anything from the death of a parent to the death of a dream; the reaction to a trauma such as a financial crisis or a bereavement; and it can range from the sowing of insidious seeds of self-doubt to the dreadful blooming of a self-detesting and suicidal despair. 'It' can be an external event or an internal one. 'It' can arrive precipitously or in a slow dawning. 'It' might be a reaction to an event, or 'It' might have a life of its own. 'It' may start out as a small niggle and over a period of time turn into a life-consuming crisis. 'It' can take many forms and indeed 'It' is as varied as the people suffering from it. 'It' is a tremendously individual experience and yet a universal human complaint. We may not even be able to define 'It' when we are going through 'It', but we can recognise 'It' in others. 'It' is suffering and pain and hurt and despair; 'It' is grief and unhappiness; 'It' is sorrow and sadness.

And 'It' stops us in our tracks, turns us around and forces us to think, maybe for the first time, about 'life, the universe and everything'. We don't ask ourselves, 'Who am I?' or 'What am I?', but we do ask ourselves two basic questions: 'Why am I unhappy?' and 'What the hell can I do about it?' The tremendous thing about hurt and unhappiness is that it leaves no room for anything else in our lives; it dominates us and imprisons us in its web. Our only thoughts are to end 'It', for 'It' to cease at all costs, even if that means that life itself should cease.

What is the answer to those questions? The answer is both breathtakingly simple and incredibly complex. It is very easy to say or write down, but much more difficult to carry out. The way out of prison and the road back to the way we once knew, our pathway and our guide to happiness is within us.

The U in the U-turn is for Understanding. Not simply understanding the world, the people in it and the way it works; not simply understanding the people around us and the way they work and the way they do things. The understanding required is very deep and not at all as simple as understanding those around us. The answer to both those questions – 'Why am I unhappy?' and 'What can I do about it?' – can be encapsulated succinctly in the word 'self-understanding'.

Self-Understanding

The key to understanding why we are unhappy is to understand ourselves, truthfully and completely, warts and all. The key to overcoming unhappiness is making a journey through self-understanding to self-appreciation, from self-appreciation to contentment, and from contentment to happiness. The journey is by no means as simple as it sounds, because it involves work – work in an area we are not used to. It also involves facing up to reality, but reality of a different sort from the everyday trivia of life – this reality is an internal, hidden reality. Only by educating ourselves about this internal reality will our discontent become comprehensible and eventually resolvable.

Imagine that Hurt is perched on the top left-hand side of the U, and Happiness is on the top right-hand side. It is only by making a journey into the depths of U, and through the Understanding that lies at the very bottom of the U, that we can make it up through to the Happiness at the right-hand side of the U. It is an arduous journey. During the journey we have to look at things we might not want to recognise, and face up to things we might not want to face up to, but it is the only way we will eventually succeed. It is possible to regain our previous happiness temporarily without making any journey at all. It is even possible to rebuild our lives without any emotional journey of any depth, and we may succeed – but only temporarily. The key to long-lasting happiness is work, often harder than any other kind of work we have known.

Take Bob Geldof, one of the most unusual heroes of our age. In a profession not particularly noted for its altruism and selflessness, he stands as a shining beacon of decency and conscience. He was the lead singer of the Boomtown Rats, which had considerable success on this side of the Atlantic in the heyday of the punk era in the late 1970s and early 80s. His greatest achievement, however, was masterminding the Band Aid concert of 1984, a concert that eventually raised over $100 million for the starving millions in Ethiopia and the rest of Africa, almost solely through sheer force of will and guilt – his will and everyone else's guilt. His achievement will stand as the memorial to his generation of music-makers long after their music fades away. But that's not why I'm mentioning him now. In his autobiography, *Is That It?*, written in the aftermath of this great effort that galvanised millions of people for a simple altruistic aim, he mentions his habit of rigorously analysing himself before he goes to sleep at night. He goes through everything he did that day, asking himself why he acted as he did, and whether he was right to do so. If he is being honest (as he unfailingly is throughout the rest of the book), he has the key to happiness in his hand. And he has unlocked himself, for the self-understanding that he has gained over the years is the guiding light steering him through life. It was this self-analysis that led him to realise that he simply couldn't bear to see the pictures of dying children on the television at night and not do something about it.

So what is this inner reality? Where is it? Can we touch it? Well, we may not be able to touch it, but it's there all right. It governs us much more than governments or the EU, and it controls us more than our parents ever did. It dictates our actions far more than we would like to believe. It is our 'core' and everything else revolves around it. The fundamental thing we need to do about this inner reality is not to define it or categorise it, but to understand how it works, how it lives and breathes, how it controls our lives and talks to the rest of our being.

Core Instinct

An old friend told me a story about when she was a young woman. She grew up in a large town in Ireland, and being very good-looking and having a warm, friendly personality, she attracted the attention of a large number of 'gentleman callers', who would take her out socially. She lived with her widowed mother, a strict and staunch Northern woman, who greeted these gentlemen with a huffy 'Hello' and a searching glance from the corner of the kitchen when they came round. Over the years, most of the callers came and went, but there was one chap, let's call him Daniel, who remained on the scene, gently and patiently, while my friend grew tired of various other boyfriends. Her affection for and friendship with Daniel grew over time, and she became convinced that he was the right one.

One night, after taking her for dinner, while walking her home through the old cobbled streets, he proposed to her. Flushed, excited and grateful, she accepted, and they parted, happy, at her doorstep. But that night, she woke up at three o'clock and couldn't get to sleep again. Everything went round and round in her mind and she couldn't get it to stop. It wasn't anticipation but apprehension that filled her and made her restless. She got up the next day and talked to her mother and told her about Daniel's long-awaited proposal. Her mother was pleased, because she knew he was a kind person who loved her daughter. But then my friend said, 'I can't accept'. Her mother, surprised, asked why. 'Because something inside me tells me not to. I just feel deeply that it is wrong for me' was the reply. And she didn't marry Daniel. Two years later, she married another man, and was very happy for many years.

Many of us can relate to that type of experience, a feeling that something or someone is very right or very wrong for us, and we often follow the dictates of this 'irrational' impulse. Many of us base our most fundamental life decisions, like choosing our life partner, on simple feelings that have no explanation and an uncertain origin. We entrust the course of our lives to them, yet when asked what they are and where they come from, we simply say things like, 'It felt right' or 'I just had to do it.' Instinct tells us what is correct when things are going well, but it is when things aren't going so well and the instinct begins to fail us that we realise we know very little about what makes us tick, and hopefully we realise that the only way out of the impasse we have got into is to gain a much better understanding of just what this fundamental feeling is.

Emotions

How does this 'inner being' talk to the rest of our mind? How does it let us know what it wants, what it feels, what it thinks? How do we know what we fundamentally desire, and how do we know what our core is telling us? It talks via instinct and feeling – our emotions! So the key to understanding ourselves – and then turning that understanding into control – is not just to be aware of but to understand our emotions, to use that knowledge to wrestle against them and then turn that control into contentment. This is the essence of the U-turn: we cannot learn anything if we simply repeat the same old story, and simply relive the same old emotions, again and again. We cannot change our lives if we simply acknowledge our emotions and then do nothing about understanding them, let alone changing them. The key to starting the journey is to break the vicious cycle and start trying to find the pathway that led to the current emotional spiral.

Half the battle of changing our life and, especially, changing our dissatisfaction with it, is understanding *why* we are unhappy. It is also vital not only to understand why we are unhappy now, but also to understand the various internal and external forces that act upon us now and may even have brought us to this point in the first place. None of us is an island: we don't exist in isolation. We are all part of groups, families and cultures that play a major part in how we feel about ourselves at any one time.

Many years ago, I went on a hitchhiking tour of the United States. In retrospect it could be regarded as foolish and, indeed, as I spent many an hour sitting on the highways and byways of America waiting in vain for a lift, I often felt that I was engaged in a rather foolish exercise. For my troubles I ended up in Orlando, Florida, where I was mugged. I have myself to blame to a fair extent, because I let a total stranger give me directions around town to a youth hostel, and then let him lead me there. Inevitably, as we hit a quiet part of town, he looked around him, pulled a knife from his back pocket and asked none too politely for my wallet. I gave it to him in two seconds flat, and he emptied the six dollars and forty-two cents in it with a practised hand. He also took an alarm clock, a pair of jeans, and my brand new Quartz watch, worth about eighty dollars. He turned to walk away, and then – frighteningly – came back to ask for more money, not believing that a tourist could have so little cash. I explained to him that all my money was in traveller's cheques, and he rifled through my personal belongings in the middle of the road at ten o'clock in the morning looking for more. Eventually he went away, and I ran in the other direction, finally finding my way back to town. I reported the crime at the police station (which the mugger had been stupid enough to point out to me before he pulled the knife) and, much to my surprise, they picked up the man within a few minutes. I got back my money, my alarm clock and my jeans, but he had already got rid of the watch. I went home and tried to forget the whole thing.

Weeks later I began to wake up every night at three o'clock in the morning in a dreadful panic, sweating and frightened and feeling that I simply had to find my watch. I would fumble and stumble my way out of bed until I got my old watch into my hand and then it would take me ten minutes to calm myself down. It took weeks of absolute fear before I figured out that the best way to prevent my panic was to wear my old watch on my wrist during the night, so that when I woke up I would immediately feel a watch on my wrist and realise that I had one. It took me a while to recognise that what I was feeling in the panic and fear of the early hours was the same fear of being killed that I had experienced when the mugger pulled the knife on me. The watch was a symbol, but the fear was real. It was only with that realisation that I stopped waking in the middle of the night, and I got one of my first lessons in the power and pathways of the emotions that lie at the core of all of us. It was through understanding that the fear diminished and I regained control over myself.

What does that story tell us – apart from the fact that I was rather naive to be led through the streets of Orlando by a complete stranger? It tells us something about how the mind communicates within itself. It teaches us that we have a communication system running from the 'pithead' on the surface – the face we present to the world – to the 'coal face' down below. The 'coal face' is our 'core', our fundamental self, and the emotional centre of our being. The 'mine shafts' that run between the surface and the core are our emotions; but, unlike mine shafts, they don't run in straight lines and they are not straightforward things!

Looked at anatomically, the emotional segment of the brain is in a place deep under the surface of the brain called the limbic system. The limbic system, in evolutionary terms, is in one of the oldest segments of the brain. That means that not only do we humans have one, so do chimpanzees, and so do squirrels; and not only squirrels, but squid! Almost every animal, down to the developmentally primitive creatures that would barely generate a blip on a brain scan, has some form of limbic system. But what does that mean? Do squirrels weep when they hear a Mahler symphony? No, but dogs do howl on their master's grave. Do squid shed a tear for a deep-fried friend? No, but penguins are monogamous for life, and don't mate again if their partner dies. Research on animals such as whales, dolphins, elephants and gorillas show that these animals have a full and rich communication system and patterns of social interaction that indicate deeper and more varied emotional lives than we may like to admit. As children we all thought that animals were like people and shared the thoughts and feelings of ordinary humans. As science progresses we are finding out that animals display a lot of behaviours and types of communication that look very similar to our own, and a lot of behaviours and types of communication consistent with a full emotional life. Any pet owner will tell you that his or her pet experiences various human-like emotions. So it should come as no surprise to us to know that emotions are very deep down in the evolutionary line, and that the limbic system, the emotional base in the brain, is a very basic system indeed.

Survival

So primitive animals do have some form of emotional life. It may be restricted in depth and expression by their lack of intellect or higher brain function, but it is definitely there in some limited form. So what is it for? What use is it to them? And, indeed, what use is it to us? The answer is survival. Emotions are crude and rather badly-formed things. They tend to be repetitive and non-progressive, reflecting our basic selves and our basic desires. Things that threaten us and challenge our potential survival elicit negative emotions, such as anger and jealousy. Events that encourage us and confirm our ability to survive produce more contented and happy emotions.

Survival in our highly-developed human context is not purely a matter of getting enough food and water, not just a matter of existing from day to day, but something that can also be threatened by non-physical things. Humans, like many other animals, are highly social, so threats to our social survival are felt as deeply as threats to our physical survival. The death of a beloved friend, for example, elicits a tremendously deep emotional response because it threatens our own survival in our structured social world, as well as reminding us of our own mortality. Episodes of depression and anxiety often revolve around feelings of despair for the future and fear of not knowing how we are going to get by, feelings of not being able to survive in our own personal social context. There is more to all of us than our bodies, so survival means much more than existing physically.

Emotional arousal, positive or negative, can be elicited as often by personal interaction as by a physical need, such as hunger. What might have been a primitive survival instinct in a less developed animal becomes refined through the course of evolution into a fully developed human emotional life that is fundamentally associated with our core being. Our emotions are the major determining factors in how we live our lives and how we view the world. It is easy to forget when things are going well just how crude we really are at the centre and especially how our emotions govern us when things aren't going so well.

Sol Wachtler was the chief judge of the New York Court of Appeals in the late 1980s and early 1990s. A highly respected judge, married with four children, he had a distinguished personal profile that could have led to high political office. After thirty-five years of marriage he started an affair and quickly fell hopelessly in love with a high-flying New York socialite. He wined her and dined her and was her lover for four years. She broke off their relationship when it became clear that he wasn't going to leave his wife for her. His emotional life fell apart after this break-up and in the space of one short year he destroyed his entire lifetime's work. He began writing his ex-lover anonymous threatening letters and making phone calls in the middle of the night. His demands became more and more intense, culminating in a written anonymous threat to kidnap her fourteen-year-old daughter. He was eventually traced by the FBI after making an obscene phone call to her from his mobile phone, and they stalked him for many months before eventually arresting him. He made a full confession and is now serving time in prison for his crimes. His reason for this bizarre behaviour? He said that after his mistress broke up with him he was in the throes of a deep depression and he was still deeply involved with her emotionally. This led to his irrational and obsessional behaviour and eventually to a prison term. This highly controlled, intelligent man was a slave to his emotions, and it was his emotions that destroyed him.

Once we dig deep into the emotional well and begin to comprehend the different forces that act on us and shape us, we have a chance of taking that knowledge and using it. For although the key to happiness is self-understanding, the gate is only fully opened when that self-understanding is put to good use. If comprehension is the bud, and happiness is the flower, behaviour is the fruit.

Behaviour

How we think of ourselves and how we behave are as intimately intertwined as the strands of a piece of string. Separating the two in terms of cause is very difficult: we may think badly of ourselves and thus not live up to our own standards, and vice versa. Separating the two in terms of how they affect us is not just useful but vital in our progress towards our ultimate goal, which is not the pursuit but the achievement of happiness. For if we end up pleased about our inner being and totally displeased with how we look, speak and act, we have a recipe for a rather short period of contentment. Equally, if we act and behave perfectly, like well-mannered Victorian aristocrats, without any genuine comprehension and with only a 'duck pond' depth of feeling, we will end up shallow, vain and bitter, with no sense of purpose to our existence, and a feeling of having been somehow cheated in life.

Increasing the purposefulness of our behaviour and increasing the depth of our self-awareness are two vital paths on the way to furthering our personal development and happiness. It is unfortunate that in psychiatry, a 'political' split has arisen between the old psychoanalytical school and the cognitive behaviourist school. The psychoanalyst maintains that comprehension is everything and that the only goal of a psychiatrist is for a patient to understand their symptoms, which will then disappear and the patient will automatically be happy. The modern cognitive behaviourist says, 'If you do well, you can become well.' Neither approach is completely true in itself because any one person is a being of many parts, not just a mass of emotions or a jumble of frenzied and useless activity. Thus, neither single approach can fully deal with an individual's numerous components; if the whole person is not treated their symptoms sometimes 'fall through the holes'. However, if the two approaches are combined, either by a therapist 'graduating', as it were, from their own school and incorporating the benefits of both approaches with any one individual, or indeed by an ordinary individual developing in emotional depth and in behavioural control, the possibilities are endless and the real goal of true happiness achievable.

Insight 1039,448 | 158 1

A highly strung young man arrived at hospital one evening in an extremely distraught state. He had a bundle of obsessive thoughts and compulsive repetitive actions that would have driven a saint to distraction. He couldn't walk through his own front door without turning around five times, and he couldn't enter his own living room unless he ran up and down the stairs five times. If he didn't obey his own tortuous rules, he was convinced that some disaster would befall one of the five members of his family. His life was crippled with repetitive exercises and various mental tortures, which he was unable to fight off by himself. And, interestingly, he had been 'cured' of exactly the same problem four years earlier. He had seen a dedicated behavioural therapist, who had helped him to fight his behaviour, repetition by repetition, ritual by ritual. The compulsive actions and the crippling repetitions slowly disappeared over time, and the man went home happy. The disease was cured, but not the unease. I met this man on his second admission into hospital when his original symptoms and worries began to recur. Meeting him taught me a valuable lesson about the nature of psychological problems and the ways of fully overcoming them.

There's more to any human than meets the eye, because we are all greater than the sum of our actions. 'Curing' this man's 'problem' stopped the outward manifestations of his deep-seated anxiety and unhappiness, but didn't prevent the problem recurring some time later. In order to become truly content, we must not only tackle what everyone else sees, but we have to dig deep and discover what only we ourselves can see – our emotional being, our true selves, our core. What we need, in a word, is *insight*!

At the beginning of every old *Star Trek* episode, the narrator's voice boomed out that the crew was 'to boldly go where no man has gone before'. That, in a sense, is what each of us has to do in order to truly progress in life and in happiness. We have to explore wider, and dig deeper, than on any previous occasion, in order to learn about and understand ourselves; and then we can take that knowledge and use it to take charge of our lives, rather than remain as victims of circumstance.

The Individual Journey

In this context, finding psychiatric categories and labels to 'diagnose' ourselves is less important than our own individual journey of self-discovery. Psychiatric diagnoses such as 'depression' or 'panic disorder' are not actual diseases, like diabetes, for example; they are just descriptions of a collection of symptoms. When a doctor says that a patient suffers from 'anxiety neurosis', all he or she means is that all the symptoms described by that patient resemble a set of feelings and symptoms described by another patient, which resemble a set of feelings and symptoms described by yet another patient, and so on. There is no broken bone in the limbic system to correspond with a particular emotional pain. No one has yet defined a psychiatric 'disease' that can be picked up on an X-ray or with a simple blood test.

It is the similarity between suffering people that doctors can recognise, categorise and often successfully treat. But it is the individual differences in lives, in events and in reactions to events, that determines what each individual experiences, and no two people's experiences are the same. The similarity of certain responses to experiences can be helped by doctor and psychiatrist, but the individuality of the response to an experience can only be helped by the individual themselves.

Some people are fortunate enough to have that individuality examined and explored with the help of a friend or therapist, but most people have to make the journey alone. The journey is often painful because it involves exploration of emotions, both positive and negative; it involves stripping away layers of self-delusion that we build up over the years, to arrive at a self-portrait which is at once sympathetic and accurate. It then involves using the hard-won self-knowledge to turn those very things that were tormenting us into things of the past. It may also involve setting new limits on our expectations and setting new goals for achievement. It ultimately involves self-acceptance and, through that, contentment.

The whole purpose of this book is to help guide you on this journey, around the U-turn from hurt to happiness. It was only by my own progress in deepening my understanding of myself, together with developing techniques of dealing with the world as it is and especially with the people in it, that I began to ascend the second half of the U-turn and learn the true meaning of contentment. When I became a psychiatrist, I recognised where many people are on their own journey, and saw that they too were without a map to help them get out of the place they felt stuck in. I was also able to learn the techniques of modern psychiatry, the ways and means of helping people who are lost in various ways, and applied these techniques, together with my own hard-won lessons, to find a way around the U-turn. For there is always a way out; there is always a lesson to be learned that will help us in the future; and there is always a path to happiness to be followed. This book is designed to act as a guide for that journey.

The place to start this journey is at the bottom, at the fundamentals. In order to know ourselves, we must know, understand, and appreciate our emotions!

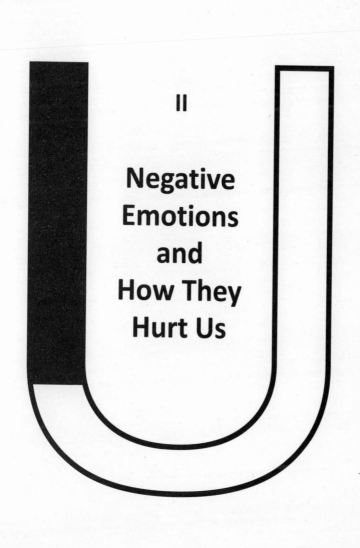

II

**Negative
Emotions
and
How They
Hurt Us**

2

Anger

Understanding our anger is vital to learning how to control it

Anger doesn't need to be defined. We know what it is. It is the most violent and destructive of emotions, and at its worst it corrodes inwardly as well as destroying those around us. It can be extremely selfish and indulgent, but it can also be a very positive and confidence-building emotion, if used properly. There is more to anger than meets the ear, so to speak, so let's examine it in detail.

When thinking about anger and considering its origins, 'hurt' isn't the word that jumps straight into the mind. 'Hurt' is what happens to little boys and girls when they fall and scrape their knees; 'hurt' is what happens when a lover leaves us and we end up miserable, dejected and alone. 'Hurt' sends us backwards into the helplessness of childhood with no power over our own fate, and a clawing need to be comforted and cosseted by 'Mummy'. To be hurt is to acknowledge a capacity for vulnerability, and it can be taken as an admission of defensive weakness, a letting down of the guard. Hurt can be caused by almost any range of human interaction, from a casual unintentional personal remark to repeated sexual or physical assault. What is not important is the intention of the offending party, which may be malign or just the opposite. What is important is the reaction of the recipient, which differs only in depth of pain and humiliation, but not in the actual nature of their reaction.

Universally, when people are hurt they react with shocked numbness, a kind of limbo state, and then with mortified embarrassment, followed by the hell of deep degradation. This state of desperation can last from a few minutes to many years, depending on the cause of the hurt and the reaction to it.

Hurt was one of the intense emotions felt by Paul Hill, a young, rather aimless, working-class man from the back streets of Belfast in Northern Ireland. He was picked up by the British police after what became known as the Guildford bombings, a horrendous terrorist attack by the IRA on a couple of public houses in Guildford, England in 1974. A large number of totally innocent civilians were killed and maimed in a series of bomb explosions in one night. Paul was picked up by the police, along with three friends, and a 'confession' was beaten out of him by angry police officers. He was convicted, along with his friends, and sentenced to life imprisonment many times over. He steadfastly maintained his innocence and refused to bow down to the prison regime imposed by the prison officers, as a result receiving many beatings and spending many months in solitary confinement. It took sixteen years of hurt and many failed appeals and campaigns before the British judiciary finally accepted that he and his co-accused had been wrongly convicted. His hurt and pain over those years of wrongful imprisonment are too deep to imagine. Now, years after his release, he is happily married. He wrote a book about his experiences, and he has dedicated his life to the fight for international human rights. How he deals with his hurt will determine his happiness for the rest of his life.

Useful Anger

Hurt occurs on many levels, ranging from the seemingly trivial insult of a casual put-down to the deeper, longer-lasting hurt caused by the ongoing trauma of physical or sexual abuse, or the emotional stress suffered by the spouses or children of alcoholics. Suffering of that degree, pain of that depth, produces a gaping hole of misery that is widened at every contact with the torturer. This type of intense suffering initially produces not a strengthening of character or resolve, but an inability to deal with the situation, a spiral of self-doubt and, finally, a hatred and anger directed at the cause of the suffering and, to a lesser extent, an anger aimed at our own frustration at not being able to deal with the situation. That is one cause of anger – hurt turned outwards. Most people can only take so much suffering, can only sink so low, before they hit the bedrock of their own personal foundation stone, and turn the pain and hurt around into fury.

To do this, to turn the hurt into anger, not only diminishes the pain but is also the first step in healing the wounds caused by the pain. It is a good anger. It turns the negative, self-destructive, inward-looking thoughts and emotions into outward-looking ones. It is a healthy anger. All the intensity is exploded on to other people and things, and this rids the mind of pent-up frustration and feelings of self-deprecation.

An elderly lady once confided a secret to me. She was a respectable middle-class lady who had married a small businessman seven years her senior when she was in her early twenties. As was the custom then, after her marriage she gave up her job and tended to home matters. She soon noticed that her husband started to come home later and later each evening, and she began to get the smell of drink from him. She questioned him, but he gruffly shrugged off her enquiries. She became pregnant and gave birth to her first child, a boy. Her husband's support diminished, and she began to see less of him. When he came home late and drunk, she would feel the hurt and frustration welling up inside her, and then when she interrogated him, he would beat her up. The pattern continued through the birth of five children, poverty, and thirty-five years of marriage. She told nobody – even her children didn't know what was going on. She suffered silently until all her children were raised.

One day, she went to the bank, withdrew all her husband's money, went home and locked him out of the house. He wasn't let in for one month. During that month he changed from an aggressive bully into a sober realist, begging her forgiveness and asking to be given another chance. She relented, took him back in, and he was as good as his word, never raising a finger to her again. Not surprisingly, however, she began to get bouts of depression and, for the first time in her life, went into a psychiatric hospital. She stayed in bed for three weeks, deeply depressed and barely eating, before admitting her feelings and then telling me all about it. 'I don't hate him,' she said, 'He's very good to me now. I'm just so angry at him for what he did to me for all those years.' She spent the next few weeks venting her anger more and more until she began to feel liberated from the hurt and shame of those pain-filled years. She recovered, left hospital and went back to live her life her own way. Releasing her anger had helped her overcome the years of pain, and expressing that anger was the key to her success.

Anger can be relieved by screaming and shouting at the hurter; it can be relieved by telling someone who is genuinely interested about it; or it can be cried out. However it's done, it is worth doing, and realising and then releasing anger can be life-transforming.

Temper

But there are other types of anger, and they don't tend to be as beneficial to the psyche as the type we've just described.

Anger is generally the most selfish and self-indulgent of emotions. It is essentially a regressive and childlike trait that is allowed to get out of hand, causing both internal and external explosions. The origin of this type of anger is simple – it is thwarted self-indulgence that sparks the combustion. It is essentially no different from what we adults derisorily call a 'temper tantrum' in a child.

When a child is about to throw a tantrum, there is a certain point when we can see in the child's face that they have made the decision. There is almost a wilful glee, just after the child has been refused permission to have something nice, in the way that he or she wallows in a reckless abandonment of control and goes for glory. Every parent knows just the change in tone of whinge that precedes the tantrum, and either gives in at that moment or puts up with the ensuing display.

As we 'mature' and grow older, the knowledge that losing our temper is a voluntary action gets lost in the back of our minds. We lose sight of the fact that we are in control and that anger involves letting go of the reins of control that we have over ourselves. Anger is a habit learned early on, and as it ages with us, it can take us over more and more. Anger is also a power game; it is an attempt to gain control or assert superiority over those around us. Thwarting of that control, or threats to that power, prompt us to indulge ourselves in a demonstration of that power, and thus we bully people into doing what we want. Not a very nice thing to look at in the mirror, is it?

Anger is also the thwarted expectation of something that we have grown accustomed to. It is the thwarted expectation of someone else's behaviour and the lack of appreciation of the other person's approach to life. Not everybody lives by the same rules as we do, and it is an important thing to remember when trying to figure out why some people act in ways we find difficult to handle. I remember as a young doctor getting very angry with a group of hospital nurses who decided that they would no longer administer any drugs intravenously, and that they would leave that job to the doctors. This meant that some doctors had to spend hours of their day going around hospital wards getting drugs out of cupboards, drawing up the drugs, finding needles and syringes, injecting the patients and then cleaning up after themselves. It was no trouble to do this a few times a day, but some doctors had twenty patients, most of whom needed injections four times a day. And the nurses had a point: they had never received training in how to give injections, and they had being doing it for years without proper supervision. But the anger I felt had nothing to do with the rights and wrongs of the decision: I had to do more work as a result of it, and I was angry about it. And, as usual with anger, nothing useful came of it.

We doctors stomped around the wards giving out about the increased work we had to do and creating bad 'vibes'; the nurses snapped back; and the whole thing degenerated into a bitter dispute. It is only in retrospect that I can see that it was my *expectation* about their behaviour that was the reason for my anger, and not the question of whether they should have been doing this task in the first place. My expectation was that they should do that work and, as far as I was concerned, the fact that they did it had become written in stone. It was the thwarting of my expectation – and nothing else – that led to my anger.

Indeed, it could be said that the degree of anger is almost inversely proportional to the merits of the case in hand. The angrier you get, the more unjustified your position. One of the angriest people I ever met was a man who came into my hospital in handcuffs accompanied by two local policemen. He had, for the first time in his life, slapped his wife around the bedroom, kicked her and punched her on the ground, and then, when he heard his fourteen-year-old daughter picking up the phone and dialling for help, he went downstairs and hit her on the head with the telephone, making her bleed profusely from the scalp. And he came into me furious at the way he was being treated by the world, his wife and even his blameless daughter. Nothing was wrong with him, he reckoned, and everything he had done was absolutely justified. As you can imagine, he took quite a bit of calming down before it was possible to deal with him, and, as you can also imagine, it was quite a while later before it was possible to get his family to meet him again. Eventually he got over his anger, and he settled down on medication. But he left me with a permanent image of the physical and mental destruction that can be wrought by anger, and with the observation that the size of his anger was as vast as the 'crimes' committed against him were small.

The origin of this anger can sometimes be more than just habit. Alcoholics, for example, often end up bitter and angry people, resentful of the friends and family who 'betrayed' them over the years. The anger they wallow in is all the sadder for its actual origin – displaced guilt. It is a hard task for an alcohol misuser to face up to the disappointment and destruction he or she has wrought around themselves. It is much easier to ignore that and blame those around them for all the crimes of rejection they eventually commit. This ignorance of fact is not necessarily a conscious thing, it just betrays a mind that is out of tune with and unaware of itself.

Turning Point

'Habitual' anger, derived from childhood behaviour, can often be as difficult and taxing to deal with as an alcohol problem. The essential crux is the realisation that control over ourselves does not disappear totally when we get angry – it is simply temporarily lost. By focusing on the actual point when we lose our temper, by making ourselves believe that it is not something that takes us over, but something we give in to, we then have a chance of overcoming the powerful habit we have built up. That belief does not come easily, especially if we have grown used to losing our temper and believe it is something we can do nothing about, that it's just a part of our make-up.

A friend of mine, Frank, told me about an argument he had had with his fiancée over a relatively trivial matter. Frank's fiancée lost her temper explosively, not for the first time, and found herself ringing her parents late in the evening to tell them to stop Frank from doing whatever he was doing to annoy her. She was twenty-eight at the time. In the middle of the phone call to her distressed mother, she suddenly realised what she was doing, stopped in mid-flight and calmed herself down. There was a certain point beyond which she could not go, even in the midst of her worst outburst. She gained control over herself, put down the phone, went back to Frank in the next room and said, 'This has got to stop.' And she meant it. From that day on, she never lost her temper, at least not with Frank. She learned a vital thing about anger right at that point: no matter how bad it feels, we always have some control over it, even if we feel we don't.

Adolf Hitler, a superb psychological manipulator as well as a psychopath, learned the trick about losing his temper in a different way. One day in 1937, before the start of the Second World War, he was surprised at lunch by the arrival of a British emissary carrying some sort of message from the British government. Hitler initially refused to see him and had him shown into the next room. 'I can't see him yet,' he told his lunch guests, 'I'm in too good a mood.' And in front of his astonished guests, Hitler began to work himself up into a frenzy of anger. His face flushed, his brow furrowed and he marched up and down by the dinner table, his rage visibly deepening. Eventually he stormed into the next room where the poor emissary was waiting and raved and shouted at him, refusing to listen to his message and demanding that his government grant more concessions in the negotiations that were ongoing. He then stormed back into lunch, and in front of his astonished friends, he forced himself to relax again, and within a few minutes was laughing about the look on the messenger's face. Hitler, the evil genius, knew that even in the midst of fury there is control, and he used this remarkably successfully for his own ends.

Repetition

The situations in which we lose our temper are often similar from day to day. A long-standing belief in the incompetence or insubordination of an employee, pupil or family member prompts us to have our hackles up when we encounter them. A retort, remark or action by this other person is taken by us as a provocation, a justification, and we promptly blow our top as a 'reasoned' response to what was said or done. We can all be very objective about other people who indulge themselves like this, but become totally unable to reasonably judge a situation when it comes to ourselves. At the point when we realise that we have just lost our temper, it is too late; the damage is done, and we find it impossible to stop the emotional tsunami that engulfs us.

The point at which we can help ourselves comes before that. We must realise that we don't lose our temper spontaneously: we are primed by our personal history or personal antagonism. If we realise we are primed we have a chance of remaining in control. If we don't – we go bang!

The only way of finding out about our emotional state at the time we lose our temper is to look at ourselves afterwards. Habitual or repetitive loss of temper is quintessentially different from that 'useful' type we spoke about earlier. In the repetitive type, we are genuinely at fault, and if we want to do anything about it, we have to accept a large dollop of blame – something that is probably outside our normal frame of self-regard. The hardest part about dealing with it is to say, 'I was wrong' – without adding a 'but' at the end of the sentence. Saying it, not only inwardly but also outwardly – to the victim of the tantrum – is a very useful way of making ourselves believe it. A little bit of humiliation does us no harm in these circumstances.

Negative Impressions

There is a certain point at which repetitive loss of temper induces not respect but derision. I'm sure that the first time tennis player John McEnroe lost his temper on the centre court at Wimbledon there was a lot of stepping backwards done, and a lot of notice taken. But by the time he had lost his temper for the umpteenth time, the respect disappeared and was replaced by contempt and derision for his child-ish displays. The admiration everyone felt for his superb tennis ability was swamped by the negative impression left by his rude behaviour. As he lost his temper, so he lost our admiration.

The same applies to anyone who loses their temper to show us who is 'in charge' of a situation. Initially people are impressed and generally take steps to prevent a repetition of the episode; after two or three occasions they simply blame the person who is losing their temper and tend to ignore the message given in the midst of their fury. It does nothing to heighten respect for the 'loser', and whatever small benefit is made in terms of getting a job done more quickly is lost in the long term by the disrespect and dislike for the temper-loser by the victim. A 'loser' indeed.

Energy

Anger is a very energy-rich emotion – it is fiery and vivid. When we get angry we release a vast amount of energy and end up mentally exhausted. That same energy is best released in a safe and controlled way, rather than letting it simmer and eventually boil over. It is much better to dissipate the energy in strenuous activity or exercise than to let the energy build up inside. It's very hard to muster up the tension to lose our temper when we are physically exhausted. Taking up physical exercise, such as swimming, or a physical relaxation method, such as yoga, t'ai chi or mindfulness, takes the sting out of our tails and prevents us from letting go in the wrong way.

A young man came to me in the clinic with a recurrent problem of losing his temper. He was an only child and had been 'spoilt rotten', as he said himself, during his upbringing. He knew he was his mother's darling and the apple of his father's eye, and like most children in that situation, he exploited it to the full. Whatever he wanted, he got, and when he didn't get it, he lost his temper. Things went like this for years until he met a young woman, and they soon decided to get engaged. For the first time in his life, he simply couldn't get his own way, and he found himself losing his temper with her when they were discussing things like curtain materials and holiday destinations. She reacted badly to this, and he realised he would have to do something about his temper if he wanted to keep her.

He began to exercise control over himself and took up rugby, training three nights a week and playing matches at the weekend. Things eased off a bit, and gradually he lost his temper less and less: until the end of the rugby season, when he suddenly had nothing to soak up his energy. His temper worsened, and gradually his relationship soured all over again – despite all he had learned about self-control. The solution? He joined the relaxation classes in a local hospital during the long summer break – and it worked! The last I heard was that he had regained control of himself, and he and his girlfriend had just bought a house together.

Anger, repetitive anger, is at its worst a very destructive emotion. It saps the affection of those around us and alienates us from them. It corrodes relationships and prevents others from seeing any positive qualities in us. No matter how aggrieved we feel about something, no matter how hard done by we feel, the only excuse we should ever give ourselves for losing our temper is appropriateness. And the only way we can judge that is by being very thoughtful and very objective about ourselves – not an easy task!

Dealing With It

Once we accept we have a problem, we need to deal with it. Realisation can help a lot, but it is not a cure. The insight must be put to good use.

The first way we can help ourselves is by finding out what 'baggage' we bring to the situation, which may have only an indirect link to the situation in which we lose our temper. When I was a young doctor, a consultant – normally a mild, pleasant and easy-going man – lost his cool about my failure to check out a patient over whom we had given responsibility to another medical team the previous week. Chastened and crestfallen, I duly checked the patient's condition and reported back. It was only later, when I discovered that a patient of his with the exact same problem had died some time previously, and that his unusual loss of temper probably reflected his own disappointment and anguish at the previous patient's demise, that I was able to understand the situation. We are emotional, not rational, beings, so in trying to comprehend our own behaviour in a situation, we must try to find the 'vibes' the situation brings out in us. That simply involves digging and thinking, and this must be done in the quiet of our own home after the emotion associated with our loss of temper has faded.

Once we are in a situation with someone or something that has made us 'let go' before, we have to make ourselves aware of it and take precautionary measures. What it takes is simply forcing ourselves to be patient, and avoiding jumping straight into confrontational areas. That involves a lot of hard work, because one of the hardest things we can do in life is break a long-ingrained habit. An effort of will at the right time prevents any explosions and makes us feel better, not at the time but later on, when we are away from the provocation.

The alternative method is simply to leave the situation when things get too hot and are about to boil over. Getting away, going out, or taking a coffee break for five minutes defuses the situation and calms the jangling nerves. If we constantly find ourselves in situations where we lose our temper and – despite being aware of the repetitive provocation – we do nothing about it, we have to ask ourselves if we actually enjoy it. Losing our temper can be a wonderful self-indulgence when we tell people what we think of them and we demonstrate our power over them. Therefore, we have to be sure that if we are not avoiding it, we aren't at least enjoying it in a peculiar kind of way.

If we find ourselves losing our temper for some inappropriate reason and not being able to find a way out when the temper has gained momentum, the only solution is to get out and take a breather. There is nothing to be gained from staying and blowing off further – just get out and stay out until the feeling blows over. That at least limits the damage to some extent. Staying until you have 'mastered the situation' generally means staying until you have gone too far.

How to Control It

The best way to combat a bad habit is first of all to recognise it, then to learn about it, and finally to find the techniques to combat it. In this chapter you have read about anger; now use the following techniques to master your temper. The techniques described are part of the U-turn – the journey from Hurt on the left side of the U, through understanding at the bottom of the U, to Happiness on the right side of the U.

The fact that you are reading this suggests that there must be something happening to put you on the left side of the U. This chapter should have given you an insight and understanding that will help along the most important part of the journey – heading up towards the right-hand side of the U. The basic principles involved in this are: gaining an intellectual understanding of the emotions involved; then gaining a fuller and deeper understanding of these emotions through self-analysis; and then changing the behaviour that causes the unhappiness in the first place. This is the real U-turn in life.

The U-Turn: Self-Mastering Techniques

1. Sit down in a quiet place where there are no distractions, and take a pencil and paper with you.

2. Think about the last time you lost your temper and with whom you lost it, and write their name down on the paper.

3. Write down the reason you lost your temper with them.

4. Pause and wait for the feelings of annoyance about the person or situation to calm down.

5. Now look at the situation from the other person's point of view and write down why they might think you lost your temper. If this feels impossible, take a short break and try again. It is important to write down 'their' opinion and not just repeat your own.

6. Compare the two opinions and see which is closer to the truth of the situation. Beware of self-justification, which

frequently rears its ugly head at this point. The harder you are on yourself, the closer to the truth you probably are.

7. Repeat this procedure every time you lose your temper.

8. Apologise to anyone you have lost your temper with and realised after a proper analysis that you were wrong. This, while being the most humiliating component of the exercise, is the most effective method in the long run. Half-hearted apologies do not count.

9. Keep analysing and, if necessary, apologising. The amount of apologising will go down over time, but only if you force yourself to apologise every time you lose your temper, after analysing the situation. It is the emotional upset that you go through when apologising that makes you less likely to lose your temper the next time.

10. Take up a physically tiring pastime and make sure that you don't lose your temper because you simply have too much energy.

Anger as an emotion can sometimes mask and be mixed in with other emotions. We shall deal with one of these in the next chapter – feelings of hatred.

3

Jealousy and Envy

> Jealousy reveals more about ourselves than the person
> we dislike

Jealousy is not a matter of definition; it is a matter of degree. We are all jealous – of things, of people, of people's property and people's attributes. We all want what we haven't got. We all desire the unobtainable, especially if we see someone else with it. We all crave sex, possessions, beauty and power, base, mean-spirited creatures that we are. Every time we praise somebody for an achievement of some sort, somewhere deep inside us a little voice growls at us, 'It should be me.'

Envy is perhaps a better word than jealousy when applied to these inherent desires. We are envious of our superiors, even those we like and genuinely admire. We cover this up as best we can, even to ourselves, saying, 'Isn't she a marvellous boss?' and, 'He's very good to me,' but somewhere inside we are saying, 'I could do that better than them.' It comes down to a very basic principle of how we regard the world: we believe ourselves to be superior to those around us, and if we don't it's because our natural self-belief, our 'superiority complex', has been damaged by circumstances and experience. It is not a particularly attractive view of humanity, but it is borne out by how we treat each other individually and collectively.

Superiority

Where does this self-belief and feeling of superiority come from? Individually it goes way back into childhood: how we were treated when we were growing up, and how nourished and cherished we felt.

Infants and children are inherently selfish creatures. They demand, take and insist upon things without regard to those around them. As they grow up, the limits of selfish behaviour are learned through discipline and example. If a child feels emotionally secure in the affection of their parents, especially their mother, and gets the feeling that they are special and exceptional, that stays as an underlying sentiment in their make-up throughout their life. If, on the other hand, a child is neglected or mistreated when being raised, it leaves a raw gaping wound, a cavity that emphasises the missed love and affection.

One way to fill that gap is to strive to be worthy of the love not granted, to prove to the world and to the parent that we are good enough to be loved. How do we do that? We damn well show them just how capable, excellent and better than everybody else we are! And then, just because we stop striving and give up the battle to prove what essentially cannot be proved – namely 'I am worthy of your affection' – it doesn't mean that we stop regarding the world in terms of superiority and inferiority. We don't. We simply quit the battlefield in a huff, and petulantly proclaim our indifference to the fray.

So it almost doesn't matter which angle we are coming from – from a dearth or an abundance of affection – we still have a jaundiced and tainted view of ourselves: either we really are superior or we're going to prove to others that we are! None of us can claim an upbringing of total love, and I hope few of us can claim an upbringing totally lacking in comfort and affection. So most of us aren't at either of the extremes described above, but encompass traits of both. The view is the same, but the angle of the viewer may be different.

When I was a student, I spent a number of months studying psychiatry in Canada. As part of my work experience, I spent a day accompanying some chronically mentally disabled people on a day trip to a local park. We separated into a number of small groups, and each group played a game. Our group's game was to look back on our lives, take four significant moments and draw little pictures representing them. Then we had to pass the drawings around the group and tell everyone what each drawing meant, and what its significance was to our lives. After each person spoke, the group gave a small but enthusiastic round of applause.

One man spoke of his father's death, and showed us a small drawing of a funeral. He then spoke about buying his own home and showed us a little drawing of a house, and so on. At the end of his little talk, he received a round of applause and duly squirmed, smiled and looked bashful. The group leader talked of her marriage and her twin babies and how they affected her life, and showed us little drawings of bald babies with smiles on their faces. She duly received an enthusiastic round of applause and smiled herself.

Then it was my turn. I found myself talking about getting exams and receiving an award or two, and telling of my joy and pride at being a student doctor, and saying how important it was to me. I then received my round of applause, which was as warm and genuine as the applause the others had received. And suddenly I felt strangely humble and very touched at the same time. Here I was, seven thousand miles from home, being sincerely applauded by a group of strangers, congratulating me on my 'achievements', not because *they* considered them important, but because *I* did. In exactly the same way, each of the others was congratulated for their 'significant moments' because they were important to each of them, not necessarily to the rest of the group.

I was also humbled because I realised that until they applauded me, I had seen myself as different from them, even superior. I was the one who was on his way to a 'great career', and they had essentially lost their way in life. I had gone to them feeling that I was on a different level and not even knowing it, and only their sincerity brought me to this realisation of it. It was an educational experience and a humbling one.

Envy

It is precisely because of this attitude – of being superior or inferior – towards each other that we become envious about each other's attributes and possessions. We may be born equal in the sight of God, but we are most definitely not equal in the sight of other human beings. Our abilities and achievements become not things to be thankful for, but things to use against others to prove our superiority to them.

The lust for power, for example, so consumes many of the politicians in this world that they tend to sacrifice honesty and idealism on the way to achieving it. Human life is sacrificed daily around the world in an effort to demonstrate the power and superiority of one group over another, and ultimately the superiority of the leader of one group over the leader of another. Richard Nixon, when he was President of the USA, became so deluded by his ambition and lust for power that he let every vestige of morality disappear from his own actions and those of his minions. He had no personal difficulty about appearing on television and blatantly lying to millions of people in statement after statement: 'I knew nothing about Watergate,' 'I knew nothing about a cover-up' and, most blatantly, 'I am not a liar.' It was the public revulsion against this naked display of amorality that led to his political downfall. His own defence? In his autobiography he sticks to his guns, apologises to very few and says, essentially, 'I played by the rules of the game as I found them.' Even in retrospect he could not see himself or understand himself, or share the world's view of his actions.

The drive towards proclaiming and proving superiority over others is fuelled by the insecurity we have, deep down, about our own abilities and attributes. These two contrasting feelings – superiority and insecurity – feed off each other and ideally produce drive and ambition, tempered and checked by the realities of the outside world. Don't get me wrong – drive and ambition are wonderful attributes; they encourage effort and development of talent; they force people to explore themselves to find abilities they were not aware they possessed; they provide ways to develop that lots of people can benefit from. What a dull world we would have without ambition, without envy and without competition. We would live in a Soviet Communist-like place of drudgery and misery, with no prospect of change.

There is nothing wrong with drive and ambition as part of our make-up and part of our world; there is nothing wrong with striving to overcome our defects and insecurities and trying to gain a better place in the world. The important thing is to balance ambition with kindness, and to understand what we are doing.

Turning now to look at jealousy, it is important to understand the balance of forces that lie within ourselves and how they affect our view of the world.

Jealousy

It is the excessive wallowing in envy that is the fundamental problem with jealousy. If envy can be considered appropriate, then jealousy is excessive, inappropriate envy. When envy plays not just one of many parts but the leading role in our emotional life, it becomes jealousy. Whatever attractive things can be said about envy, whatever positive angles can be found, just about nothing positive can be said about jealousy. It is as destructive as anger, and it is much more corrosive to the sufferer than the object of jealousy. Real jealousy never focuses on inanimate objects but on people. Real jealousy starts insidiously, poisoning trust and contact between people, builds slowly into a malodorous obsession and ends as a seething crusade against reality. By its very nature, jealousy reflects not on the object of attention but on the sufferer. The degree of inadequacy and powerlessness of the sufferer is reflected in the degree of irrational emotion invested in the jealousy. It becomes, quite simply, a *raison d'être*.

When jealous feelings creep into the back of the mind, they take root and spread insidious messages of doubt across every perspective. Every event, if viewed with a jaundiced eye, can produce collateral evidence of a lack of loyalty or of infidelity, be it only of an emotional kind. Every 'fact', when looked at from this biased angle, not only increases the store of resentment, but distances the sufferer from reality, thus making it more difficult to return to an objective point of view. The mind becomes more and more obsessed – more single-minded – and nothing can deflect it.

It is this corrosion of objectivity that is the most important aspect of the problem. It is this that leads to the inevitable deterioration in relationships that characterise persistent jealousy. If you are looking for something that will bring you and those around you to the 'Hurt' part of the U-turn, pathological jealousy will surely do it, and not only bring you there but those around you as well. The sufferer is then left with only invective, irrationality and solitude for company. The problem outgrows the person with the problem.

Take Joseph Stalin, the leader of Russia for forty years. He lived in the system that he had created, a system of police rule, paranoia, backstabbing, insecurity and death. Right up to his death he remained the supreme ruler of a vast nation, and the master of 180 million people. He appeared to have everything any person could want but constantly required more and more extremes of grovelling and supplication by his 'adoring' people. He was proclaimed a living genius in such various areas as military strategy, economics, science, linguistics and Marxist theory. Yet he was fuelled in his thirst for power by the inadequacies of his own intellect and his feelings of inferiority about his rough Georgian country upbringing. He could not rest content in his power until every old Communist Party member who had been around in the 1917 revolution and knew him from the old days had been killed by his minions in the KGB. He purged untold hundreds of thousands of party members and had literally millions killed because of his jealous guarding of his power. In the end he confided to Nikita Khrushchev, his successor, that he was utterly alone and that he could trust no one – not even himself. He died unhappy, jealous and inadequate, in his own bed, probably of natural causes.

Focus

Jealousy is not usually directed at a large number of people or objects. Jealousy most commonly springs up between husband and wife, partner and partner, lover and beloved. When we proclaim love for another, we proclaim our affection for them, and we also proclaim our dependence upon them for our emotional wellbeing. Our partners and spouses have a tremendous hold upon our happiness, and while a loving word can fuel our affection and love, so a harsh one can bring the walls of Jericho tumbling down and send us into a deep sadness. The dependence on another can be a positive or a negative thing, depending on the relationship between the two people. Jealousy springs from creeping doubt and uncertainty, but also from being wrapped up in the other person, and the feeling of being unable to exist without them and their affection. A threat of withdrawal of that affection by one partner brings an emotionally charged response that is often out of all proportion to the action or 'crime' itself. Thus, the reaction reflects not the crime but the dependence.

A middle-aged man once told me about his changed fortune over a long number of years. He had started life as a musician and earned his crust during his formative years by playing the saxophone in various bands around the country. He developed his talent and began playing in recognised bands and large venues. He returned home, met and married a younger woman, and on the basis of his international reputation, settled down to a successful career, playing in different places every night of the week. Not unusually in the circumstances, he began to drink heavily, coming home later each evening, and began to lose touch with what was going on at home.

In his isolation, he became convinced that his wife had taken a lover, and began to accuse her, check her clothing for signs of suggestive stains and made life very difficult and unpleasant for her. When she could take it no longer, she barred him from the house, and his marriage was effectively at an end.

I met him a few years later, after he had attempted to kill himself in a state of drunken depression. The alcohol had damaged his brain: he would forget simple, everyday things unless constantly reminded, and he became totally incapable of looking after himself. However, when it came to his wife, he proclaimed a deep love and affection for her, even if it wasn't reciprocated; he was obsessed with his jealous denunciation of her 'lover', and he was starting a legal battle to prove that she had wronged him. In short, he had become an obsessed and jealous drunk, and despite my sympathy for him, I couldn't help feeling that his jealousy hadn't served him well. Last time I met him, he gave me details of his forthcoming legal action, and all I could do was wish him well and secretly hope he failed. What had started off as a small niggle of jealousy in the back of his mind had grown out of all proportion to any basis it had in fact, and this eventually consumed all of what hadn't been destroyed by alcohol.

Objectivity

The only way to come to terms with a problem like this is to attain that laudable goal – objectivity. If a jealous emotion takes root, the way to combat it is first to step outside the situation and look at the facts. The realisation that there may be a problem and that it may not simply be the 'other person' is an indication that the situation is potentially retrievable. But it is not enough just to acknowledge a problem and then do nothing. That realisation must be capitalised upon, and put to good use. 'Gosh, is it just me?' is a good place to start, but not if you only get as far as 'No, it couldn't possibly be.'

How is it possible to stand outside looking in, and still be inside looking out? One of the best ways is to literally turn things around and try to look at things from 'the other' point of view. Literally imagine that you are the other side of the couple; try to think and behave as he or she would in the circumstances, without acting as a self-apologist at the same time. If this is done genuinely, it can give invaluable insight into another person's actions and reactions, and open up alternative views to those so powerfully held. This is not easy: it requires persistence and practice, and, above all, a willingness to acknowledge that there may be another point of view.

Another way of gaining perspective on the situation is to seek the advice and opinion of a friendly neutral such as a doctor, therapist or friend. A sound mind applied to the sound body of evidence supplied should give at worst an alternative view, and at best an appropriate view, of the situation. When seeking advice it is important to choose well and also to make up your mind to take the advice as given and not reject it out of hand just because it doesn't agree with what you want to hear. The key to benefiting from advice is the willingness to see an alternative viewpoint, and resistance to advice can be very damaging.

Insecurity

Jealousy is almost always rooted in personal insecurity. None of us is a fully rounded individual, none of us has a fully developed personality, none of us can fully compensate for the various traumas of our upbringing – in short, we are all human. We all have deficiencies, gaps and insecurities in ourselves which, if we are honest, we recognise and should try to overcome. Jealousy is a projection on to another person of those insecurities, simply because not only is the 'relationship' threatened, but we as individuals feel under threat as well. It is much easier to project this personal inadequacy onto someone else, focus our feelings outside ourselves, than it is to acknowledge our own problems and even, God bless us, face up to them. If we find ourselves wallowing in jealousy and even 'hatred', it is time to look at the blemishes in our own mirror, not at the spots in someone else's!

The U-Turn: Self-Mastering Techniques

If we feel that we are consumed with jealousy and that it is taking over our life, it's time to do something about it.

The principles involved are the ones that are used throughout this book – the U-turn principles of *feel*, *think* and then *act*. The focus of these exercises is to increase our objectivity about the people around us and especially our views of them.

1. Sit down on your own with a pen and paper and make sure you are not distracted.

2. Divide the paper into three columns headed Feel, Think and Act.

3. Think of the last time you felt jealous or envious of another person, and remember the emotions you had about that person at that time.

4. Recall those emotions in detail. Relive the powerful feelings you had about them by imagining yourself in that situation again. Now write down the four most powerful feelings that describe different aspects of your emotions. For example, if you see someone going out with your ex-boyfriend or girlfriend and you imagine yourself staring at them across a room at a party, you might feel *anger*, *envy*, *hurt* and *sadness*. Write these emotions down in the Feel column.

5. Now move on to the next column, Think. Divide the column into two headings: Them and Me.

6. Under the heading Them, and beside the first of your named emotions, write down the reason why *they* elicit this emotion in you. For example, beside the emotion *angry* you might write 'Because he is with her, and he is mine.' Beside the emotion *hurt* you might write 'Because he dumped me.'

7. Now focus on the reasons why each emotion affects you *personally* – not objectively. Write down in the column Me the reason for each emotion in terms of your own image of yourself. This is probably the hardest part of the exercise, but it is the key to resolving the problem, and it is worth spending more time on this than any other section. Instead of looking outwards at the situation in front of you, look inwards – at what the situation makes you think of yourself. For example, beside the emotion *anger* you might write, 'Because I feel helpless about trying to get him back.' Beside the emotion *hurt* you might write, 'Because it makes me feel so inferior to other women.'

8. In the last column, Act, you need to make a resolution about the jumbled emotions and thoughts that precede it. The way to take an appropriate action to resolve the situation is quite simple. Look at the Think/Me column and think of a way to reverse the thoughts about yourself by acting against them. This can be done through *confrontation* or *sublimation*. When we act to resolve a complex emotional situation, we must act according to one of those two principles in order to reverse the feelings about ourselves each cardinal emotion evokes. For example, beside the emotion *anger* we could write – and not only write but also do – 'Go right over to him and ask him out all over again.' This might not succeed, and you may not end up going out with him again, but you will help resolve the feeling that 'I feel helpless about getting him back.' This would be acting according to the principle of *confrontation*. Beside the emotion *hurt* you could write – and not only write but act on – 'I'm going to chat up other guys and ask one of them out.' This would be acting to reverse the feeling that 'I feel inferior to other women.' This is an example of *sublimation* – using a negative stimulus in a positive way.

The important thing about this process is to do it whole-heartedly. In order to resolve deep feelings like jealousy, it is necessary to work your way through the U-turn, and *feel*, *think* and *act* out of the dead-end street. Only half doing it will resolve nothing.

One of the worst feelings that we can have is feeling down and depressed. It is these feelings we deal with in the next two chapters.

4

Depression: The Experience

> Depression is a horrible experience: but you *can* learn
> from it

When psychiatrists or psychologists try to define depression in psychiatric terms, they seek to place limits and descriptions on what is an emotional experience. Words like 'guilt', 'despair' and 'fear of the future' are used not to describe the experience, but to define whether or not what someone is going through is depression in a 'psychiatrically acceptable' sense. Textbooks spend pages specifying the parameters of 'clinical depression', yet do not mention a word about what the experience is like to someone going through it, nor what meaning the experience has to that person. Essentially, the emotion, the suffering, the awful experience of depression itself gets lost in the definition of it.

That's not so bad if you're on the outside of the depression looking in. As a psychiatrist, looking at the problem objectively, it is necessary to define limits to an experience and to set parameters for what is or is not depression in order to treat the problem properly. It is vital for doctors to have a common definition of what a 'disorder' is like in order to communicate to each other about different treatments and their successes and failures with a particular 'disorder'.

While that may seem impersonal and clinical it is vital to be objective as well as sympathetic in order to give a patient the best possible treatment. You don't have to go through a depression in order to sympathise with someone who is. You don't have to live through a depression in order to sense the life of someone who is living in one. It is not even entirely necessary to have had an experience of depression in order to treat it properly as a doctor. It is, however, necessary to go through a depression in order to fully understand it.

Some years ago I went through a period of significant stress and unhappiness. In retrospect I believe that I was depressed, but at the time I had little knowledge that what I was going through was a common experience. To me it felt utterly unique. Every day was unpleasant, almost every waking moment anxious, and the future was a frightening continuation of the present. When I emerged from that period some time later I resolved to make sure that I would never go through the experience again. The lesson I learned from the experience was that there was a cause of my 'depression' that could be resolved with insight, followed by dedication and constant effort. The methods described in this book are partially methods I used myself to avoid having to go through the experience again, together with coping mechanisms that I learned from the best teachers available.

The great advantage, in general, that a patient has over a psychiatrist is that the patient is going through the experience and the psychiatrist isn't. The patient with the depression is on the inside looking out, and the world looks very different that way. It is the depth of this experience which lends the patient the motivation to develop self-understanding later.

The Experience

Brian Keenan is a Northern Irish teacher who spent four years in captivity as a hostage in Beirut, at a period when the

Lebanon was going through a civil war. He was captured by a fanatical Muslim group who wanted to use him as a bargaining tool in their relations with western governments. For most of that entire four years, he was kept alone, blindfolded and in chains, fed minimal amounts of dreadful food, and told nothing of the outside world. He was threatened and occasionally assaulted. He described his experience of suffering and his depressions in his powerful book *An Evil Cradling*. His description of his life as a hostage, and of his own mental response to it, is unbearable in its intensity and absolutely desperate in its sadness. At a press conference soon after his release he said:

> A hostage is crucifying aloneness. It is a silent, screaming slide into the bowels of ultimate despair. A hostage is a man hanging by his fingernails over the edge of chaos and feeling his fingers slowly straightening. A hostage is the humiliating stripping away of every sense and fibre of mind and spirit that makes you what you are. A hostage is a mutant creation, full of self-loathing, guilt and death wishing. But he's a man, a rare and unique and beautiful creation of which these things are no part.

Brian Keenan's life became a constant battle against wallowing in the depths of depression. He used every trick and device he could think of – talking, going over old stories in his mind – to prevent himself slipping. His battle was not only courageous but also determined. Quite often he would succeed, distracting himself from his own reality and keeping his spirits buoyant. But quite often, he didn't.

Different Aspects of Depression

Brian Keenan's experience is clear and vivid. He battled against depression and occasionally lost. His description brings the dreadfulness and suffering of the experience home to us all. For him and for everyone going through a depression, every individual moment is a pain and a suffering, in which existence becomes narrowed down into a band of revolving thoughts, all negative. Certain aspects of the past or present become magnified, guilt about a misdemeanour or impotent fury at a grievance echoes through the mind, and it is impossible to escape from the repetitive cycle of sadness. Doubts about self-worth are magnified and we feel useless, limp and alone. Life becomes pointless and it becomes irrelevant to think about the future, because the future only exists as a repetition of futility, or simply doesn't exist for us at all.

The precipitating factor for the depression may become a focus or an obsession that cannot be got rid of, or it becomes lost in a haze of dulled experience. Daily routines change from the usual range of pleasant to monotonous and become uniformly laborious. Performing simple daily tasks requires an almost superhuman effort of will and energy. Coping ability falls asunder, and minor tasks take on awesome proportions and are filled with unforeseen complications and consequences. Pleasure and enjoyment evaporate from our existence, and no smiles, jokes or laughter can penetrate our gloom. Love and affection, hugs and kisses are viewed as if through a long tunnel; they are observed at a strange kind of objective distance, but their warmth doesn't reach us. We are prone to panics and fears, which can grip us, vice-like, around the throat and don't let go. What they are about we can't say, but they terrorise us when they are present. Cicero said it all: 'Nothing is pleasant to him over whom some terror hangs.'

The suffering may not be constant: there may be periods of relative coping, when it is possible to feel reasonably capable and fairly objective about ourselves and our situation, only to find ourselves plunging into the depressive abyss with dreadful regularity. The attractiveness of taking to or staying in bed often wins in the fight to maintain control over our lives and take part in daily activity. In contrast to our physical lethargy, our mind is a seething mass of repetitive thoughts and emotions, which for some unknown reason we cling to or can't let go. Our own personal history is rewritten, Communist-like, with an overwhelming emphasis on crimes, misdemeanours and pain, and a total neglect of any pleasures and joys we have experienced.

The depressive experience varies from one individual to another. Some people have a tremendous battle with one aspect of depression, for example the physical feelings of exhaustion and dullness, and have no recollection of problems of self-worth or low self-esteem. Physically, we can be taken over by an extreme lethargy and have no physical energy to do our normal daily tasks. We look dull and depressed, and our faces are sad and void of expression.

I met a profoundly depressed Dublin woman, with a large extended family who took great care of her, on the night she came into hospital. She sat immobile, dishevelled, with an expression of extreme sadness, and was totally unresponsive to questions even from her own son, who was with her. After a short while in hospital she began to recover and, much to my surprise, was able to tell me all about the interview I had had with her that night, down to the details of what I was wearing at the time, and what had happened to her before and after she talked with me. Even though she had appeared dull and almost not there at all, her mind was working and she was listening to and memorising everything that was said to her and about her.

Some people find themselves able to carry on doing the superficial, basic things in life, like getting the groceries and going to work, but find they hate themselves and think everything they do is worthless and that everybody despises them. Others are tremendously anxious and hyperactive, rushing around the place but getting very little done, all the while feeling brittle and on the brink of tears.

We can totally focus on any negative aspect of our lives, past or present, at the expense of objectivity. An elderly Irish farmer, who was admitted to hospital when in the depths of a deep depression, was totally obsessed with a small strip of land he had given to a good friend and neighbour seven years earlier. It was a tiny piece of land and he had given it to his neighbour to allow him to build a wall for a shed. He felt very down about this, even though it had taken place so long ago, and he blamed all his current trouble on his 'stupidity' in giving the land away. His family utterly refuted this, pointing out how little he needed the land, how small it was in the first place, and how much use it was to his neighbour, but he remained adamant that it was the cause of all his trouble. When his depression lifted, he forgot about the land, and when reminded about it he said it was irrelevant. He was aware of the importance he had placed on it when he was depressed but when he felt better it was simply irrelevant to him.

Depressive thinking not only clouds reality, it clouds our perception of what we are going through. It is quite possible for us to fully believe that the reason we are depressed relates to a particular situation or person and then realise when we are in better shape that this simply isn't true and our anger and blame was misplaced.

Depressive thinking is a circular process – thinking old thoughts and fighting old battles – and if the genuine precipitating factor isn't on the depressive 'circuit', we are entirely capable of missing the crux of the matter. We cannot dismiss the thoughts and insights we gain when we are depressed, because they can be invaluable in helping us out of ourselves, but we must also re-judge them when we are better, to make sure of their truthfulness and accuracy.

An attractive, middle-aged beauty therapist came into hospital, suffering from a bout of depression that had lasted three months. She was listless, dull, unable to cope, and agitated about everything. She complained bitterly about how cruel life had been to her and she confessed deep-rooted guilt about neglecting her children. She had been separated from her husband, with whom she had had two children, for a period of five years, and had a new relationship in her life. Things were tight at home, but she was convinced that she was facing bankruptcy and ruin. She sank further and further into her black mood until she couldn't concentrate, she couldn't sleep, and she became convinced that she was an evil person and that she 'smelled bad'. No discussion, no objective opinion and no counselling would convince her otherwise. She sank into a tortuous round of self-denigration and hatred of herself for what she was and what she had done. It took four months of medication, psychotherapy and eventually shock therapy to get her out of the mood and back on an even keel.

And the outcome of it all? Despite all her worry and fears, her children assured her that she hadn't neglected them; her finances were straightened out to her satisfaction; and she went back to her new relationship with a new lease of life. Months after her recovery, she and her own doctor were unable to come up with the real cause of her depression. In her case, all the causes and worries she had when depressed disappeared when she was well. Her situation remained the same, but her outlook was transformed. And in her case the verdict was 'No psychological cause found'!

Awareness

The reason why psychiatrists find it necessary to define and delineate 'depression' is not just to measure it and to determine the success or failure of various therapies, but to actually decide what is and what is not a depression. Strange as it may seem, sometimes going through the experience is not the best way of judging the experience objectively. It is quite possible to go through a depression and not even know what it is or what it was about. It is also quite possible to go through a second period of depression and still be unaware of what it is, despite being told what the first episode was.

As we get older and more physically infirm and worried about our health, we can go through a depression fully convinced that there is something physically ailing us, and are only reassured of physical wellbeing when the depression lifts. One elderly man I knew became convinced that his bowels were rotting away inside him. He saw every eminent physician available, and they all reassured him that there was nothing physically wrong with his tummy. His wife had died two years before, after forty years of marriage. They had had an up and down marriage, with good times interspersed with periods of arguments and separations. At the time of her death they had been going through a bad passage and he had been angry at some things she had said to him, hurtful things that remained with him after she died. During his time in hospital he talked about her and their life together and the things they did together. Gradually, as time went by, he began to feel just a little bit better about his situation and to acknowledge how much he missed her. It was only when he recovered from his deep-rooted grief and depression that his worry about his bowels lifted and he proclaimed himself cured.

It is at times like these, the depressed times, when the mind can deceive us in many different ways and our worries are not always what they seem to be at the time.

When Depression Is Not Depression

It is also quite possible to convince ourselves that we are depressed when something else altogether is ailing us. We can refuse to recognise reality in various different ways, putting a label of depression on it when the truth lies closer to a problem with alcohol, or selfishness, or perhaps life-long laziness and lethargy, that we are simply not prepared to face.

A very depressed middle-aged man came into hospital one night. He was a businessman, married to a very respectable, self-contained woman, and they had two beautiful children. The night before he was admitted, he had been in the sitting room watching television when his younger girl came in. She wanted to change the channel, so she took the remote control and flicked the switch. He responded by losing his temper, roaring at her that she was a 'silly bitch', and struck her across the face with the remote control. She ran from the room crying and screaming, and locked herself upstairs in her bedroom. His wife returned, found out what had happened, and insisted he go to his doctor, who had him sent to hospital the next day. The man himself felt dreadfully sorry and guilty about what he had done. He told a tale of increased feelings of isolation in the family, of bouts of depression and tears, of feelings of futility and desperation and even ideas of doing away with himself.

Talking to his wife, however, produced a different picture. Her husband's depression was interspersed with periods of heavy drinking, which had happened on and off for many years. Between bouts of drinking, he became increasingly crotchety and irritable, picking fights with family members and refusing to go out socially with them. He would inevitably go back to his drinking despite numerous heartfelt promises to his wife and daughters that his drinking days were over. He made life a misery for those around him and he couldn't see it himself. Hitting their daughter was the final straw for his wife. She decided that she wanted him out of her house, on a trial basis at first, but probably for good. After many tears, many pleas for forgiveness and many more promises to reform, the man eventually agreed to leave. The last thing he said to me as he left hospital to start a new and lonelier life in a small flat was: 'You know, Doc, I should have known.' And he was right – he should have known. In his case the problem wasn't his feelings of depression and sadness, but the years of alcohol abuse and bad temper that he had simply denied and ignored. A sad but all too common story.

The key to helping this form of self-deception is to dig deep and to try to come to terms with the processes that make up our internal reality. The only time when this may not necessarily be beneficial is when we are actually going through depression. If we comprehend exactly the precise nature of what we are going through, when we are going through it, it is likely to make our suffering greater, as we have a heightened awareness of our torture. If we remain in blissful ignorance of what we are going through, as we go through it, the physical discomfort, the physiological consequences will remain the same, but the intellectual agony of the depression will be lessened, to some extent anyway. The time to do the digging into ourselves and our own nature may not be at the depth of depression but in the period after recovery, when the memory of what we have been through is still fresh in our minds and the motivation for changing ourselves is all the greater for it.

So it is important for us to be aware of what we went through to encourage us to try to find out the reasons why we went through it. When we have mastered our emotional resources we have a solid motivation to dig in and probe ourselves and come to terms with what we have gone through, and try to find ways to prevent it happening again. If, however, we remain ignorant intellectually of our depression, we run the risk of walking right back into the situation that precipitated it in the first place, repeating the entire dreadful exercise, and coming out at the other end none the wiser. It is much better to suffer, to be aware and maybe to learn from it than it is to suffer moderately and remain ignorant.

Why Me?

When we have gone through an appallingly painful experience, and after coming out of it we ask 'Why did it happen?', there is really only one answer. The only reason to suffer is to understand! If we could gain understanding without suffering, the world would be a happier place. The main reason we must try to understand is to prevent further suffering. Unfortunately, it seems we can't have understanding without suffering; but what a waste of an experience it is to suffer and not to understand.

Understanding Needs Effort

When we are actually going through a particularly difficult experience is not always the best time to learn about what it really means to us. This is not always the best time to try to gain insight into ourselves. Sometimes our emotional resources are too compromised by the bewildering shock to the system that a depression is to allow us to sit back and take stock of the situation. Sometimes it is necessary to wait until the level of stress and pain lessens in order to focus on the personal meaning of the experience. There is a great temptation, however, as soon as the suffering begins to diminish, to simply switch off about the whole thing, to say 'I'm glad that's over,' and make a conscious effort to forget everything. To call that attitude a mistake is a glorious understatement. We owe it to ourselves, and to those around us, to glean as much understanding and insight from the experience as our intellect will allow us.

In Oscar Wilde's play *The Importance of Being Earnest*, Lady Bracknell says, 'To lose one parent ... may be regarded as a misfortune; to lose both of them looks like carelessness.' There is just enough truth in that statement, if we look at it in relation to depression and suffering, to make us take note. If we go through such a dreadful experience, we have to commit our mental resources to the idea of learning from it. If we go through a second episode of pain, and we haven't made any effort to learn from the first, we are at least partly to blame for the second episode. There is no excuse for mental laziness, because we generally pay for it later – and pay double. But if we do try hard, and face up to ourselves with some degree of truth, then we are less likely to suffer later on – that is the pay-off.

Types of Depression

However, if we do learn and do understand and still experience episodes of depressive pain, we may have to accept that sometimes there is just no reason that we can understand. Sometimes we suffer because of an internal chemical process that we are powerless to control. In these circumstances, we can search and dig deep, we can look for meaning within ourselves and still not come up with an answer. And this leads us to the conclusion that there is more than one type of depression. One type is the result of deep-seated emotional difficulties and reactions to stressful events; and the other is a chemical imbalance in our brains, which can only be treated with drugs such as antidepressants.

One young man of twenty-three had spent two years of his life in a psychiatric hospital because of depression. He and his doctors had repeatedly explored his upbringing, his relationships, his despairs and his hopes in order to try and find a reason for his depression. No cause could be found. In the end he was given a new medication, and within four weeks he was much improved. Even when he was better, no precipitating cause could be found for his depression. He left the hospital and got on with his life. And then his battle was not to comprehend but to accept. His focus became one of tolerance, not comprehension, a battle of acceptance, not of understanding – a different battle altogether.

Chemical or Reactive?

How do we know which type of depression we have? How do we find out what to focus our energy on? The answer is simply that we must first learn about ourselves. Only when we have faced the truth about our emotions and our desires, our capabilities and our limitations, can we judge whether our suffering comes from the resolvable within or the unresolvable outside of ourselves. Because we can never fully understand ourselves, we can never be fully 100 per cent integrated.

There should always be some room to learn about ourselves. It is only after we have exhausted our intellect in a search for comprehension that we should give up to some degree, and focus our energies on coping rather than digging. We can never know enough of ourselves, but sometimes the law of diminishing returns applies, and we would benefit more from learning techniques of fighting back against depression and of self-management, than learning techniques of self-examination. The other fact is that many depressions are mixtures of the two types of depression and thus it may be impossible to differentiate which is which in any given situation. The only way to treat someone in a situation where the cause of the depression is unknown is to treat them as if they had both types simultaneously.

What to Do About It

When we are in the middle of a profound depression and feel absolutely lost, and don't know what to do, we must remember that there is always a solution and there is always a way out. What that solution is and what the way out is is often an individual journey that involves change and adaption to circumstances, both internal and external. In fact the journey is a U-turn: not only do we turn our minds around, but we turn our whole lives as well. What we can do in these circumstances is make a decision to start out on that U-turn. What I will describe in the next chapter is the process of going on that U-turn: how to start it, how to keep at it and how to complete it. It may be a long journey, but it is worth it.

5

Depression: The Escape

> There are many ways of helping depression: the worst
> thing to do is nothing

When we are trying to start to reverse the spiral of depression, there are some vital things to learn about the nature of depression. When we are faced with a downward spiral of mood and the sinking physical feelings that go with it, we are generally left with a major question: How can it be stopped, and even reversed? The first important thing to remember in this situation is that a problem and its magnitude is a question of attitude and not of fact. Depression can sometimes be of a physical nature, but it always manifests itself in psychological processes. Problems and situations are not viewed from a position of cool reality, but from a viewpoint in which the worst outcome is invariably expected, the clouds have already gathered and the storm has already begun. Depressive thinking precludes objectivity, it has its position worked out already, and it does not allow any other points of view. It cannot view a situation from anything but the worst position. Problems become exaggerated and the good things vanish.

When we are in this frame of mind, the first thing to find out is what the problem is – and the problem is the state of mind and not the situation.

Perspective

If you deal with a person with Down syndrome for any length of time, you begin to get a sense of their extraordinary placidity and good nature. They have a sense of fun and a great capacity for affection – both receiving and giving it. Because of the nature of their disability, their coping skills are often impaired, leading to occasional tantrums and upsets; but they invariably return to their former state of happiness without undue delay. Objectively speaking, their situation is one of the worst a human being can find him or herself in, but subjectively they feel no angst and are not aggrieved. A certain amount of their positive attitude is due to ignorance, but their mood and manner is often significantly better than people who have the same degree of mental disability but don't have Down syndrome. Why it is like that, nobody knows, but it is a blessing to go through life with an ability like it.

They can teach us a very important thing – it's not reality itself that's important, it's how we look at it that counts. Reality is an internal state, not an external one. When our version of reality begins to crumble around us, the most important thing we need is another view of the external world. A friend who cares enough to listen without prejudice, or a professional person to whom we can turn for advice is the most important tool to help deal with the situation. Trusting them and not being afraid to speak out to them is vital in getting a handle on a depressive spiral. Not only does speaking out and getting an unbiased view of things help us to change our thinking, it helps unburden ourselves of the great weight of battling alone. There is a great emotional lift that comes from unburdening ourselves to another, which cannot be found on one's own. Generally, the only thing that stops us from looking for help in this way is our own pride, and that is just plain stupid when the depth of suffering is taken into consideration. Seeking help from a professional, especially a doctor or psychiatrist, is one of the major steps to swinging the whole situation around. It is not an admission of defeat; it is an admission of need.

Changing the Way We Think

Depressive thinking consists of little fragments of thought, with an emotional downward spiral attached. Something may happen, someone may say something and – bang! – we're off on a merry-go-round of thought processes that end up with us down in the depths. If we can only nip that original event, that original thought, in the bud, and hit it with a cold dose of objectivity, we could prevent the ensuing self-destructive thought processes. Our main problem is that we don't separate our emotions into the thousand thoughts and statements that depressive thinking consists of. If we can see the triggering thought – and that takes effort and concentration on our part – we have a chance of dealing with it before the depressive spiral sets in.

For every negative attitude there is an equal and opposite positive attitude; for every negative thought, an opposite positive one; for every negative action, an opposite positive one. If we can take the negative thoughts, turn each of them around and look at them positively, we have half the battle won. If we can take our negative attitudes and turn them around into positive attitudes, we have won the major battle. If we can finally take our negative opinions about ourselves and turn them into actions that defy those opinions, we have won the war, because those actions eventually determine our opinions of ourselves. The process of doing that is difficult, long and tedious and involves working out a lot of our thought processes and a lot of our own attitudes to ourselves that have built up over the years. The U-turn process is a difficult one, but one that eventually changes these long-held personal opinions about ourselves. These personal attitudes about ourselves are greatly entwined with our self-image and self-confidence, and we will discuss these in later chapters.

Action, Not Words

John Profumo was an English cabinet minister in the early 1960s. He was a young man on the rise and he had a great future – maybe he could even become prime minister if he played his cards right. However, he became too cocky and began to believe he could get away with anything. He began sleeping with a younger woman, and when this was discovered by the press, he stood up in parliament and denied it completely. Eventually the truth came out and there was a massive scandal. In the end he admitted the truth and had to resign. There was a long-drawn-out trial, which revealed the truth and led to the suicide of Stephen Ward, the man who had introduced the young woman to Profumo. The government fell at the next election, mainly due to what became known as the 'Profumo scandal'. The whole story was made into a movie called, appropriately enough, *Scandal*.

But that wasn't the end of the story. Shamed and depressed about what he had done and the consequences of his actions, John Profumo looked round for a way of making amends to those he had hurt and of trying to end the self-hatred that he felt for himself. He founded a shelter for homeless boys in London and for the next twenty-five years he worked tirelessly to help those less fortunate than himself. Eventually he was forgiven by the British establishment and was awarded a CBE, an important honour, by Queen Elizabeth in 1975. And when he accepted it he smiled for the cameras and the press that had followed his downfall in the 1960s. He was relaxed and friendly and at peace with himself. By acting directly against his low opinion of himself, by giving to others where he had previously been so selfish, he was not only forgiven by society, he forgave himself. We can all learn a lot from him.

Change

When we are in the middle of a learning process about ourselves, when we are digging deep and coming up with rather nasty little truths we don't want to face, it is quite common to get depressed by our insights. Alcoholics, for example, when facing up to the reality of their ruined worlds and self-inflicted wounds, often sink down under the weight of this awful reality. Subjectively, it is a time of great suffering, but objectively it can be a time of great hope, when there is a chance to turn one's life around and rise again from the ashes. That is extremely difficult to see if you've just seen your marriage, job or financial security go down the river, or have just woken up to the realisation that they've gone, but it genuinely can be a turning point, a time for great change and self-renewal. This does not deny the pain involved, but puts it into the perspective of the prospective gain. There is often simply no comparison.

The only thing we can hope to gain from a bout of depression is insight – not only into personal perspectives we may not have had before, but also into a new *depth* of perspective or emotion. Unrealistic ambitions may be dropped, appreciation of the importance of those close to us may be enhanced, and a fuller view of what we truly want from life can ensue. The difficulty a large number of people have with gaining insight from depression and from suffering is that the reward gained is less than the degree of suffering involved: the intensity of the negative experience doesn't justify the gains – it's a poor 'return on investment'.

Well, this may be true. There may not be a great pot of gold at the end of the rainbow. But it is a very individual thing. It is impossible to predict who will gain from their experience and who will not. However, we owe it to ourselves to try to learn from our suffering, not because we are guaranteed a major life transformation, but because the consequences of *not* trying may be so great. It is quite common for people to go through a period of depression, emerge on the other side and resume normal life again, only to plunge back into depression at some time in the future and not even recognise the experience as depression the second time round! Not only do a large number of people go through the experience without learning about the reasons for their depression, they often learn nothing at all either about themselves or about depression. This is a monstrous crime against themselves, an utter waste of a potentially enriching experience and an utter negation of their suffering.

Individuality

Depression as an experience is a very individual one. No one can ever fully appreciate what it is like for someone else to go through a bout of depression, simply because everyone has their own background and experience on which depression acts. Likewise, it may be very difficult to determine whether what we are going through is a bout of depression, or of anxiety, or of panic – or of all these. Quite often the experience is a mixture, with a predominant flavour of one type or another.

After meeting and treating a large number of people suffering from depression or anxiety, I have yet to meet someone with an 'ordinary anxiety' or an 'ordinary depression'. They simply don't exist. So it can be quite difficult to say clearly to a patient or a colleague, 'Mr X has a "definite depression" or a "straightforward anxiety".' But a couple of words cannot convey adequately the depth of experience and range of suffering that any one person goes through. Inadequate as these words are, however, they are useful to those working in the area to help exchange information.

As a professional it is quite easy to get caught up in labels and definitions and miss out on the individual going through his or her trauma. It is very important for any doctor or thera-pist not to get lost in defining something and giving someone's experience a diagnosis and then neglect the full experience. It is also important that the person caught in the experience does not get obsessed with diagnoses or labels – these are not the problem to be attacked. Having a great debate with your doctor about whether what you are going through is truly depression, or an unusual form of depression, or an atypi-cal depression is likely to avoid the issue rather than hit it on the head. Labels and diagnoses are useful, but they are not comprehensive, and it can be a waste of time to get obsessed with a definition of the experience. It's enough to know that we have suffered and need help. The definitions can be left to others.

Getting Out

When you are going through an intense and horrible expe-rience it is very hard to know how best to get out of it. The primary focus is often on simply getting the suffering to stop rather than working out *how* to do just that. A blind panic can consume us, preventing us from taking simple ordi-nary measures that would be obvious to us in less distraught circumstances. Simple everyday decisions can start to appear overwhelmingly complex and our ability to cope with them plummets.

Talking It Through

I have already mentioned the vital step of admitting the need for help and seeking it from a trustworthy professional, someone who commands our confidence. Friends and neighbours, relations and those close to us can be a wonderful help, assisting us through and sharing the suffering with us. The emotional relief this gives us may be all that is required to turn the situation around and free us from the depression.

The only problem with an ear and a mind that is close to us is simply that it may be *too* close to us to give us an objective, rounded view of the situation. A person who is overly sympathetic to us can give us warm and genuine support but not necessarily the best advice. The most sympathetic? Yes. The most realistic? No. For it is the latter – the objective advice and hard-headed analysis – that is often the most useful for us in the long term. Objective psychological exploration in the form of some sort of psychotherapy can often help us arrive at conclusions, understand ourselves and make us change faster and more definitively than if we tried to do it all alone. It's not that some other person imposes their will or their opinion on us, but that we do it ourselves, with someone else helping us along the way.

A lovely, middle-aged housewife used to attend my clinic a few years ago. She told me a story that would make the devil weep, and unfortunately it was all too true. Her respectable plumber son got involved with a married woman (let's call her Sarah), who left her husband and moved in with him. Sarah's husband had been an intravenous drug abuser and she in time had become one too. She in turn got her partner, my patient's son, on to drugs and they used to get high together. She became pregnant and, despite her drug use, gave birth to a healthy baby daughter. Then Sarah found out that her husband had recently died of Aids-related complications, so she got tested and was found to be HIV-positive.

Over a period of months she became sick, neglecting her daughter and her partner – who turned to his mother, my patient, for help. Being a mother, she gave it unconditionally. She looked after her granddaughter most days of the week, she looked after her son's partner as she got gradually weaker, putting up with her irrational tirades and her bitterness. She also had to cope with the hatred she felt for the woman who had destroyed her son's life and turned him into a junkie and a jail bird.

Eventually Sarah died and my patient had to take her granddaughter into her home to look after her full time. Then, heartbreakingly, her son was diagnosed as HIV-positive, and she had to face up to the prospect of his impending death, and the prospect of raising her granddaughter herself. All the while she came back to me week after week to tell me the next instalment of this gothic horror story, and I was impotent to help her in any other way than listen to her. When I had to leave that job and move on, she was very sad and said that I had been a great help to her on her difficult journey and that a lot of the sadness she felt was relieved by simply talking about it. And despite doing nothing apart from listening and giving support and advice, I think I had been a help to her. Sometimes that is all that can be done – but it can be a lot.

Various therapies or strategies can be used by a therapist to try to tease out an individual's mental processes and their meanings and bring them out into the open. The particular strategy used is not as important as the relationship that builds up between client and therapist, and therein may lie the heart of success.

Medication

Another advantage of approaching a professional in the field is their access to remedies that friends wouldn't have.

Antidepressant medication can be a vital step along a path to recovery. There is a certain point at which introspection and analysis become inadequate to deal with a situation and it takes tried and tested formulae to help us. Antidepressant medication is remarkably successful – far more so than the popular image of 'happy pills' would have us believe. The vast majority of people with a bout of depression can recover from it with a simple medication in a matter of weeks. It is not an artificial cure involving dangerous substances, it is simply a removal of the excessiveness of the depressed mood, leaving the individual's mind whole and renewed. In the most severe cases, shock therapy can be used to help relieve the worst ravages of the depression, and this too is remarkably successful, and has almost no side effects. Once more the popular image (who can forget Jack Nicholson writhing on the table getting shock therapy in *One Flew over the Cuckoo's Nest*?) belies the wonderful benefits of successful therapy. Fear of these types of therapy can prevent someone from approaching a doctor or psychiatrist when they may be the most beneficial things around for them – so it's important to keep an open mind.

Self-Help

In recent years, it is becoming apparent that some self-help remedies are more successful than originally thought. Strenuous exercise can act as effectively at lifting a mood as a good antidepressant. Unfortunately, research shows that the type of exercise required to be genuinely antidepressant is about forty-five minutes of sweat-inducing cardiovascular exercise three times a week. That is quite a lot of exercise, especially if someone is not used to it and is leading quite a sedentary lifestyle. The exercise can be jogging, power walking, swimming, cycling, tennis, etc. Gentle exercise – such as walking around the block for a few minutes once or twice a week – is not adequate.

Other research now shows that practising a deep relaxation exercise, such as mindfulness, can also help with depression. Quite a number of people I know find it very helpful. Although it sounds easy, and there are many CDs and books that describe mindfulness, it takes constant practice to get to an effectively antidepressant level of expertise with mindfulness. Ideally it should be practised for about thirty minutes per day, and it may take weeks of effort to get to an adequate level of expertise.

The U-Turn: Self-Mastering Techniques

The U-turn principles of *feel*, *think* and *act* can be used to deal with depressive thoughts and ideas. The exercises aren't easy, and if you think they are after you do them, you aren't trying hard enough to get to the truth of the matter!

1. Sit down with a pen and paper and make sure you won't be distracted for some period of time.

2. Write at the top of the page 'My U-Turn'. Divide the paper into three columns headed Feel, Think and Act.

3. In the Feel column, write down the four emotions you felt when you last felt depressed. It is important to first think of the situation in which you last felt depressed and remember exactly the emotions you felt at that time. As the feelings of that time wash over you, write them down. The list might look something like *sad*, *lonely*, *ashamed*, *humiliated*.

4. Divide the Think column into two headings: 'When and Why'; and 'Myself'. In the 'When and Why' column, ask yourself, 'When did I feel this way before and why did I feel it?', and think long and hard about every aspect of your

feelings before writing down an answer. The way to find out the true answer is to find the resonances that the particular emotion has with your past. If you remember the situations in the past when you felt this way and you can get a clear recollection of those past situations that resonate with the present difficulties, you have the answer to why you feel that way now. For example, if you wrote *sad* in the Feel column, you might write, 'Because I feel like I did when I was twelve and my mother died.' If you wrote *lonely*, you might write, 'Because it feels like when I started my new school and I didn't have any friends.'

5. In the Myself column, write down the opinions of yourself that these feelings evoke – both the past feelings and the present feelings. For example, beside the feeling *sad* you might write, 'I hate myself because I was responsible for her death.' Beside the feeling *lonely* you might write, 'I don't deserve to have any friends.'

6. In the last column – Act – look at the opinion of yourself expressed in the Think column and do something about it. This can be by *confrontation* or *sublimation*.

   With *confrontation*, the idea is to choose an action that is a direct thrust against the self-ideation (the thoughts about yourself) in the previous column. If that column said 'I hate myself', go and do something that you would only do for yourself if you really liked yourself. Treat yourself to a present, or ask yourself, 'What would I like to do if I liked myself?' and then go and do it.

   Alternatively, instead of confrontation use *sublimation*. If you wrote, 'I don't deserve to have any friends' in the Think column, find a way to help other people make friends, for example joining a volunteer group that visits the elderly and helps them make friends with someone. The important thing is that the action is related to the opinion of yourself revealed in the Think column, and that the action you take fights back against it. It is not enough to say, 'I don't really hate myself' or 'I really do have good friends'; the point is to act as if you don't believe your low opinion of yourself, and by simple repetition of that act you will come to believe that your former opinion of yourself is false.

7. The trick of the situation is to work through each stage of the U-turn. A quick, glib answer at each stage will only produce false solutions that will not work in the long term. Use the depressive feelings you have had to reveal what you truly think about yourself, the underlying opinions of yourself that govern your daily existence, and until now have determined what you can and cannot do. Then choose actions carefully, ones that confront the issues raised by those opinions. If the actions you choose are too easy, they probably aren't the right ones to help you complete the U-turn. There is an element of courage required to do things that don't match your opinion of yourself, and that courage must come from a desire to change and a need to rid yourself of the pain you are suffering.

Depression as an experience is profound, intense and debilitating. It can take over our lives and dominate them. The point about it is not what the experience is like, which is uniformly bad, but what can be got out of it, which is very variable. We owe it to ourselves not only to recover, but also to learn. Otherwise the entire experience and the suffering are meaningless. What a waste. What an opportunity. When we go through a period of depression it is often emotionally mixed up with tremendous feelings of anxiety, and we will deal with anxiety in the next chapter.

6

Fear and Anxiety

> We do not have to lead our lives crippled with fear: there
> are ways to defeat it

The Origins of Fear

Little children like a light left on in their bedroom at night
so that they don't get frightened in the dark. What are they –
and, indeed, we – frightened of in the dark? We don't really
know. The bogeyman, the banshee, and all the other monsters
that populate the nether regions of children's minds, represent vague notions of evil and malice rather than specific
ghoulish beings.

Somewhere between birth and self-awareness comes along
a badly-formed but definite sense of fear and apprehension
that transcends culture, types of people and generations. We
all know exactly what it is but we are unable to explain it
completely. We can all describe the cold sweat, the palpitations, the dry mouth, the surge of awareness that fear and
anxiety bring, yet are less able to describe its psychological
component, the despair and dread, the dreadful apprehension and the conviction of doom. And there is a conviction
of doom, of a terrible trauma, of grievous harm, of dreadful
change or even of death.

Where in our own psyche this fear originates is a matter of much speculation. Some talk of the terrors a young infant experiences – the separation anxieties that cement mother–child relationships – and claim that these lead us on to other fears. Others talk of birth anxieties, of fear originating at the time of birth as we are abruptly expelled from the warm enveloping pool of our mother's womb into the cold, harsh realities of external life, along a rather crushing pathway and after a lot of stress. Even more extremely, some talk of traumas encountered in previous lives, of negative experiences and upsets from many years and many lives ago. Some 'therapists' advocate rather exotic experiences like rebirthing (reliving the pangs of birth) or 'former life therapy' (awakening the traumas of our former lives in order to rid ourselves of the origin of our present-day fears and anxieties). We can do no more than speculate as to the truth or otherwise of these interesting theories. No one can say for sure if these exotic origins of our 'natural' fear are true or not, just as nobody can prove that God exists. The only comment I would make is that if someone wants to have a rebirth, they should call on another doctor to deliver them!

Original Fear?

Stephen King is a world-renowned author. His many horror stories have made him one of the world's best-selling writers. He writes about vindictive automobiles, pyromaniacal schoolchildren, mad men in old hotels, mad women with homicidal tendencies and just about every variation on themes of horror that his fertile imagination can muster. He wrote a long and detailed preface to one of his books outlining his own development as a writer, his fascination with fear and his theories about the origin of the fear aroused by horror stories. He believes that the fear is essentially a fear of death, which is manifested in numerous ways and distributed widely in the depths of our brain. It is an interesting thought and may explain some of the terror evoked by his weird imagination, but it doesn't explain the fears that originate and are manifest at an age when we don't have a concept of death, or indeed a full concept of life or our own existence. Thus we can accept that some or a large part of our adult fears may come from a fear of death, a fear of no longer existing, of our being not carrying on, but it is going too far to say that it is a complete and comprehensive answer to the question of the origin of fear. Certainly in the midst of a panic attack, the fear of impending death may be a major focus, but that is not the same as saying that it is the actual real fear at the centre of the panic attack.

Many experiences in our lives produce fear and anxiety and are a necessary part of growing up and of change. We are all afraid before an important exam and the fear is legitimate, for we might fail and harm our career. We are all afraid of embarrassment and of humiliation in public and we all start off with a fear of public appearances and public speaking. If we have suffered in a particular manner, such as being the victim of a violent husband, we are left with a fear of physical violence and often of being alone and vulnerable. If we have lost someone who was close to us, by death or separation, we are left with a fear of further loss of others close to us and of ending up being alone. Almost every fear we have is linked to our own experiences and how we reacted to them.

There is no doubt, however, that the fear of death *is* a biggie, and it may be a fear that underlies many others. Many years ago I went on a holiday to Spain with three friends. Two of the four of us went swimming one day and without being aware of it we were swept out to sea by an underlying current. I realised that something was wrong and started to swim back to shore, which by now was about a hundred metres away. I looked around for my friend and eventually saw him struggling about twenty metres away from me. I started shouting and waving my arms, trying desperately to get the attention of someone on the shore. After about five minutes of shouting and screaming for help, a Spanish man on the shore noticed and started swimming out to us. By now my friend was in serious difficulty and began to go under. I reached him and, with great difficulty, held him up until the man was close by and then I let him go. Now I knew my friend was safe, I started back to shore. But I found myself getting more and more tired and I too began to slip under the turbulent waters. I was going under for the second time when I felt my legs brush against something and found I was being washed onto a crop of rocks. I slithered and fell on the rocks and was pushed back and forth for what seemed like an eternity, until my legs and arms were cut and bleeding. Eventually I managed to haul myself onto the rocks and then over them on to dry land. Exhausted, coughing, spluttering and half covered in blood, I lay on the beach and got my breath back, eventually recovering enough to go over to where my friend lay semi-conscious on the beach, and to help call an ambulance.

My friend recovered in hospital and was discharged two days later none the worse for his ordeal. As for me, I never forgot the experience and how close to death we both were. It affected me in a way that was both subtle and profound. Somehow things never seemed to be as bad after that experience. While some things that people said or did to me were upsetting and would often make me anxious, nothing ever fundamentally disturbed me as things had before the experience. It was as though I had faced death and seen what it was like – and it really wasn't all that bad after all. Death became just an absence of life and a much easier concept to handle. A lot of my fears about many things in my life and my future died that day, and when times get tough I just think of the alternative to living, the alternative outcome to that day, and things just drop back into perspective. I don't regret the experience, frightening as it was. What I learned that day was that if you face the worst and it isn't that bad, you can face anything.

Learning Fear

The real origin of fear and anxiety is often lost in the welter of physical and psychic sensations that surround the experience. The real origin may indeed be in childhood ghosts and ghouls or in later major jolts such as parental death or separation, or may even be in our present-day stresses and anxieties. There may indeed be no real origin or focus for them and they arise in us as simply and straightforwardly as our joys and pleasures. We may even pick up the tension and anxiety of those who surround us, especially when we are growing up and absorb them, sponge-like, into ourselves and call them our own.

A 25-year-old man once told me his story. He was intelligent, articulate and well educated. He had left school at sixteen and had been unemployed and practically unemployable since. His entire existence was crippled with anxiety, fear, palpitations, sweats and panics. He could barely go outside his own home without suffering intense misgivings and worries about his own safety. He hadn't committed any crime or misdemeanour, and hadn't offended people around him – he was simply afraid of being alive. He had a history of dreadful panic attacks that came upon him at various irregular times and no specific places. He would suddenly become crippled with fear and anxiety and have to go home. Even at home, where he felt reasonably safe and sound, his life was made a misery by his indecision and doubts – he was so afraid that he could barely go outside the door to get a loaf of bread. And he had had no major upsets to deal with in life: his parents were alive and treated him well; he had not had an unhappy childhood; he was not beaten up and abused; he wasn't on drink or drugs. It wasn't until I asked him in detail about his family that I got a clue as the potential origin of problems. 'What's your father like?' I asked. 'He's just like me,' he replied. 'He hasn't been outside the house in years because of his nerves. I just picked it up from him.' He may well have been right, for I was unable to find a better explanation.

Trying to identify the fundamental cause of anxiety can be very difficult. It is often lost and obscured both in other numerous fears and the emotional cul-de-sacs that pervade the mind when very anxious. Not only do worries get lost in the maze, they may actually transform themselves totally and we can end up saying 'Eureka! I know what it is!' at totally the wrong problem. For example, I have known the understandably anxious and uptight wives of alcoholics to expend a vast amount of energy worrying about their neighbours' and relations' awareness of the problem rather than focusing on the actual cause of the anxiety itself – their husband's drinking. One very anxious lady was absolutely obsessed and visibly distressed about a scar on her left shin while her children were out on the streets joyriding and stealing from shops. It's not that she didn't care – she just didn't see the tricks her mind played, twisting the stress from one problem and turning it on to another lesser one.

Useful Anxiety

There is a place for stress, fear and anxiety in our lives. If there were none, we would still be living in caves, eating raw meat and wearing mammoth skins. It's what gives us an edge, it's what gets things done, it's what gets us off our ass and doing things. If we were perfectly content, we would be perfectly lazy. Anxieties represent badly-formed but necessary coping mechanisms for the vagaries of the world. Life requires us to constantly adapt to change, and fear and anticipation of change help us to become aware and cope with it when it happens. In small quantities it's great; in large ones it's crippling.

There is a certain point an anxiety crosses when it ceases to be useful and becomes a liability. That point is quite hard to define and varies from person to person and from situation to situation, but it is nonetheless a definite point. Subjectively we may be the worst judge of where that point is. We are often far more capable of putting up with anxiety than we care to admit and thus if we had our own way we would suffer little or no anxiety and consequently get little or nothing done in life. It is not too difficult to see when anxiety gets the upper hand in someone else's life; it is usually written in their faces and in their actions – they are miserable. It is not so easy to say when it gets the upper hand in our own lives, because it feels quite similar when we are close to the 'safe' side of the dividing line and when we are on the other side, but the degree of function and control we have over our lives differs greatly. When we are too anxious we simply can't do anything because of it.

A tax consultant I knew led quite a stressed life. A quiet, reserved man, he found it increasingly difficult to cope with the demands of his clients, his work colleagues and his family. He was made a partner in his firm, and took on more responsibility. As his anxiety grew, his work performance began to deteriorate, and he had to put in more hours to achieve the same amount. Eventually it all became too much for him and he ended up in a psychiatric ward. His partners were astounded. 'How come you never told us how stressed you were?' they asked him. 'I've always been anxious,' he replied. 'It was only recently I found out how bad I had got, and by then it was too late to bring myself back. I had no idea it was getting so bad.'

Types of Anxiety

The world of psychiatry divides fear and its accompaniments into a number of different headings – generalised anxiety, panic, phobias, and obsessions and compulsions. They are all variations on a common theme; they are similar in their subjective experience; and they often blend into one another. They differ in the outward manifestation of the inward fear and the degree of that manifestation.

Generalised anxiety is another name for pervasive, deep fear; its psychological and physical components are intertwined. *Panic* refers to an intolerable degree of anxiety that often comes in waves or attacks and usually later fades in intensity. It readily shades into anxiety. *Phobias* involve avoiding objects or places due to an association between that object or place and fear. It could be regarded as a coping mechanism – avoidance gone wrong and taking over a person's life. *Obsessions* and *compulsions* are constant intensive repetitive thoughts and actions that represent another coping mechanism gone wrong – the effort to avoid fear by repetition of various thoughts and actions becomes as big a problem as the fear itself.

Thus the coping mechanisms become problems, and the anxiety gathers momentum through an inability to tackle and, often, an inability to recognise the causal fear. How each of us develops and tackles (or fails to tackle) a fear is determined by our personality and our previous coping mechanism, not by the circumstances we find ourselves in, or indeed the type of stress we undergo. The source of these stresses is varied but their expression or manifestation tends to run along lines that are ordained by ourselves, or at least by our character traits. All of us experience great stress and anxiety at some points in our lives, usually involving fear of the future, fear of the consequences of actions or omissions, and fear of the unknown. It is how we cope with that stress that determines the manifestation of that anxiety on the surface.

Generalised Anxiety

Ordinary fear – or generalised anxiety – and panics are slightly different from phobias and obsessions. Here the fear is non-specific and its manifestations more varied. If a phobia is a singular fear, in generalised anxiety the fear becomes universal. Fear is like flu – it spreads rapidly. Anxiety about an exam raises the body's and the mind's arousal level, and the anxiety spreads to include fear of the future, fear of losing your friends, fear of being embarrassed, fear of being disliked, in short fear of everything and about everything. Concentration goes, and the ability to think clearly disappears. The world becomes malevolent instead of friendly, and problems become insurmountable. Every molehill becomes an Everest, and every task a trial. At a crescendo this can be panic, but a generalised anxiety can be almost as unbearable and much more prolonged. The spiral of fear is not only feeding itself, but it also defeats itself and its purpose. If anxiety is the body's defence mechanism against stress – designed to heighten awareness and arousal and prepare us for fight or flight – when it gets to this stage it is clearly counter-productive.

Panic

There is a component to fear that is akin to holding on to a cotton thread hanging over a balcony on the forty-third floor, and then letting go of the thread – before it breaks. There is an element of letting go, of giving in to fear, that is at the origin of a full blast panic attack. There is almost a voluntary component to it all, if a horrible experience like a full panic attack can be called a voluntary experience. Panic has all sorts of definitions but it basically involves a dreadful set of physical symptoms together with an immersion in a sea of fear that feels like Armageddon. Waves of unbelievably acute suffering engulf the mind and all reasonable control over the self is abandoned. Panic is as appallingly difficult to go through as it is easy to say. The entire mind is as suffused with fear as the body is drenched with sweat. The origin of the panic is utterly lost in the experience, and it is the intensity, not the origin, that remains in the memory later. The sufferer completely gives in to the fear and there appears to be no escape from it. There is no thought but the desire to get it all to stop.

Pauline, a thirty-year-old researcher, described a panic attack to me:

> I stood in the supermarket and began to feel a wave of anxiety coming over me. I felt as if everyone was looking at me and I became very embarrassed. I felt my face flushing and my skin began to tingle. A feeling of tremendous fear came over me and I felt as if something terrible was going to happen. I was going to die or something. I began to hyperventilate and I felt like screaming, the fear was so strong. I felt I had to get out of there immediately, so I rushed to the door and didn't even bother to pay for the few things I had in my basket. I got outside into the parking lot and I didn't even know where I was, and I barely made it to my car. I fumbled with the keys and got in, and just sat there for what seemed like ages. Eventually things calmed down a bit and I got it together enough to start the car and get home.

The one certainty about a panic attack is that it will definitely cease and fade away, but it leaves a residue of apprehension and anxiety behind it, which is focused on not having to go through one again. Panic is the ultimate fearful experience, but it differs from other fears and anxiety not in quality but quantity. Panic is fear gone wild, out of control, and it is the lack of control that is the central experience of panic. The fear overtakes us as the self-control leaves us.

When an attack is over we have learnt little about the causes but a lot about our ability to tolerate one. Facing another one is a prospect we wouldn't wish on our own worst enemy, and especially not on ourselves. And yet we feel unequipped to prevent another one and we don't know the exact reason it came on us. So instead of finding out why we had a panic attack, we simply avoid the place or circumstances in which we got it. If the prospect of hanging is supposed to concentrate the mind wonderfully, then the prospect of a panic attack concentrates it just as well.

The second worst thing about panic and fear is that it can take over our lives, leading us to do certain things – and more commonly to avoid certain things – so that life is simply an existence centred on fear and avoidance. The worst thing about it is the fear itself!

Phobias

A phobia, or a very specific anxiety, is one in which the fear is focused on one object or one situation. The origin of the fear and where it ends up may have little to do with one another. Some phobias start as a result of a specific event that occurs at the same time as exposure to the phobic object, and the fear becomes crystallised upon that object. In post-traumatic stress disorder (a type of anxiety), a fear-inducing event such as a car accident leads to a subsequent fear of cars or of travelling. The logical mind might dismiss this association, and say that your chance of having another accident is one in a million, there is no need to be afraid of travelling in a car, but the mind is not a logical thing; it relies on its own emotional logic.

A telling thing about the origin of various fears comes across from looking at their cures. Fears and anxieties that come out in a specific way – such as a phobia – can be dealt with quite successfully by facing up to the feared object, and relaxing through the panic that it induces. Behavioural therapy for phobias is based on the principle of facing the feared object, either bit by bit or all at once, either with or without relaxation techniques, either accompanied or alone, and overcoming the fear by confronting it. Once it is fully realised that the feared object is not as fearful as it once was, the phobia can disappear into thin air, as if it never happened. In a similar way, panic can be helped by practising relaxation techniques before or during episodes, and these can relieve the worst excesses of the experience.

What this tells us is that fears as they are gone through may be unrelated to their origins, because they can sometimes be relieved without reference to and without resolution of their origins. Facing up to a life-crippling phobia such as agoraphobia – a fear of outside places and open spaces – can be very traumatic, but it can give the sufferer a vast reservoir of confidence and ability that should fuel them should they have to face such an experience again. The thing that really has to be tackled is the fear itself, not merely the object that is feared.

The success of techniques that involve gradually facing fears bit by bit and getting used to the object of fears shows us that fears build up in steps. They aren't a solid block. There is a spiral build-up of fear and the anticipation of fear, which starts as a simple squeak but gathers momentum and becomes a roar. The anticipation is probably the biggest component; this is the fuel for the momentum of sensations that eventually becomes impossible to face. If we are capable of tackling something we are afraid of when it is small, we simply extinguish this 'building up' in its infancy. If we avoid tackling that something, or if there is no apparent way of dealing with it and we don't want to face it, we miss an opportunity to prevent the crippling ascendancy of fear.

Courage is not tackling something the world finds fearful, but tackling something that *we* find fearful, and finding courage sooner rather than later can prevent a lot of misery. Courage has been famously described as 'grace under pressure'. I think that is rubbish. Courage is facing what you fear most, and that is a different thing for each of us. The most commonly used mechanism to treat phobias – systematic desensitisation – involves little amounts of courage being used on each occasion to tackle a hierarchy of fears in order to achieve a hugely courageous tackling of a major fear at the end.

One man I met had a terrible fear of spiders. He couldn't go out into his garden for fear he might meet one. He was initially shown a small photo of a small spider, and got used to it. He was then shown a photo of a large spider, and got used to that. Next he was placed in a room with a spider in a jar at the other end of the room, and after some initial panic, he became relaxed about that. Eventually, by taking things bit by bit, he was able to let a spider crawl over his hands without so much as sweating. He had overcome his fear, bit by bit, and was overjoyed at his own success.

Obsessions

When I was a boy scout I used to go on lots of hikes and walking expeditions. On one occasion a group of eight of us went for a day trek in the Wicklow Mountains south of Dublin at around Easter time. The weather started fine, but – being Ireland – it soon deteriorated into a mixture of squalls and sleety showers. The second day found us trekking over a mountain and getting caught in the most ferocious snow-storm, pelting us in the face and making us dive into our rucksacks for our warmest jumpers and best wet gear. The storm lasted about seven hours and we spent that seven hours trudging around in three feet of snow completely blinded by the swirling flakes and ubiquitous grey cloud. Every step was like weightlifting with your legs and every minute passed slowly, like a watched clock. Fatigue ached through every muscle and joint, and every time we took a little break and just collapsed in the snow for a few minutes, it required a gargantuan effort to start over again.

The previous Saturday night I had seen the comedy duo of Morecambe and Wise sing a silly song called the 'Alphabet Song' on the television: 'A – you're adorable, B – you're so beautiful, C – you're a cutie full of charms ...' and so on. Gradually, as we marched on, I sang that part of the song over and over again in my head to relieve myself from the utter misery I was going through. It just repeated itself after each line and eventually I was able to drift away mentally, to some extent, from my surroundings. Well, I survived – just about (we ended up half a mile from where we had started after a fifteen-mile hike) and gradually recovered my physical and mental strength. But it took weeks, even months, to get that ridiculous song out of my head. It simply wouldn't go away, and popped into my mind almost every day, all day. Even today, many years later, it still comes back into my head recurrently and insistently whenever I'm undergoing some mental or physical stress. If this particular obsessional thought served its purpose all that time ago, it has certainly overstayed its welcome!

If the treatment of phobias and avoidance is to face up to the fear, the treatment for obsessions and compulsions is a bit more difficult. One method is to drown an obsessional thought with another forced conscious one. Every time I heard that silly song in the back of my mind, I immediately forced myself to think of a few lines from another silly song and, concentrating on that, I forced the two obsessions into competition. The equilibrium thus established seemed to help them fade from consciousness and stop intruding into my thoughts. It was a remarkably successful manoeuvre and I have used it successfully over the years with various repetitious worries and obsessions.

Stopping compulsions – repetitive mannerisms or actions that are difficult to stop – often involves another person, usually a therapist, stopping the sufferer performing the ritual whenever the urge gets too great. Thus the compulsion is tackled in itself, and the underlying motivating stress can then be tackled in its own right at a later time.

A more intractable example of obsessive thoughts and compulsive actions was a young woman who came into hospital complaining of an inability to get anything done in her life. She was a forty-year-old single lady who held a responsible post as an administrator in a hospital. She did her job well, with an attention to detail that would leave most administrators far behind. She was consumed by cleansing rituals in her home that ruled her life and paralysed her ability to do anything outside her work. She kept her house spotlessly clean, and spent hours cleaning the bathroom, the kitchen and the bedroom to remove all traces of dirt and all the 'germs'. She spent at least half an hour in the shower both before and after work, scrubbing herself clean, convinced that she was contaminated and dirty. She washed her hands twenty or thirty times every day until her hands were red and raw from the soap and water. Her thoughts and actions were consumed by fear of dirt and of cleansing rituals, and she was incapable of dealing with all the normal facets of daily existence.

All through this she worked at her job and somehow managed to perform at this to a very high level. Eventually, however, it all got too much and she sought psychiatric help. It took a short stay in hospital, some antidepressant medication and behaviour therapy before this lady began to cope with her problems. The solution in her case involved hard work in not giving into her rituals, which she had originally developed to cope with little stresses, and focusing her energies elsewhere. She did very well in the long run, but it was an uphill struggle.

Curing the problem of a 'coping' mechanism gone wrong gives temporary, even extended, relief. It may even 'cure' someone of their phobias or compulsion. A resurgence of the underlying stress, or even a difficult period that causes the same degree of emotional turmoil, can produce a relapse. It may even return out of the blue, with no apparent precipitating factor. The reason the problem comes back may be hard to find, but we should not be particularly surprised if it does. Our coping mechanism is quite simply built into our personality make-up, and that can be reactivated, just as the ability to ride a bicycle can be reactivated even after a long time.

Dealing with It

A thirty-year-old man I once treated told me how he grew up in a very deprived area of Dublin, and he spent all his life in the area. His family were very close to him and were individually and collectively involved in drugs, drink and crime of every sort. He himself was a drug addict who abused heroin and had a series of convictions for petty crime. All the time he was highly anxious, fearful and depressed. Indeed it was his childhood anxieties that made him drink heavily in the first place, as he found that drinking alcohol relieved his social fears.

One day, during his twenty-fifth year, he decided that he had had enough. He threw the various friends and family who were sponging off him out of his flat and thought about his life. He stopped drinking, stopped taking drugs and took control of his situation. He gradually became less anxious and fearful and more content with the way he was managing his life. When I met him he was single, unemployed and still living in the same area. But he wasn't being trodden on by anyone. If his family tried to borrow money from him, he told them where to go. He wasn't crippled with anxiety or a victim of stress, he was doing fine, thank you. He had got rid of the things that caused his fears and he was fighting fit for the rest of life. He had a long way to go, but he was determined to make it. This is an example of managing the situation to manage the reaction.

What can you or I do when we are stuck in the throes of a dreadful and crippling anxiety, an all-pervasive fear, and we don't know the first place to start to tackle it?

The first thing we have to do is to acknowledge that there is a problem, and accept it. If we are in a situation where fear is dominating our lives and our thoughts, we have to admit to ourselves that this is the truth of the situation. After we accept that there is a problem, we should want to do something about it. Not doing anything means that the problem festers and grows and becomes more difficult to tackle in the long run.

The essential thing about combating fear is knowing that there are two parts of the journey. Before we start, we need to divide fear into the meaning of fear and then the fear itself. Then the first part of the journey is the facing down of the fear itself and of its various manifestations. The second part is the journey to understand the meaning of the fear and the reasons it comes to a head. We can use the principles of the U-turn to turn the situation around from one of helplessness to one of control of the situation and ourselves. There are four ways of starting off on the U-turn – relaxation, advice, escape and exercise – and once these have been done we can start on the second part of the journey.

1. Relaxation

The first thing to do is relax. Learn to relax and practise it. There are numerous ways of doing this, and finding the way that best suits us can be a lifesaver. Relaxation courses are run from local community centres, and often psychiatric hospitals. Yoga, t'ai chi, and Pilates are all methods of relaxation that involve movement as well as calming down. Relaxation books, CDs, tapes and exercises are all highly useful if used regularly. Meditation, especially if learned correctly and practised regularly, can be wonderfully relaxing. Mindfulness, really a form of meditation, is a modern method of an ancient technique. All these techniques are designed to calm the mind and body and help put the brakes on the spirals of anxiety and fear. Learning a technique on a course or from a book, CD or download can be wonderfully beneficial, and can be practised until perfected and then used either regularly or simply when 'stressed out'. They are wonderful in the short term and quite useful in the long term.

The best way to practise relaxation and start on your anxiety U-turn is to try this method. First lie down on a comfortable bed or couch and stretch out. Make sure that the room you are in is quiet and that you will not be disturbed by anyone for half an hour. The first aspect to get right is your breathing. Clear your mind of any extraneous thoughts, and focus completely on your breathing. Close your eyes and try to relax. Notice the pattern of your breathing and concentrate on the rhythm of the breaths in and out. Slow the pace of breathing down to a quiet, slow pace that is enough to give you oxygen. Start to count with every breath: 'one, two' with every breath in, 'three, four' with every breath out. Keep coming back to that simple count every time your mind wanders away from the simple breathing pattern and starts to think about your worries. Keep a mental picture of the air flowing in and out of your nose as you count in the gentle pattern 'one, two' and then 'three, four'.

Next choose a part of your body, say your left leg. Squeeze the muscles of your left leg very tightly for a count of four, right through the breathing cycle. Then slowly relax the muscles in the left leg completely, letting the whole leg sink slowly into the bed, heavy and relaxed.

Now concentrate on that leg, and on making it completely relaxed. Mentally picture the leg as it slowly becomes heavier and heavier and sinks further and further into the bed. If you are being successful at this you will experience a kind of faint pins and needles feeling in the leg, as your mind releases control of it and allows the tension that is always there, and which you don't normally feel, to slip away. When the leg is completely relaxed it should feel heavy and almost useless, and activating it becomes a bother. This whole process may take a few minutes and it is important to keep concentrating on your 'one, two', 'three, four' breathing all the way throughout.

Now move on to the next part of your body – perhaps your right leg – and start the whole process again, first tensing the muscles, then relaxing them, then concentrating on letting the whole leg go. Work your way up your entire body: the left and then the right thigh; the buttocks; the abdomen; left and right forearms; left and right upper arms; head and neck; and finally the face. The whole process should take about twenty minutes if done properly. Don't skimp on the process by simply doing the muscle relaxation – be sure to do the full 'letting go'.

The last part of the process is to return to the first part. Concentrate on your breathing, counting your breaths and visualising the air passing in and out of your nostrils. If the whole exercise is done properly you will not feel sleepy, but alert and fully relaxed, and concentrating not on worries but on breathing. You should do this exercise once a day for the rest of your life. It will fuel the mental motors that will get you round the U-turn.

2. Advice

The second way to start off the U-turn is to get sound advice and, if necessary, proper medication, be it tranquilisers or even antidepressant medication, from a doctor or psychiatrist whom you can trust. He or she may be able to see and point out to you things that aren't immediately apparent to you in your heady onrush of anxious turmoil. It may be possible to get some practical hints from him or her about handling different stressful situations that feed the anxiety. At worst, even an objective opinion can take the sting out of some of our more outlandish but subjectively realistic fears. Appropriate medication can be extremely useful for taking the edge off anxiety and diminishing fear. Even if the response is only temporary, it can calm us down enough to begin to try to tackle the fundamental causes of our worry.

3. Escape the Situation

The third thing we can do sounds very simple but may be very difficult in practice. We should get away from the situation that is directly causing our fear and anxiety. We can do all the courses we want, we can take all the pills in the world, we can get all the good advice we can take, but if we are stuck in a fearful and anxiety-provoking situation, we will never get fully better – we will only cope better. We do not need constant mental or physical battering at any stage in our lives – life's too short. We simply have to get out of the situation, if only for a while, to relieve the stress and put things in perspective.

Sometimes the solution to fear and anxiety is staring us in the face, and we owe it to ourselves to at least try it. In a later chapter I will deal with tackling what is often the biggest problem of all – the fear of change. Inertia is one of the biggest factors in maintaining anxiety and if we tackle a situation rather than letting sleeping dogs lie, it can turn our life around. Not tackling it not only maintains our anxiety but makes us hate ourselves for not dealing with it, which only feeds the cycle further.

4. Exercise

The next component of treatment is exercise. Not gentle exercise, but robust, regular, sweat-inducing cardiovascular exercise. The level of exercise required is at least forty-five minutes of significant exercise three times every week. The type of exercise can be simple, such as running or jogging on the road or in a gym; it can be cycling, swimming or rowing; it can be tennis, squash or badminton; it can be a team sport like soccer or basketball – but it has to be very regular and it has to be strenuous. Just walking the dog slowly for fifteen minutes every other night simply won't be enough. Of course you may have to build up this level of exercise over time – you don't want to get a heart attack while you treat your anxiety – but in this situation quantity is quality. Frequent, sweat-inducing, effortful exercise banishes anxiety.

The Next Stage

The four stages mentioned above are the components of the start of the U-turn, but by no means the whole journey. The next part of the U-turn is both the easiest to say and perhaps the hardest to do. *We have to find the real cause of the fear and anxiety and face it.*

If the fear doesn't come directly from an obvious situation, like some of those mentioned above, it can be quite difficult to find the real source of the fear. The most pervasive fears known to human beings are the fear of change and, especially, the fear of the unknown. Even the fear of death can be defined as fear of the unknown. Fear occurs at transitions, changes from one situation to another, progress and explorations. Fear of the future, of 'what might happen if ...' is universal. Fear of the unknown is so strong that it prevents millions of people grasping a situation and changing it. 'Ah, the divil you know', we say, 'is better than the divil you don't.'

Grasping that fear, facing up to possibilities and probabilities of a situation, having a realistic assessment of what can or cannot be done – this is the essence of managing fear and anxiety.

Facing up to the possibility of the worst outcome of a situation enables us to look at the situation with a realistic, not an emotional, eye. If we are aware of the worst, we are better equipped to decide what is best. Refusal to see reality, refusal to face the unacceptable and undesirable leads to unnecessary anxiety and increases our fear of change. If we wallow in it, if we are aware of it, we can't be frightened of it. The wonderful thing about all this is that it can be done mentally, before it needs to be done physically. Thus we can pre-empt any emotional disappointments or problems associated with the unknown by making them known.

The U-Turn: Self-Mastering Techniques

We can help ourselves face our fear by a very simple U-turn technique.

1. Find the usual quiet place where you can be alone for a period of time.

2. Take a pen and paper. Write at the top of the page, 'Fear – My U-Turn'.

3. Divide the page into three columns: Feel, Think and Act.

4. Under the heading Feel, try to recall the feelings you had the last time you were in a fearful situation, or the last time you had a panic attack. The best way to do this is to imagine yourself in the same situation and try to recall the events that led up to the feeling of fear. It is important to distinguish between the physical feelings and the psychological feelings that you went through. Make a list of the psychological feelings. For example, the first feeling you might

have had was *fear of death*. The next one might have been a tremendous feeling of *embarrassment*. The next one you might write down could be *anxiety*, and so on. You only need to list the first four feelings.

5. Under the heading Think, think about the worst thing that could provoke each feeling listed in the Feel column. The object of this is to try to discover the things we fear most and to find out the worst thing that could happen to us. In doing this we may recall the frightening incident that produced this fear in the first place. We may recall a traumatic injury, a fearful incident of physical or sexual abuse, or childhood anxieties about school or parents that can resonate across the years even when we have left our childhood far behind.

   We must take the fear that we find when we look for it and then take it to its logical conclusion. For example, if the feeling listed in the first column is *fear of death*, the worst thing that could happen to us is *death*. If the first column has *embarrassment* listed, we must think of the most embarrassing thing that *has* happened to us and then the worst thing that *could* happen to us. This might be, for example, 'Being unable to remember the words when speaking in public.' If we have put *anxiety* in the first column, we would have to think of the worst situation we could be in that would cause us anxiety. For example, that might be 'Being alone in the world.' The way we find out these things is by exaggerating the feelings we wrote down in the first column and then putting those dreadful feelings in a tangible context, a real situation.

6. In the third column, Act, we have to turn those situations around. Using the U-turn principles of *confrontation* or *sublimation*, we have to propose ways of facing those worst fears or of integrating them into our lives. If we have mentioned a fear of death in the Think column, we must devise ways of confronting death and making it vivid and meaningful for us. That may mean visiting graveyards and burial places of

long-departed relations. It may mean reading about death, about the way it can happen, and about death's spiritual meaning. It may mean visiting the scene of the death of a loved one and trying to find out what happened rather than blocking it out. If we have put 'Embarrassment when speaking in public' in the Think column, we have to go out there, find a public speaking course and practise speaking in public. If we have put 'Fear of being alone in the world' in the Think column, we have to spend time alone and confront the feelings of loneliness that that might cause in order to deal with it.

We have to wallow in the feared situation, become comfortable with it, and become familiar with it for us to face it down and overcome it. It is only if we cannot face the fear directly that we should try to sublimate it, and not face it directly but integrate it into our lives. For example, if we have a fear of being homosexual, it is not necessary to actually sleep with a partner of the same sex to be comfortable with the concept, but it is necessary to find out about homosexuality and talk to gay people in order to overcome that fear. The confrontation need not be total, and the sublimation need not be total, but it is necessary to become totally familiar with the fear in order to stop it ruling our lives.

Fear is anticipation gone wrong. If we face the fear, we take control. Thus the management and control of our fears and anxieties, our phobias and our obsessions, our stresses and our worries, is essentially in our own hands.

One fear that can be especially hurtful is the fear of criticism. We deal with what criticism is all about in the next chapter.

7

Criticism and Hatred

> Criticising someone reflects more on us than them

Criticism is considered an art form in some countries. In Soviet Russia, critics used to have to go to a critics' school for a number of years before they were allowed to inflict their views on the world. These were, of course, art and literary critics. In our part of the world, anybody can put pen to paper, start a blog on the internet, and waffle on about a play, movie, book or indeed a person, and then they too are 'critics'. What distinguishes these critics from the rest of the population is that they generally confine themselves to their own area of expertise. The rest of the population feels no such inhibition in our personal lives and we gaily criticise our fellow man and their actions in our daily conversations. We are all critics and we all criticise.

Why Do We Do It?

When we offer a critical opinion of someone, their actions or words, we are attempting to do a couple of things to them. First, if we say it directly to them, we are trying to make them change what they did or said, because it is our opinion that they were wrong and we are right. Second, and more important, we are trying to establish our superiority over them, and the degree of emotion we invest in the criticism reflects our personal feeling of being threatened that is inherent in what they did or said. It is because of our personal sensitivity and vulnerability in any one area that we bother to criticise somebody at all. The question of objectivity doesn't enter into it – it is purely opinion versus opinionatedness.

So when we feel like criticising somebody or their actions, we must first ask ourselves: why do we feel the need to bother? If we can understand the reason we need to bother, we begin to understand the motivation behind the vehemence of our opinion. If we are truly aware of the motivation, we may be better able to judge the opinion – our opinion – and see whether it is actually valid. If we still feel that our opinion is valid, then and only then do we have any right at all to criticise someone else. Generally, however, we never stop to judge the degree of rationality in our criticism and we just blast on regardless. This reflects not the correctness of our opinion but the degree of our emotional reaction. Criticism, especially heartfelt criticism, is never objective and it reflects on the critic much more than the criticised. The problem is that most people listen to the criticism rather than objectively regard the critic, and thus it becomes an established view in the listener's mind – even if it's complete nonsense.

A colleague of mine, let's call him Michael, was particularly critical of his boss, behind his boss's back. As far as Michael was concerned, his boss could do nothing right, and everything he did just showed how ignorant he was. Every day Michael was sniping and picking away at any action or decision the boss took, to such an extent that he undermined the proper functioning of the team we all worked in. Most of my colleagues believed Michael and began to have serious doubts about our boss's abilities. Finally someone was promoted from among our ranks. This produced a bad reaction from Michael, and gradually he began to criticise and pick at the new appointee. It was then we all began to realise that Michael's opinion wasn't as objective as we had thought, and that it reflected jealousy of his superior's position rather than an unbiased opinion as to his competence. However, it did take quite a while for us to realise just who was at fault – it is quite easy to look at someone else, especially a superior, and pull their performance to pieces. It is only when we are in that position ourselves, and have to perform as well or better than our predecessor, that we realise that our criticism may well have been unjustified.

How to Criticise

If we are the boss in a large workplace and we wish to instil fear and loathing in our staff, we can, of course, call them in, shout and rant at them, throw them out and get away with it – if that's what we want.

But if we feel the need to pass critical remarks about the appearance or actions of someone we know, and we are convinced that it is because we want them to change for the better – not just because they annoy us – we have to do it carefully. The one thing we cannot do is show the degree of emotion that prompted us to take action in the first place. Tact is what it is all about, and tact is all about hypocrisy. We must rid ourselves of our vitriol and concentrate on gentle and apt phrases to communicate what we want to get across. The object of the exercise is not to rid ourselves of emotion but to persuade someone else to change. That involves ensuring that we control our emotions or our irritation and that we don't inadvertently let them out through sarcasm or even an aggressive tone. If we can persuade someone that our primary concern is their good, and not venting our irritation, we have some hope of getting our message across without getting their backs up. Self-control is vital and self-indulgence is not on.

In ancient Greece they used to kill the messenger who brought bad news of lost battles. In modern days we don't usually get killed for making criticisms, but that is only because we have a thin veneer of respect for the law. You can rest assured that the recipient would often like to kill the giver.

Cecil Parkinson was a member of the British cabinet during the Margaret Thatcher era. He was a good-looking scoundrel with a modest amount of talent. He famously fathered a child with his mistress during his tenure, and essentially dumped both child and mother to save his career. The tabloid press in Britain hounded him for months, even years, demanding his resignation because of the scandal. He didn't resign and Mrs Thatcher didn't fire him. He was saved because of his loyalty and his ability to get on with one of the most notoriously difficult women of our time. She repeatedly appointed him to high office, despite the scandal. He was credited with a smooth tongue and an ability to suggest alternative opinions, and even criticise Mrs Thatcher without earning her enmity. By making it obvious to her that he had no resentment or dislike for her, and that he was unalterably loyal to her, he made it possible to drop in an idea or criticism that differed from her view without getting her back up.

Criticism Sticks

Criticism gives a false sense of superiority to the critic. We are at once enthralled by the words used to put down another human being, and we take them seriously. We are also in awe of someone who puts another person down, and we are impressed by them. We are also just a little bit afraid of them – we may not like them, but we generally respect them. Criticism is a quick way to a kind of social status but if it is overindulged in, it isolates the person as a crank.

Critical opinion sticks, perhaps partially, but definitely. If we wish to damage another person, we can start rumours and say negative things about them, and eventually a sullied reputation gets established. There are always two ways of looking at someone, especially someone exceptional or different. They can be regarded either positively or negatively, and it isn't very difficult to change a public opinion about a person from a positive to a negative one. Adolf Hitler realised this principle when he started persecuting the Jews in Nazi Germany. He took non-Jewish people's dormant anti-Semitism and so inflamed it by rumours and propaganda that he was able to institute first a pogrom and then an extermination plan against them without so much as a peep from the vast majority of the German people. This was raising criticism to the level of a philosophy, and using it to manipulate millions of people to bend to his will. And the frightening thing about it is that it wasn't that difficult to do. All it took was an institutionalised propaganda campaign of hate that was crude, simplistic and repetitive. Indeed, on one occasion, Hitler's anti-Semitic zeal got the better of him and he ordered a film to be made comparing Jews with rats – dirty, vile and hanging around sewers. This was too much for even the Nazi propagandists and they persuaded him to drop his insistence on this film's distribution in Germany, fearing that the audience would laugh at the analogy, and thereby ruin the carefully constructed campaign of hate. You can't fear and hate something you laugh about.

When George Bush Sr was running for the White House, he instituted a campaign against his opponent, the Democrat Michael Dukakis, based on associating him with a convicted murderer and rapist, Willie Horton. When he was Governor of Massachusetts, Dukakis had started a weekend release scheme for prisoners. Horton, who at the time was serving a life sentence for murder, took part in the weekend release programme. During one of those weekends, Horton committed assault, armed robbery and rape. The association between Dukakis and Horton's crime, which was established by a sustained series of television advertisements, stuck in the public mind and almost solely because of this Bush won the election. Most intelligent people looking at the advertisements would say that they presented a ridiculous analogy – that by voting for Dukakis they would be freeing more rapists and would become victims themselves. Yet Bush reversed a seventeen-percentage-point deficit and turned it into a four-point lead at the election a few months after starting the campaign. He succeeded on purely negative advertising. The architect of these ads, Lee Atwater, later apologised for his misrepresentation of Michael Dukakis, but only when he was terminally ill. This should serve as a very powerful reminder of the sticking power of a critical or negative opinion, and what occurs in politics can just as easily occur in private life.

Giving Criticism

Interestingly, the ability to criticise another, to that person's face, without building up steam and letting out a shriek of bad temper, is a very self-confident one. Generally we are so nervous and upset about crossing the socially accepted norms and being antisocial enough to make a personal criticism that we lose sight of what we actually want to achieve. We resent our victim for making us do this to them. We dislike being 'forced' into criticising them, and we generally take it out on them. We get caught up in our own self-righteousness and lose our objectivity. If we had enough confidence to let our opinion be known early on, before the problem built up into a major one, we wouldn't have gathered any emotional momentum at all.

Kingsley Amis, the British novelist, tells a story about interviewing an aristocratic fellow author on the radio. The radio producer, wanting to get some sparks into a rather banal interview, began interrupting them and telling them to do things differently. The aristocrat, nonplussed, simply told the producer to stop interrupting them or he would leave, immediately. The producer thought about it, realised that if the interviewee left he would have no show, decided it wasn't worth the risk, and shut up. Amis was very impressed with this display of aristocratic confidence. 'I would have to lose my temper in order to do that,' he recalled afterwards. Too often we have to lose our temper to get over our reluctance to criticise and then we end up throwing out the baby with the bathwater and achieving nothing.

Taking Criticism

If finding an easy way to give criticism is difficult, finding an easy way to accept criticism is well-nigh impossible. We all err, we are all human; therefore we are all due, and indeed need, criticism and correction throughout our lives. The fact that we need it doesn't make it any easier to accept when we actually get it. We are all just a little shallow, or vain or egotistical, and we want to believe we are better than we are. Criticism of any sort from any source is an affront to our own good opinion of ourselves, and this is very hard to take. If we are very depressed or lack self-confidence, criticism can drive us further down into ourselves, and make the path back even steeper. No one is exempt from a sensitivity to criticism and no one can take too much of it.

Valéry Giscard d'Estaing was President of France for seven years. During his time in office, a scandal erupted about his accepting diamonds as a gift from a corrupt African leader, the self-styled Emperor Bokassa of the Central African Empire. For four years after he left the presidency, he tells us in his autobiography, he was unable to look at a newspaper or watch the evening news for fear that somebody might be criticising him about that gift. Many years later he admitted in an interview that it had plagued him for years and had made his life a misery. It can scarcely have been a pleasant experience.

And that is what it can be like for someone who is the victim of sustained personal criticism: it is devastating. When we hear something negative about ourselves, we are stung. There is no way we can avoid the feelings of hurt and outrage that hit us. We cannot avoid the feelings, but we can control their expression. The first thing to do when we are criticised is to be quiet and listen. If we absorb and deflate the outrage, we have a reasonable shot at really hearing what is being said, and we might even learn something. If we react to the simple idea of actually being criticised, we learn nothing – we probably explode angrily against the critic, and end up hating them. A big waste of time for all concerned.

Judging Criticism

When judging a criticism, an hour or day or a week later, when our hurt subsides, we must also then judge the critic.

If they are a political opponent, a mortal enemy or an ex-spouse (is there a difference?), they may have an ulterior motivation for their criticism. They may wish to lessen people's opinion of us, and this is the reason behind what they are saying about us. They may also be saying something worthwhile, despite their antagonism, and they should be listened to and then dismissed if they are just spewing meaningless venom.

If they are our friends, however, or strangers who don't have any apparent reason to dislike us, we should sit up and pay attention to what they are saying. If at all possible we should ignore the way they say it, because if it is ungraciously expressed, they themselves have a problem. But that should not hinder us from listening to what they say. We owe it to them to at least pay attention to what they say and then judge it. We have no guarantee that their criticism is valid, just because they said it, and we shouldn't change dramatically at every small shadow cast upon us, but we should exercise our powers of reason to analyse what they are saying. Then, if we choose to ignore their criticism, at least we are ignoring it for the right reasons. We have no monopoly on correctness, so we might just learn something.

Two friends of mine, Jane and Patricia, had been friends for years. Jane was homely and sweet; Patricia was outgoing and a socialite. Jane would regularly invite Patricia round for dinner, but she never received an invitation in return. Patricia would get out and about but wouldn't bring Jane along with her when there was anybody else of interest around. One day it just became too much for Jane, and she sat her friend down and told her what she thought. 'You're a selfish cow,' she said. 'You've never invited me out with you after all the times I invited you.' Patricia stormed off in a huff, but thought about what her friend said. The following week she invited Jane for dinner – which she herself cooked. It was a start. She got past the hurt of receiving the criticism to get as far as judging what was said, which was quite an achievement for the selfish cow.

Hatred

We can learn a lot from well-motivated, or at least not purely vitriolic, criticism. As we get older, we tend to become more settled in our ways, less changeable, and we tend to become less tolerant of other opinions, and less gracious. If a criticism has the effect of stopping us in our rather rigid tracks and making us see actions and words more objectively, we actually ought to be grateful to our critics – they educate us. In general, however, we reward our critics with the one thing they surely don't deserve – our hatred.

It's no surprise that a multi-millionaire pop singer who takes his craft seriously – George Michael – should call an album *Listen Without Prejudice*, talking directly to the minuscule number of his critics and not to the hordes and legions of his fans. Similarly, some forty years after the Beatles broke up, Paul McCartney still resents the critics who claim that John Lennon was the musical genius, and McCartney the simple tunesmith. Criticism of any sort, even if it is well deserved, slices our self-confidence into shreds, and unless we are mature enough to handle our shattered pride and our volcanic resentment carefully, we invest all that emotion into dislike for the critic. 'How dare he say that!' overcomes 'Why did he say that?'

Facing Up to It

By turning all that hurt and resentment into dislike for the critic, we avoid facing up to the possible truth of what they are saying. What's more, we end up forgetting the reason for our dislike, and end up just hating the person or group blindly but intensely. If we are asked why we dislike them, we generally reply by describing the emotion we feel rather than the real reason.

One of the few people in life I have definitely disliked was one of my superiors in a hospital job I had a number of years ago. Having successfully irritated him once or twice, I was subjected to a degree of criticism and abuse far in excess of what I felt the misdemeanour warranted. Hurt, more at the tone than the words, I doubled my efforts and tried harder. When that produced no change in the level of criticism coming my way, I felt utterly undermined, lacking in confidence and unsure about the tiniest thing I did at work. The only comfort I had was that plenty of others shared my opinion of him, but that wasn't sufficient to piece myself back together. After I stopped working for him and moved on, I found myself unable to shrug off the intense dislike I felt. Despite recognising objectively that some of the criticism was appropriate, I was unable to absorb the emotion that came at me and I returned it as dislike. Let's face it, it's not easy to be truly objective about ourselves.

Criticism, both giving it and receiving it, are real emotional minefields. If we give it too strongly or receive it too strongly, we can end up ruining friendships, creating enmity and bitterness that end up lasting a lifetime. We owe it to ourselves, our critics and our victims, to give thoughtful consideration to what we say, and what is said to us. Then, and only then, can we abandon all reason and thoughtlessly indulge in all those wonderfully antagonistic emotions that lurk in the recesses of our minds.

How to Turn Criticism Around

There are a number of simple principles that you can adopt when receiving any sort of criticism that will make the criticism easier to bear and also deflect it away from you.

The first one is very simple but very difficult to actually carry out.

1. *Listen.* Deflect criticism with attentive listening. It takes a real boor to go on with continual criticism when you aren't answering back. Shutting up is vital. Not a word!

   If you are being criticised in the workplace or in a personal social context, ask the critic what you can do to improve or change the situation. Turn the situation round to a positive one. It is very hard for the critic to sustain criticism if you are agreeing with them and saying, 'What can I do about it?' *Never* allow the phrase 'But I only ...' escape from your lips. That can come later, when you have had ample time to adjust to what was said and to judge it objectively. Never try to defend yourself in the heat of the moment – unless it is a battle for power in which you have to strike back. In all other situations, sit back and take it. It will be better in the long run.

2. Pre-empt the criticism with a self-criticism: 'I know that you aren't happy with what is going on, and I want to change things – with your help.' Agree with the criticism, at least in public, and nod intelligently until the barrage is over. You don't have to agree with it in the long run, just the short run; and that makes it end all the quicker, as the 'giver out' feels less need to justify the criticism by repetition and emphasis.

3. Don't nod as if you agree and then give off irritated vibes as if you would like to strangle the critic. People pick up vibes like aggressive movements and angry gestures, and this may force them to double their criticism for emphasis. So sit tight and take it.

4. Don't reply immediately, unless you absolutely have to. Go away, absorb the information and the criticism, and then come back. If you respond straight away, the first thing to happen is that you will react with your emotions and not your sense. Take time out to judge the words spoken and not the manner in which they were spoken.

5. Always look at it from the other person's point of view. Look for a reasonable idea as to why they might want to criticise you, such as trying to get your job or revenge for something you did to them, and if there isn't a clear and explicit motivation, forget it and listen to what they say. You can probably learn from them.

The U-Turn: Turn Criticism into Education

The basic principle is simple. If you want to criticise someone, you have to remove the emotion and simply give the message that you want them to change. Having just examined how people find it difficult to take any criticism at all, how is it possible to give criticism without getting their back up?

1. First, decide if it is vital that the other person be criticised at all. Judge your own motivations, and if there is any hint that

you are doing this simply to dump on someone else or to try to get one over on them, forget it.

2. Remove all emotional components of the criticism before you give it. Make sure that what you have to say is completely dispassionate and not emotional barrage. One way to do this is to run it past someone outside the situation and see what they think. This can prevent you going too far in what you say or do.

3. Praise, then criticise, then praise again. Always think of how you can say something positive about the person before you say anything negative. If it is only a small positive thing, focus on that and exaggerate it if necessary before giving out to them. It is easier if you find something that is good about them and talk about that rather than invent it, because you can be at least partly sincere when praising them. It is absolutely vital to show the person that you are not just picking on them, that you don't 'have it in for them', and that you are criticising what they do, not who they are. You have to reassure them that you don't hate them before you can criticise with any hope of the message getting through. After you have criticised them you must praise them again to reassure them that the message is practical and not emotional: you don't hate them; you hate what they do.

4. When getting down to the nitty gritty of the message, always use the phrase 'I would have done it differently', not 'You did it wrong.' Using yourself as a standard takes the emphasis away from the person you are criticising and on to a manner or style of working or doing something. It removes the personal from your comments. The object is to get the message across, not to destroy the person. The object is to get the person to realise that there is a better way than what they have done until now. The object is to get the message across without getting the person's back up to such an extent that the message doesn't get implemented. Depersonalise their situation as far as possible and personalise

117

your own situation as much as possible. Use phrases like, 'If I were in your situation ...', and 'What I would do is ...' Gentle suggestion is far more productive in the long run than creating intense resentment by using a sledgehammer.

5. Separate the message from the person receiving it. Not 'You're a bad driver' but 'You drove badly on this occasion'; not 'You're lazy' but 'You could have worked harder on this job.' Emphasise the reasons for your disapproval, and do not emphasise the disapproval itself. Always give a reason for what you are saying – it must not be just your own opinion. Explaining the reason for what you are saying, and not lying in the process, will make it easier for the other person to accept your message in good faith.

6. Once you have got the message across, praise the person again.

7. If you have tried this method at least twice, and had no change or response, then just lose your temper at them and see if that gets you anywhere!

Giving and taking criticism is one of the minefields of life and of relationships. Doing it gracefully is a testament to good manners and effective communication. Taking it gracefully is a testament to good self-control.

In order to learn more about just what it is that predisposes us to many of the troubling emotions we have dealt with above, we have to deal with a major problem that afflicts many people throughout their lives – a negative self-image. We deal with this in the next chapter.

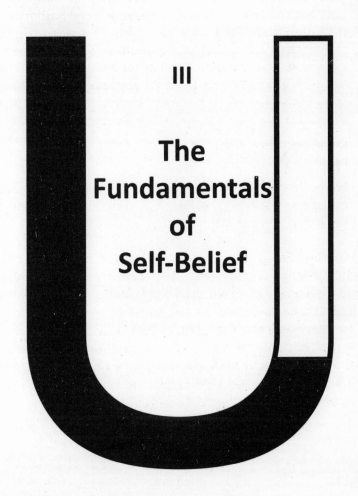

III

The
Fundamentals
of
Self-Belief

8

Self-Belief and Inferiority

> What we think of ourselves underlies everything we
> think and do

What do you think of yourself? What do I think of myself? Well, it all depends on what I'm doing and how I'm feeling at the time. If I have just had an argument with someone I love, I feel low, not very proud, and unsure of myself, and I generally don't have a very high opinion of myself. If, on the other hand, I have just told a great joke at a party and followed it up with an amusing tale of an encounter with my old boss, and everybody in the group is looking at me with shining appreciative eyes and laughing at what I said, I feel great; I feel good about myself and generally I feel very secure. What does that prove? That our opinion of ourselves follows the mood we are in?

Well, yes – but only in the short term. Much deeper and more important, our moods are a consequence of how we fundamentally feel about ourselves.

Self-Consciousness

'Self-consciousness' is a term that can only begin to convey a whole existence based on self-regard, on intensely monitoring other people's reactions, and searching for evidence to back up a negative self-opinion. Self-conscious people are not happy people; they live life with an added unpleasant icing over existence. Nothing is particularly pleasant because they can't drop the layer of self-consciousness to allow themselves to indulge in and enjoy any particular activity freely. Relaxation provides only temporary relief – even when it's achieved, which isn't easy or frequent. Every aspect of life is coloured and nothing is viewed objectively. Everything is viewed from a personal perspective, usually a negative one.

A pleasant young man in his early twenties came to me at my clinic. He had had a decent upbringing, supportive parents and a good education. He came from a modest background, but was trying hard to get on in life without causing too much trouble to anyone. He was enthusiastic about things, rather naive in his view of life, and he had a lot of problems.

His main problem came from his relationships with peers, and his difficulty in understanding where other people were coming from and what they wanted from relationships. Typically he would enter into a friendship with a lot of boyish enthusiasm, overwhelm his friend with too many demands and too much affection, and eventually alienate them by his overwrought efforts at being friendly. He had been bullied and teased at school, and didn't know how to fight back. He was thus left with a permanent fear of other people and with a self-consciousness that bordered on the paranoid.

He could not walk into a room where there was anyone else, either stranger or friend, without turning bright red and getting panicky. He was intensely obsessed with being well thought of by everybody and he tried too hard to be likeable. If he received even the mildest suggestion that could be taken as a criticism, he would be upset for days and unable to sleep or to function properly. His life was an absolute misery, and he was unable to start off either at a job or in a friendship without investing so much into its success that he took the slightest setback as total failure and would quit. Not surprisingly, when I saw him he was jobless and practically friendless. He was in a state of perpetual misery, and he couldn't escape from the feelings of self-consciousness that plagued his existence. He required a lot of help over a lot of time to get better.

Our opinions of other people are not objective things, no matter how clinical and detached we pretend to be. The vital factor in our opinion of other people is how we get on with them and, more important, whether we actually like them. If the ugliest, dimmest person in the world makes us feel they like us, we can forgive them a lot. When we relate to people, there is an unspoken but definite quality to the relationship that determines whether or not it will progress, and whether we like the person or not. That non-verbal quality is a projection of 'liking'. It is not simply pretending to like someone, not acting it, but actually feeling it. And that means we must take a genuine interest in other people in order to like them. It is not a matter of smiling at everyone you see, it is not a matter of being a good listener, it is not a matter of trying to be 'likeable'. These are good and useful characteristics and they might increase our short-term popularity, but the only way to get people to like us in the long run is to have an interest in them and to genuinely like them.

It is from a genuine affection for others that we begin to display those characteristics, such as consideration for others and thoughtfulness, that makes us attractive to others as an individual. It was very interesting that when I asked my self-conscious friend above what he thought of others he revealed that he was incapable of thinking about others without thinking of their opinion of him. It was almost as if he never even thought of what they were like as individuals or what they thought of life and the world around them, apart from what they thought of him.

How is it that murderers have friends or even lovers? Quite simply, if they convince somebody that they genuinely appreciate them, they can become friends despite the other person's knowledge of what they have done in the past. If the murderer hates himself, however, he won't be able to project any affection for another person, because he has no affection for himself.

A famous English serial murderer, Myra Hindley, who was convicted more than forty years ago of the most heinous and vicious child kidnap, torture and murder crimes in the history of British law, befriended a famous humanitarian peer, Lord Longford. He visited her in prison, became convinced of her new-found Christian faith and began to campaign for her release. The outcry against this campaign was understandably huge. Lord Longford himself could not understand why his campaign produced such a strong reaction, because he himself was convinced of the sincerity and faith of the child murderer. Thankfully his campaign did nothing except make him look stupid. But Hindley could not have persuaded this eminent man of her cause unless she believed it herself, and believed in herself. She had got over her self-esteem problems, and had been able to bring him round to her point of view.

It is more difficult for a self-conscious person to project liking for a person than an unselfconscious person, because they are caught up in a negative self-hating cycle, and cannot view either themselves or that other person objectively. If the other person picks up on a lack of 'liking' coming from the self-conscious person, he will have no desire to carry on the relationship. Thus the victim of constant self-obsession will unwittingly feed into the self-deprecatory cycle of the self-conscious, and confirm what he feels certain of – that he is not worthy of affection.

There is a vast difference between liking someone genuinely for themselves, and admiring someone for their superficial characteristics – especially if these are the characteristics we feel we don't have ourselves. If we admire someone, feel inferior to them and want to become like them, we may not actually like them at all. We may just be envious of them and, as we have seen, that is totally different. Most of us can think of some boy or girl at school who was 'it'. He or she was great looking, very sociable and had lots of friends, and had enviable success with the opposite sex. I don't know if we liked them a lot but I know that most of us wanted to become them, at least for a while. In those circumstances it would be difficult to project a genuine feeling of liking for them because what we felt for them was not affection but jealousy, a very different emotion.

How Do We Develop Our Self-Image?

So where does it all come from? Where does the fundamental self-image, either positive or negative, originate? Our self-image essentially comes from two sources, one internal and one external. The internal source is unconscious; we are not aware of its origins or its effects. The internal, core personal constructs come from deep down and long ago. As infants and little children we all firmly believed that we were the only important people in the world and that the whole world revolved around us. If that feeling was backed up by warm and loving parental security, our little world was complete. There were no threats on the horizon and nothing to challenge our good feelings about ourselves. If our early years were secure, we were granted a hard-to-shake inner core of self-belief.

The realisation that we are not all-powerful and not all-important sinks in via little battles with reality, without unduly disturbing our cosy world. If, however, we are suddenly thrust into the real world, perhaps through separation from our parents, illness and a long stay in hospital or, worse still, by neglect or abuse by our parents or people close to us, it can drill holes in our core of self-appreciation that we may never recover from. If, for example, a child loses their mother and is forced to take up a more responsible role than normal at an early age, they may be able to perform up to scratch in an external way, but lose out on the slow internal path to happy maturity.

It is well known that the pop star Madonna lost her mother when she was six years old. She remembers clearly her mother dying and she remembers going to her funeral. She dates all her fundamental attitudes to life and her difficulties and behaviours from that point. She has been an incredibly successful entertainer and is now one of the wealthiest people in show business. Yet we could interpret some of her behaviour as a result of losing all sense of personal value. She shamelessly plundered her Catholic upbringing, her sexuality and her own personal life for her performances. When she put herself on display in the documentary movie *Truth or Dare* she revealed not only her selfishness but also the contempt in which she held other people. She evidently didn't have much respect for her audience, and had no time whatsoever for the groupies or wannabes who hung around and imitated her every look and move. I suspect that she has no great respect for herself either, because anyone who would expose herself on film to that negative extent when she doesn't need to simply couldn't have a great opinion of her talents or of her fundamental self-worth.

Internal Factors

When we look back into our past we don't necessarily remember the internal factors that produce a healthy or an unhealthy way of viewing ourselves. The events, feelings and emotions that occur in early childhood happen at a time when language and memory are only just beginning to function.

Our experiences then are of a different texture from those that occur at a later age when we are able to use our intellectual skills to better appreciate what goes on around us and what happens to us. However, the vague early experiences do have an effect on us that is almost invisible if they are positive, but much more visible if they are negative. The positive, warm, enveloping experiences disappear in later life almost as if they never existed, but they leave behind an inner core glowing with security and self-appreciation. The fact that they are unconscious and we are essentially unaware of how they arose makes them more and not less important in the long run. No one hates themselves if they feel enough love.

There has to be a balance, of course. If someone is given absolutely unconditional regard, allowed to do anything and still receive encouragement, it leads to selfishness, gross self-love, and essentially a 'spoilt brat' personality. The Menendez brothers, a pair of wealthy playboys who lived in Beverly Hills, killed their parents with a shotgun one night in 1989. They spent the next six months spending their parents' money in a luxury-filled binge. They were spoilt rich kids, who had experienced little suffering and few problems in their lives. It looked as if the only thing that the parents did wrong was to give their children too much love and too much money, and make too few demands in return.

Conversely, Mary, a 35-year-old housewife and mother of three small children, came into hospital complaining of depression and an inability to cope. Her husband, who worked as a salesman, had an alcohol problem, and for ten years she had had great difficulty in coping with this. She described in great detail the uncertainty that hung over her and her future, and the frustrations she had in dealing with her home situation. Unusually, though, she described her husband as being off alcohol for the previous eighteen months and said that he had been kind and good to her since he stopping drinking. During the same period, while he was getting better and putting the alcoholic times behind him, she began to fall apart and find it all increasingly difficult to handle.

On gently exploring Mary's background, it became apparent that her problems went much deeper. She came from a very disturbed background, with an alcoholic father and an uncaring mother. 'I had to grow up quickly,' she said. 'There was no other way to handle it.' She recalled a childhood of great insecurity, trying as the eldest child to keep the younger children fed and washed, while coping with violence and disapproval from her parents. She escaped by marrying early, only to find herself falling into the same trap, with her husband's drinking problem. She managed for years and was just about able to cope when her husband stopped drinking. Then, she said, 'It hit me all of a sudden. I just felt so insecure and unsure of myself.' She had repressed all the suffering she had gone through over the years, and it was only when she was in a situation where she no longer had to just cope with things that everything came to the surface. It was then we began to tackle the problem of her poor self-image and her feelings of inadequacy. It was only then, after she stopped focusing on her husband's drinking problem and began focusing on herself, that she took the first steps on the road to recovery.

Those internal factors that govern our self-esteem may be deeply hidden and indeed undetectable, but they can have strong influences that can last a lifetime.

External Factors

The second area that looms large in terms of self-image lies not in internalised but in external factors. These factors are conscious factors and arise when we begin to develop self-awareness as a young child. Our interactions with the outside world, people and events – but especially people – influence our self-image. Kids who are fat or in some way 'different' can be mercilessly tortured by their classmates and end up with appalling feelings of inadequacy, despite all the love they get at home. Lord Byron, the Romantic poet of the early nineteenth century, was regarded as the most dashing and romantic figure of his day. He was handsome, famous, rich, and led a life of wonderful adventure and excitement. But he was prone to dreadful bouts of melancholy and depression, during which he questioned his own worth and his own life in the most exquisite verse. When a friend of his was asked to explain the mentality of his amazing friend, he replied, 'In order to understand him, you have to start with his club foot.' If we find it hard to believe that one little deformity might be the fundamental reason behind Byron's recklessness and his depressions, we have to remember that it is his image of himself that is important to him, and not the outside world's. If we understand that his self-image was created around the fact that he had a club foot and that he saw the other children as 'perfect', we can partially understand the rest of his life. Little children can be the most cruel people in the world when it comes to being nasty to each other. Mind you, adults can be just as cruel, but they are generally less overt about it.

At some stage in our early life we begin to develop an ideal image of ourselves. We begin to get a feeling of what we want to be, what we are capable of, what we are good at and not so good at. We try to work hard at those things we feel we may be good at, and try to cope with the possibility that we may not be brilliant at everything. We try to dismiss those things we are not good at as irrelevant to us. We have to cope with the differences between what we felt as babies – that we were the centre of the universe and we were very special – and what the world outside thinks about us. When we meet the rest of the world and it doesn't reinforce that self-image, we have to go through some serious revision of our self-image. We develop a dynamic force, a constantly changing tension between what we feel we want to be and what the world tells us we can be. We dismiss as many of the negative events as we can as being irrelevant to us, but if we are hit with constant failure or are constantly criticised for our failures, we internalise this message and believe it to be our true worth.

If we can't match our ideal self with our perceived self, and the negative self-belief is reinforced by others or other events, we sow the seeds for lifelong feelings of inadequacy and depression. Our life becomes a self-fulfilling prophecy, as we believe that we are worthless and we don't have the self-belief to go out and prove otherwise.

Striving to achieve a certain goal in life, such as a sporting award, or a certain academic prize, can fire us with enthusiasm and give us a zest for life. We can invest a lot of our self-image in the achievement of that goal. Failure to obtain that goal, however, can whack us in the solar plexus and leave us feeling terribly inferior to those who do achieve it. Unemployment too can slowly suck the marrow of self-appreciation dry, when we are hit by job refusal after job refusal and end up with the belief that we are incapable of working. Rejection by a lover, spouse, boyfriend or girlfriend can leave us devastated for a very long time, with feelings of inadequacy and self-dislike that only mirror the intensity of the affection in which the loved one was originally held.

A friend of mine, James, had been going out with his girlfriend Michelle for a number of years. They got married and settled down in a pretty country cottage in the south of England, where they both worked, and had a large and varied circle of friends. James recalled a weekend they spent together at the time of their second wedding anniversary, when they seemed to be so happy and their life stretched out in front of them. The following week, Michelle left him. She left a note on their bed saying that she had tired of the relationship and that he wasn't to try and find her. Eventually he found out that she had been having an affair with her boss for over a year. He was devastated and even two years later couldn't find the self-confidence to approach another woman romantically. 'It's not that I still love her,' he said, 'it's that she walked out holding my whole self in her hands when she left.' It took many years, and another relationship, before he began to like himself again.

Poor Self-Image

There is a difference between the character of the unhappiness that is produced when our self-image is damaged and when our self-appreciation is left intact but we suffer in some other way. The difference is self-hatred, which lends to the unhappiness a bitter futility. A grief reaction, at the loss of a friend for example, can produce the same intense unhappiness, but without the knife-edge quality of self-dislike that other types of emotional trauma can bring when our self-image is devastated. It's a very individual reaction to each individual situation. If our self-image is poor in the first place it can be easier to give in to despair and self-hatred after an emotional upset than if our self-confidence is strong. It is quite possible to live life teetering on the knife-edge of despair, just waiting to be pushed over the edge by some minor upset. Whatever 'insult' is sustained is added to the catalogue of injuries that confirm a negative self-image.

The ultimate expression of self-hatred is suicide. When Kurt Cobain, the lead singer with the rock group Nirvana, took his own life in 1994, he was subjected to a rather vitriolic attack by the American *60 Minutes* reporter Andy Rooney, who basically said that the singer's life was essentially worthless because he was a junkie, a low life and a maker of noisy music and it didn't matter if he took his own life as it hadn't been well spent. I was so outraged at the lack of understanding of the despair and self-hatred that drives someone to suicide that I wrote to Mr Rooney:

> You gave more credit and importance to Kurt than he would have himself. His was not the story of 'the spokesman for a generation', but the story of a troubled, drug-abusing, unhappy man from an unhappy family, who had done little in his life and found the little he had done was exaggerated by the world around him. He did not like himself and thought so little of himself that he killed himself, the ultimate in low self-opinion. The reason he killed himself was that he would have agreed with your description of him, and not because he would have disagreed with it. His story is a singularly personal tragedy and we should note it only as that. He hated himself and what he saw himself as being and gave up his ultimate possession because he saw himself as being unworthy of life. How the rest of the world and the media see him is their problem.

Eventually I received a reply to this letter in which Mr Rooney grudgingly conceded some of the points I made, but he didn't alter his view of the singer's death.

Limits to Stress

Interactions with the 'outside' world that hurt us and leave us feeling small are generally not as traumatic to us as a problem emanating from our early formative years. If we are strong in ourselves, we can sustain a large amount of external trauma; we may have some problems, but not enough to shake our self-belief. However, there is no doubt that we can all be broken by external events and traumas, and we all have a certain level of stress beyond which we cannot go without altering our opinion of ourselves. All torturers practise their dreadful trade knowing how to shake an individual to the core, to shred away layers of personality and achievement that had been built around them, and leave a broken and vulnerable child behind. Patty Hearst, the newspaper heiress, suffered appallingly when she was kidnapped by a terrorist group, the Symbionese Liberation Army, back in the 1970s. She was raped, tortured, locked in a cupboard, and indoctrinated with their ideas. She was completely broken and her self-image was shattered. 'I would have done anything they wanted in order to survive,' she said afterwards. 'I did not want to think any more.' She was demolished as a person to such an extent that she participated in various terrorist activities, such as bank robberies, undertaken by the group, and she began to believe in their 'philosophy'. When she was captured by police she told the story of her torture and her suffering, but she was still convicted of bank robbery. She was eventually pardoned for her crimes, mainly because of what she went through before she committed them. Very few people could expect her to sustain her personality and self-image during such a series of hideous and dreadful experiences.

Similarly, we see in the film *In the Name of the Father*, which is based on a true story, how the British police extracted a 'confession' from a hapless innocent young man by torturing him and threatening to kill his father. The young man, Gerry Conlon, and three of his friends were sentenced to massive prison sentences for the infamous Guildford pub bombings, and the judge, Lord Denning, when passing sentence, regretted that he could not pass a death sentence on them. It took seventeen years in prison and a massive publicity campaign to get the 'confessions' exposed as fraudulent, and even then the police who had extracted the confessions were acquitted of obstruction of justice. Essentially there is nobody whose self-esteem cannot be broken if they suffer badly enough or long enough. The effects of massive trauma, for which we may be utterly blameless, are often to make us feel inadequate, guilty and self-hating.

Perpetuating Low Self-Esteem

Once a poor self-belief is established, for whatever reason, it is perpetuated by a bizarre mental wallowing in it. If someone doesn't like themselves, they seem to search for evidence of why they shouldn't, and then latch on to it as proof of their personal unworthiness. There is an avoidance of opportunity and a perverse underlying desire to destroy any achievement or success in order to back up the negative self-image. And once the new job or the new romance fails, there is a 'told you so' reaction from one half of the brain to the other. The pattern of self-deprecatory thoughts is repeated anew, and is often tolerated because at least it is familiar. There is a fear of change inherent in us that will encourage us to wallow in familiar misery rather than strike out for unfamiliar possible happiness and contentment. 'At least,' the mind says, 'in your present state you can't fall any further.' The biggest obstacle to breaking out of the mould of self-deprecation is not our families, our past or the various hurts we have suffered in the past. It is ourselves!

A very aggressive young man was admitted to the hospital where I worked. He was twenty-three years old and was feeling suicidal and depressed. He felt rootless and lost and felt his life wasn't worth living. He came from a working-class background, with a supportive mother and a rather harsh and critical father, and had done only okay at school. He had become moody and irritable as a teenager and never quite got out of that teenage 'defiance of authority' mode. He went to a welding school and graduated with a reasonable qualification. He worked for a while and then went off to England to a change of scene. He got into drugs in London but never let them take over his life. He stayed moody and unhappy, and became increasingly violent to those around him, especially when drunk. He moved to the north of England, found a pretty girlfriend and married her. He had a lovely baby daughter and felt happy for one period in his life. But the old insecurity came back, and he began to pick fights with his wife and lose his temper. He felt he couldn't be happy and eventually she kicked him out and he returned home to Ireland.

When he came to us he had received a divorce notice from his wife and was feeling very depressed and self-hating. It took a long time to get through the layers of aggression and defensiveness to find out what the experience had been for him, and what drove him to act the way he did. And at the end of the day his main explanation for his aggressive behaviour was a chronic feeling of emptiness and low self-esteem that came from a critical father and poor grades at school. He carried that feeling with him even when things were going well for him. He found himself feeling unworthy of happiness and began to create the circumstances that would return him to his familiar self-hating misery. In the process he destroyed his new family and gave himself new reasons to dislike himself. It took some time before he began to understand just what had happened to him and it took a while longer to understand that he was doing this to himself rather than simply being the victim of 'circumstances'.

Egotism

It is possible to look on self-consciousness as an inward directing of life's energy and forces. If the whole of my life is spent thinking about other people's opinions of me, and how I look to other people, no time is spent thinking about other people as individuals or about events that don't have a direct bearing on myself. That, in anybody's book, is selfish. Strange as it may at first appear, shyness is an extreme form of egotism. If I am a shy person and I walk into a room, I will blush and get embarrassed, not just because I feel everybody is noticing me, but because I expect them to notice me. It is not a pleasant experience, but nonetheless it is an egotistical one. There is a certain childish expectancy about the experience, which is a bit silly when viewed later. The pain of that type of experience is undeniable, but one of the ways of coming to terms with it is to understand its basis. If we didn't have an unexpressed expectation about how people should behave towards us, we wouldn't get embarrassed either if they paid attention to us or if they didn't. Indeed, if we didn't feel superior to those people around us, we wouldn't feel that they should dance attendance on us at all. What in fact we need in those situations is a good dose of humility and then we wouldn't suffer so much.

What is required as part of our change in attitude is a U-turn of our attention and our focus outwards. If we turn our life forces and our energy outwards, we lose the self-obsession that is required for self-consciousness. If we can invest our energy in other people rather than in how we appear to other people, we can begin to get other things – and ourselves – into perspective. If we can do something positive for other people, such as work in a charity for the homeless or visit elderly people, we can get a satisfaction and a genuine appreciation that is different from what we thought we actually wanted, but that is infinitely preferable.

Self-approval can be built on externally orientated achievement just as much as on self-serving achievement. Indeed it could be said that one of the benefits of living through feelings of self-consciousness and inferiority is that it makes us able to understand so much better what other people suffer in their lives. If that can be translated into a practical expression such as a career choice or even a more considerate opinion of others and what they go through, it is nearly a worthwhile experience – nearly.

There is an order of Catholic nuns called the Carmelites, who are a contemplative order – they live a life of complete silence and spend their time praying for understanding and guidance, mainly for others. I once met a Carmelite nun who was visiting a sick relation in the hospital where I worked and was thus temporarily exempt from her vow of silence. She was polite and friendly but very composed and by no means intimidated by her surroundings – a modern intensive care ward, with monitors, machinery, drips and bustling nurses all around her. She asked me about her aunt and I gave her the reasonably good prognosis. I rather self-importantly described the care her aunt was getting and the various medical procedures that had been performed to help her. When I was finished, expecting to have made some impression on this poor recluse from the modern world, she smiled at me and said, 'Thank you. I will pray for you.' Because she said it so sincerely, with respect but without being impressed, she showed me just how self-important I felt in charge of all this medical technology, and how self-conscious I was of my own importance. And off she went, totally self-contained in herself because she expected nothing. She was truly humble, truly unselfish and truly unselfconscious.

Fighting Back

Somewhere down in the pits of self-degradation is a little flame. It is small, it looks as though it can be easily extinguished, and it doesn't burn very brightly. But it is there. What it is I cannot really say, but it is that certain something that allows us to fight back when we have nothing to fight back with. It is that something that enables us to hope that the next day will be better, even if the day gone by was pure torture. It is present at different levels and in different amounts in different people. Some people have to hit rock bottom before they realise they have it. Some people have to escape from whatever internal pressure is on them before they feel it inside them. But we all have it and that is exactly what we must use to fight back against all that oppresses us.

Everybody has a personal force within them, and it is expressed in many ways. Turning a life around and battling against possibly a lifetime's self-deprecation is not easy, but it is within the bounds of all of us to do it. There is genuinely a point at which we are so low that we cannot go any further, a bedrock of solid character upon which our personality is built. It is not necessary to reach it to know it is there. It is enough to be aware of it and feel the certainty of it and go up from there.

A 55-year-old woman, a former alcoholic, told me her story. She had spent twenty years of her life drinking and eventually hit rock bottom. She had ruined her marriage, alienated her family, and brought herself to the brink of financial ruin. She hated herself and her drinking, and every time she reached for a bottle she felt absolutely worthless. She was eventually admitted into a hospital in a semi-conscious state after a massive drinking binge that lasted three weeks. She had previously been warned about the effects that drinking might have on her health and had ignored the warning. She was admitted from accident and emergency and was put in intensive care, with brain damage induced by hepatic encephalopathy (or liver disease). She wandered in and out of consciousness over a period of days.

At one stage, when she appeared to be unconscious, she overheard a doctor tell a nurse at the end of her bed, 'She's very sick; she has liver failure.' She lay there and the significance of the remark sank into her. The wasted years flooded back into her mind. She quietly made up her mind that she was going to fight back. Amazingly, after a few more days her liver tests began to get back to normal and she recovered fully after a substantial period in hospital. She never drank again, and she attributes her remarkable recovery to pure mental determination based on the shock she got on overhearing the doctor's comment. The message we should get from her is that it is never too late to turn around, and the only thing required is solid determination. Solid determination comes from solid motivation.

President Nixon was not the most endearing of people. In fact, he was a downright crook who fought, lied and cheated his way from nowhere to the greatest prize in politics. Once he gained the US presidency he continued using the methods he had used to get there, and eventually resigned before being impeached. He became the most reviled figure in modern American history, all by his own hand and his own mentality.

Yet when he died and was buried twenty years after Watergate, he had become the elder statesman of the USA, a man who talked with world leaders and who advised his successors right up to a month before his death. The last ten years of his life, when he was in his seventies, were spent writing books, hosting meetings and formal dinners, and generally acting as if he were a man twenty years younger. When one commentator was asked, 'Why is he doing this? Is he running for president again?' he replied, 'No, he's running for the post of ex-president.' Richard Nixon came back from ultimate disgrace – and who can think of any worse disgrace than the one he brought on himself? – and he fought back courageously and tenaciously to reclaim the respect of the world. We should all learn from him: not from his morality but from his guts; not from his bigotry but from his backbone; and not from his human failings but from his human spirit.

Being Selfish

So how is it possible to escape the self-deprecating cycles of thought and emerge with a renewed self-image? How is it possible to reverse negative thoughts and make them positive? Well, it isn't easy, and the basic thing to remember is that it won't be immediate. Beware of false dawns, instant solutions and thunderbolts from heaven; they rarely last any length of time. Any change worth its salt may be decided upon in an instant but it takes weeks, months or even years for real change in ourselves to come about.

The first thing to do is to learn how to be good to ourselves and how to be 'selfish'. It is the utter suppression of our own personal desire to the extent that we don't know what we want, that helps lead to a dreadful self-image. It is possible to spend an entire lifetime trying to please others and end up only displeasing ourselves. This desire to please others leads to an inability to find satisfaction in ourselves, and leads us to perpetually seek the approbation and praise of those around us. This only satisfies temporarily and leads to a dismal and despairing cycle of self-disgust, as praise and appreciation eventually wane. Part of breaking that vicious cycle is saying, 'I want to do this', and if necessary having the courage to step on someone's toes in order to do it. The vital first step can only be taken from within, leaning on the rock that lies there and getting the courage to do it. It can be enough to change a life, not immediately, not quickly, but slowly and decisively.

Constant battering leads to constant giving from a position of weakness, not a position of strength. 'I am giving because I have to, not because I want to' basically occurs because no alternative can be seen. This in turn leads others to impose upon us because we have given up our personal rights. This is because we don't police them or enforce them. Most people are not inherently malicious, but will take any break given them, and convince themselves that it is their right. If we give an inch people will take a mile, if they can get away with it. Any re-taking of the ground already ceded will be resisted, quite simply because it has become the norm, and has been gotten used to.

Learn to Say 'No'

Taking a stand, saying 'No', both to ourselves and to others, will lead to a change, both internally and externally. Do it, and we will be surprised by people's ready acceptance of us after a short while. It is very similar to what happens when one of a group in an office is promoted to manager. After an initial flurry of upset, the situation settles down and the person is given the respect inherent in the position they now occupy. Once the others recover from their surprise and resentment, life resumes, but very differently for the person promoted, both in how they view themselves and how the others in the office view them. Eventually, the person promoted becomes not 'the person who was promoted from among us' but 'the manager'. This happens in both the public perception and the personal one. It takes a while, it cannot be done without some upset, but it is surprisingly quickly accepted by others. It is precisely the same process that occurs internally and externally when we decide to say, 'That's it. No more of this.' There is an internal and external re-adjustment, slowly over time, and people eventually accommodate to the new us.

Escape

If something external is oppressing us, and pushing us into the miserable self-hating depths, it is not really necessary to face that person or situation head-on in order to escape or even overcome it. There is no real need to hit the bully on the jaw in order to stop him tormenting us. There is no need to 'win' battles with a drunken husband in order to stop the pain he is inflicting. There is no real necessity to tell a domineering parent where to get off in order to actually stop the domination. If we are in a situation where something is making us suffer that much, we should simply get out of it. The battle can be fought later when our internal resources are up to dealing with it. The most important thing we can do is to stop the suffering and then look at the situation from a distance. We have to get out of the house, the job, or the relationship that is dragging us down – it is not worth all the pain it is causing.

If there is no definite escape in the short term, we should use our natural intelligence either to get back at our oppressor or to limit the extent of the suffering caused. There is no person alive who doesn't have a weak spot, and finding out what that is can be the key to managing an unbearable situation. Just as in a schoolroom situation the class bully wouldn't like to be asked, 'Do you fancy him, then?' every time he laid a hand on a boy he wanted to bully, at work a sexually oppressive boss wouldn't like to be reminded about his wife when he tries to get familiar with a vulnerable female employee. Even David didn't try to handle Goliath by taking him head-on in a fist fight: he avoided a physical encounter and beat him by keeping him out of reach and throwing stones at him. There is more than one way to skin a cat, and more than one way to handle external oppression. The first step is to make a decision to stop it, the second step is to wangle out of it and give ourselves time to recover from the trauma. Manipulation in this context is not a crime but a defensive technique. The object of the exercise is to survive, not to win a war medal.

The movie *What's Love Got to Do with It?* tells the story of the singer Tina Turner. It gives a portrayal of a physically battered wife caught in the trap of a loveless marriage to Ike Turner, who eventually became a drug addict. One day, after ten years of beatings and even rape, Tina suffered a particularly brutal beating just before a concert appearance. She could take it no more. She left the hotel they were staying in with only the clothes on her back. She checked into another hotel, bruised and battered and dripping blood from her face, mustering as much dignity as she could in the circumstances. She never confronted her husband, and she never went back. The next time she saw him was in the divorce court. She survived and went on to greater heights than she could ever have reached with her husband. There's a lot to be said for getting out while you can, just to survive. In any situation where there is an oppressor and an oppressed, the oppressed just needs to be able to say 'No' to find a way to survive. Getting to that position may not be as easy as it sounds.

Facing It

The ideal method of dealing with external oppression and the internal self-disgust it produces is, however, actually to face down the oppression or oppressor in a direct way. If this can be done – and almost anything can be done if there is sufficient will – we should do it, however embarrassing and ridiculous it may seem. The important thing about doing it is not the way it is done, nor the effect it has on the situation, but the effect it has on us. Direct confrontation, while very traumatic at the time, will grant us a quick bypass into a much more positive way of self-regard. Even if the oppression does not stop immediately, standing up for ourselves provides in itself enough self-regard to be certain of relieving the problem in the long term. The courage to fight the next battle will come a lot easier next time, and any subsequent times required. The mental certainty that it is within our powers is enough to change our whole way of thinking about ourselves. From that point on it is possible to construct a new self-made persona.

In his early years, Bill Clinton was raised by a loving mother and a violent and alcoholic stepfather, whom his mother, Virginia Kelly, had married after Bill's father died in a car accident. When Bill was in his childhood and early teens, he had to witness the trauma of seeing his mother being beaten by her drunken husband. One day when he was fourteen, he could take it no longer and he stood up to his stepfather and told him never to touch her again. His stepfather looked at him and saw that the young boy was now the same size as him and could give as good as he got in a fair fight. He stopped hitting her, and with Bill around most of the time he never hit her again. It is that courage to stand up and be counted and fight back against our oppressor when we don't know the outcome that is required to change our lives around. If Bill Clinton had never done that, it is unlikely that he would have ever become president. He made himself stronger by standing up to his stepfather, and this strength in the face of adversity was part of what eventually led him to the presidency.

Facing up to oppression does two things: it stops the oppression; and it gives us back our self-respect. As I said before, courage is doing what we are afraid of doing, and facing up to what we are afraid of facing. When we have the courage to face something or someone down we place a large deposit in the bank of self-regard and make the next courageous challenge just that bit easier to handle. We have begun the U-turn.

Choices

As the fightback begins, desires, decisions and preferences become more apparent than they ever were before. The instinctive reaction to a decision-making situation would previously be to duck, to avoid it, and find out what someone else wanted. As our personal situation changes, it should become necessary to begin to dictate the course of events that happens to us, by making decisions as they come up and also by choosing and then following our personal preferences. Indeed, personal preferences and choices are no more than whims made definite. The trick is not to be caught in indecision, as that purely feeds feelings of inadequacy. If a decision has to be made, it is far better to take the least successful option available, and try it for a while, than it is to dither in indecision, and end up incapable of any decision at all. As time goes by, preferences will emerge from the background with more logic and reasoning behind them, and it will be easier to choose from between various courses of action, and then have the confidence to hold to them. It is literally a reverse of the negative spiral of self-hate and paralysis that previously carried us downwards.

In the last chapter of this book we will deal with how to cope with this 'reversal of fortune' and how to make decisions and choose directions that reflect what we truly want in life. It is not enough to just get out of a bad situation or a bad self-image; we have to use our new-found freedom and self-regard to move up and move on in life.

John, a 29-year-old sales assistant still living at home, came into hospital because of his feelings of self-doubt and anxiety. He feared his domineering mother and couldn't do anything without her approval. He gave out about her and called her many unflattering things. When he was discharged, his doctor wrote a summary of his case to be forwarded to his family practitioner. Unfortunately it was posted to John's house instead of the GP's clinic. John's mother read the summary and the unflattering things he had said about her and was not pleased. When she confronted him, he didn't deny what he had said. She was taken aback by that and really didn't know what to do. He took advantage of this letting down of her defences to make the momentous decision to leave home. He started looking for a flat and began to make all sorts of plans: to go abroad for his holidays and to learn to drive. He stopped staying at home in the evenings and sought out his own life. Quite literally, a new world opened up for him and he began to make plans and set horizons for himself that he hadn't dared dream of previously.

Dangers

There is a danger in achieving freedom from oppression and freedom from self-torture. The danger is that in freeing ourselves we impose ourselves on other people; that in escaping from inferiority and self-disdain we believe ourselves superior and disdain others. The problem with this is that it takes place insidiously and over a long time. It is much harder to recognise in ourselves, simply because we are not suffering, and thus aren't obsessed with monitoring ourselves. It is very simple to see it in other people, but dreadfully difficult to see in ourselves. The problem essentially is that instead of gaining insight from the dreadful self-hating experiences we have gone through, all we have done is changed. It's a lot better than not changing at all, but it is simply not good enough.

A middle-aged Canadian man astonished me with his egotism and boorishness in a group therapy setting. He totally dominated his meek wife, and was generally disliked at work. Interestingly, he had been a meek and repressed child who had been dominated by his father, a retired army officer. One day in his late teens he stood up to his father and shouted back at him for the first time in his life. His father was taken aback and gave in straightaway, and he never bullied him again. My patient then took this as a sign that – seeing as it had been so successful with his father – this was the way to deal with everyone in the outside world. And so he continued, shouting and bullying people for many years until he reached middle age. Eventually his colleagues at work demanded that he get help, and so he ended up in group therapy. It took a lot of work for him to get to see that he had a maladaptive pattern of dealing with other people, and what was successful in one situation would not be adequate for dealing with everyone else for the rest of his life.

The trick that he had to learn, that we all have to learn, is to constantly judge ourselves and our motivations. If we could be as scrupulous in our dissection of ourselves when we feel better and self-content as when we feel like a dog's dinner, we would be truly cured, and, like the nun we met earlier in the chapter, truly humble.

The U-Turn: Mastering Your Self-Image

When turning around our self-image it is necessary to find out just what we think of ourselves. After all, how can we change when we don't know what we are trying to change? The vital thing to remember is that our self-image is not one thing but is made up of many parts. We may invest heavily in any one part of it, and thus risk losing our total self-image if that one component is taken away from us. But the reality is that there is more to all of us than one aspect, and that our true self-image is made up of the sum of our self-image in different areas. What we will do here is to divide up our self-image into the broadest areas of life, and try to arrive at a true picture via the component parts. In this exercise, feel free to add any other areas that you feel are especially important.

The first part of the U-turn is to describe yourself both in the broadest of terms and in the most specific of areas. As in other parts of the U-turn, start off by sitting in a quiet room with some time out to think clearly.

1. Take a piece of paper and write at the top: 'My Self-Image U-Turn'.

2. Divide the page into three columns, with the headings 'My Self-Image', 'My Ideal Image' and 'My Changes'.

3. In the first column, leaving a space under each heading, write 'Work', 'Relationships', 'Social and Leisure', and 'Spiritual and Values'. You'll be examining your self-image under each of these headings, which are the cardinal areas of life.

4. In the first column, describe your self-image in each of the four cardinal areas. The way you decide what your

self-image is in each of those areas is to ask yourself appropriate questions:

- For the Work section you could ask yourself: 'Am I satisfied with the job I am doing at present?'; 'Do I consider it a worthwhile job?'; 'Am I performing in it to the best of my ability?'; 'Do I feel up to the task or am I overwhelmed by it?'

- For the Relationships section you could ask yourself: 'Am I in a satisfactory relationship with my spouse or partner?'; 'Do I treat them well and am I treated well?'; 'Do I get a sense of worth out of the relationship?'

- For the Social and Leisure section you could ask yourself: 'Am I content with my social abilities and my leisure and exercise time?'; 'Do I have good friends whom I like to spend time with?'; 'Am I fulfilled in what I do with my spare time?'; or, indeed, 'Do I have any spare time at all?'

- And for the last section – Spiritual and Values – ask yourself: 'Do I have a sense of purpose in my life?'; 'Do I dedicate any of my life to developing my spiritual side?'; 'Do I spend any of my time giving to others in a practical way?'

5. By asking yourself these types of question you should be able to define exactly what your self-image is in each of these areas. Write down a succinct summary phrase of your self-images in those areas in the first column. At the end of this exercise you should have a portrait of your own self-image, the areas where it is good and the areas where you feel deficient.

6. In the next column, look at your ideal self-image in each of those four areas. Think about just what sort of person you would like to become in an ideal situation. Don't be unrealistic; don't write down simplistic ideals ('I want to

be a millionaire', or 'I want to be Superman'), but think about the person you would like to be in an ideal world. You should make this a wish list for the different areas of your life:

- First look at one of the main areas of your life – Work – and define what your ideal job would be, what area of work it would be in, what style of work it would involve and in what way you would use your talents to the fullest.

- Look at your main Relationships – those with your partner and family. Define exactly how you think that relationship should be, and the sort of relationship you want to have with them.

- Next, look at your Social and Leisure time and describe the ideal way you would spend your spare time, and the ideal way you could make friends and spend time with them. Think about any activities you haven't yet got around to trying out, and let your imagination run free in trying to say just what you would like to do.

- Under the next heading, Spiritual and Values, define just what you would wish yourself to become as a spiritual being as you grow older. Decide whether you want to become more religious (as in being involved in organised religion), more spiritual (by exploring the meaning of life and death and embarking on your own spiritual journey, perhaps by reading the teachings of the great spiritual teachers of the past), or more giving – or indeed not giving – in terms of time and effort (for example in charitable work, helping those worse off than yourself).

What you need to define – in specific, not general, terms – is the sort of person you want to be and the different areas of your life that will make up that ideal person. You are also defining the type of person you admire; the type of person who, if you became like that person, you would think better of yourself. Define the person you believe is worthy of your admiration, and thus the person you could even like if you became them.

7. In the last section, start moving from the present imperfect to the future ideal. We have to take back the different components of our lives and make the transition between the present and the possible future. We have to make the transition mentally first and then physically. The first thing we have to tell ourselves is that it is possible for us to do this. By breaking the problem of our poor self-image into the different component areas, we can also break the solution into its component parts.

Let's look at each area and see just what we can do to transform our lives in those areas. The most important thing is *the belief that it is possible*. Everything else stems from that. While we all have the feeling of being stuck in our own little rut, we have to constantly tell ourselves that it is possible to escape that rut and do what we want to do with our lives. After all, we have only one shot at this existence and we should never have to say to ourselves at the end of our lives, 'If only'; we should be able to say, at worst, 'At least I tried', and at best, 'I succeeded in what I set out to do.' It is always possible to change, and it is never to late to try.

There are so many people who give up in life without really trying to do or see anything differently from the way things have always been. They will never change their self-image nor their lives because they refuse to see this is possible. It is that grasp of the possibilities of our own situation that makes us do what is required to change our circumstances and our thoughts and feelings about ourselves. There are so many examples in this book of people taking a hold of their circumstances and seeing something better as a possibility, and then figuring out a way to do what is necessary to make that a reality. We have to do the same for ourselves.

Now for each of the four categories, write down ways of transforming the present into the ideal. Once we see that it is possible we have to think about ways of making it possible. What we write down are the ways that get us started on the path to reaching our ideals.

Start with Work, whether you are a fireman or a housewife, a professor or a CEO, a prince or a pauper, and even if you are currently unemployed. Now that you have defined what your goal is in terms of your ideal work situation, you have to make plans to make it a reality. Look at your situation at work and begin to plan the pathway to your ideal situation. Plan it in little steps, not big ones, in small ways, not big ways – at least initially. Keep the goal in mind at all times and decide whether what you are doing is working your way towards that goal or away from it. If you are working towards it, keep at it; but if it is not helping towards your goal, find a way to change it. Once you have your final objective in mind, you will make things happen in that direction by keeping it in mind at all times. What you work at in steps will eventually transform into a whole, if you persist and work hard. And if you are in a situation in which you are not in charge and you are constantly being blocked in trying to reach your goals, it is better to confront the situation than leave it and let your ideals go to rot.

For example, if in the Work category you decide that your ideal is to own and run your own business, write down how you would go about initiating your ideas, such as buying and reading a book on starting your own business and spending some time working in a similar business to get experience in the trade.

If you have decided in the Relationships section that you want to have a kind and loving relationship that is one of sharing and giving, start by acting that way with the people around you, and then start looking for someone to continue that habit with.

If under Social and Leisure you decide that you want to become popular socially and to engage in, say, golf and hang-gliding, start by deciding whether you need to take a social skills course to enhance your social poise, and ring up the local golf course to see if beginners' lessons are available.

In the last section, Spiritual and Values, start on the passage towards what you have defined as your ideal self. Most of us are well-intentioned but are often too lazy to do anything about it. If we define just what our spiritual goals are and where we feel we have a place to offer help, we start to reach them by writing down the paths to those goals. We can start by helping out at the local church bazaar, by buying and using a book on meditation, by simply giving some of our income to charity and finding out what happens to it. The reason we have to do something of value to others and something altruistic is that unless we do, we lose the sense of purpose in our own lives and we lose the ability to find that purpose, even if it hits us between the eyes. Starting to act for others doesn't give us a sense of personal value, but it makes us able to begin to find one.

When we contemplate what it is we would like to become and what we feel we are now, it is easy to give up and say 'There's not much chance of that ever happening' and 'What's the point of even trying?' We have to attempt to match the two people: us as we see ourselves right now; and us as our ideal selves. They may be quite a distance apart, and when looking at that difference we may feel disappointed and depressed. If we can perceive the ideal as being even remotely attainable, even in the smallest way, we are on the path of turning ourselves from past negative self-regard to future self-congratulation.

What will keep us going, keep us getting out of bed in the morning, is the fact that we are working towards a goal, and many others around us are simply working. And when things go wrong – and they will at some point – we have to return to the ideal self we previously outlined, recreate that self over again in our minds, and start to work our way towards that self. All it takes is belief that a difference is possible.

In order to understand the workings of our own minds and the different components in them that work together to make up our full personalities, we need to look at these components individually. We do this in the next chapter.

9

Personality and Projection

> Our personalities are complex, but with understanding
> and effort we can change

When we see someone with 'personality' we're looking at someone we admire, someone we would aspire to emulate. It's not necessary for everybody else to feel the same wave of admiration as we do – our own opinion is sufficient. We all have different heroes and heroines from the past and the present, and those heroes and heroines have different characteristics that we admire. Often these admirable characteristics are latent or underdeveloped in ourselves and we would dearly like to acquire or enrich these traits. Our admiration is fuelled by our self-perceived deficiencies, and the size of the deficiency is often proportional to the size of the admiration.

But the real crux of appreciation of personality lies not in our opinion of others, for that is in some measure objective, but in our opinion of ourselves, which is not in the least objective. We seem to suspend all normal methods of reasoning and perception when it comes to judging and observing ourselves. We are forever apologising to ourselves for ourselves, but tempering that apology with a dose of self-justification and explanation. We can always excuse what we do or say to others, by patting ourselves on the back, and saying, 'I know why that happened. It's perfectly understandable in the circumstances!' The only way we can live with ourselves is by maintaining an internal dialogue with ourselves, connecting, explaining, excusing and, occasionally, deluding.

Layers

One way of looking at our personality make-up is to divide it into three layers. The first layer is our outer layer, the surface layer, the bit that everybody sees and relates to. I call this layer our 'public persona'. It includes how we walk and talk, how we project ourselves, how we handle various situations we are used to, and how we adapt to others. In *The Great Gatsby*, F. Scott Fitzgerald calls personality 'an unbroken series of successful gestures'. It is our image, and it is a real and vital part of us. It is essentially what other people think we are, because it is often all they see of us. It is the bit that people decide to like or dislike, often on the basis of shamefully little information. It is the part of other people that we see, and observe and judge, and we ignorantly assume we know the whole person by the little characteristics and traits they display.

The second layer of personality is the layer of self-appreciation and judgement that continually monitors our first layer. It is essentially what we believe ourselves to be. I call this second layer our 'personal image'. It makes us more rounded people than the bits on the surface; it makes our actions more plausible, our enemies more justified in their hatred, our mistakes more comprehensible. It is also quite capable of ignoring some basic facts or motivations, which are on the surface and visible to others, for the sake of inner peace, and to help us live with ourselves. The connections between the superficial first level and the analysing second level are indirect, not direct. Communication between external reality and internal monitoring could be considered enthusiastic but incomplete, rather like a new salesperson's work record.

The third level is essentially what we really are as people. It is our core, our character, and our fundamental self. I call this layer our 'inner being'. Our 'core' is not the same as the next person's. We are as varied in our inner selves as we are in our outward selves. Our core is our basic personality, and it governs our thoughts, speech and behaviour in such a basic and natural way that it is sometimes difficult to realise we actually have one. It influences our passage through life more than any other aspect of our make-up. It is the steady hand on the tiller of the ship of life. It is useful to realise that it is there, and also to realise that it is not the same as our second layer, our internal dialogue layer. Our image of ourselves is not the same as our true selves – we constantly fool ourselves.

Layer 1: Our Public Persona

Let's look at the first layer in more detail. All the things about us that people see and hear are essentially things that are within our control. We can give one impression to one set of people in one situation and give the opposite impression to a similar set of people in different circumstances. People judge each other very quickly and on very small criteria, for example how we look and how we sound.

People who are good-looking have an innate advantage over the rest of humanity. People are far more inclined to pay attention to and take an interest in a beautiful person than an ugly one. People will be more interested sexually in a good-looking boy or girl than a plain one – it's a fact of life. Beyond plastic surgery, there is not a lot we can do about our basic looks. However, there is a lot we can do about the way we present ourselves, and if we care about how people think of us, it is vital to consider how we look to them. Good grooming, keeping hair clean, choosing clothes carefully and appropriately – all that is reflected instantly in the eye of the beholder. It's not as if everyone notices the details of what the components of good grooming are – they don't. What everybody does notice, however, is the overall impression, even if nobody says anything about it, either positive or negative.

I remember first meeting a rather quiet, dowdy young woman who later became a friend. She was pleasant and polite but gave no impression of attractiveness or awareness of personal presentation when first talking to me. Like most people around me, she made very little impression on me and I tended not to pay attention to her. But when she appeared at a formal dinner, miraculously transformed, she turned heads. She had changed her looks to such an extent that she seemed a different person. Gone was the greasy hair, the dull clothes and the glasses, and out came the blonde highlights, the breath-taking ball gown and the glamorous look. She left an indelible impression on me about the way she could be. After this change she was never again ignored or looked on as dowdy. She underwent a genuine transformation that was solely created by attention to appearance.

There is a train of thought which is quite common, especially among students and teenagers, that dressing up or looking neat and attractive is somehow hiding away your true self, that in order to be honest you have to look as you do every Sunday morning when you get out of bed. It is simply not true. Looking well, if not actually stunning, predisposes people to listening to you and noticing you and having a favourable impression of you. Ask yourself what your reaction was the last time you noticed that someone looked absolutely dreadful. Unless it was someone close to you going through a rough patch, the chances are that a negative impression weaselled its way into the back of your brain without you even realising it. There is no bigger turn-off, either socially or sexually, than greasy hair, an unshaven face or dirty fingernails.

The other great thing about looking good is that we become aware of it too. We pick up people's reactions to us, and we respond to them. If they are positive, it relaxes us, makes us feel good and makes it easier to communicate. There is also a wonderful feeling about looking good and knowing it, irrespective of other people's reactions. It just makes life a little sweeter.

Projection

The other way we convey an image to others is by our manner and our speech. It's actually a lot more difficult to modify these than it is to change our visual image. If we can hit the right mark in our voice and in what we say, even if its just a few words, we can overcome numerous difficulties by virtue of conveying the right image. Impoliteness or rudeness is simply not on. Even if it's just an attempt to be light-hearted that goes wrong, it can cause an offence that is very hard to obliterate. It is always better to be a bit boring and polite than it is to be rude and memorable. People remember offensive remarks, even if well-intentioned, for years after they have forgotten a hundred compliments.

A friend started a job outside his native Dublin city for the first time. He was working in a business in a large town with people who were generally locally based. He sat down with a few of his new colleagues about a week into the job and started off by saying, 'Gosh, it's really great to be down here working with all you ordinary country folk.' The remark went down like a lead balloon, and hit exactly the wrong mark. While he knew almost none of them, they all knew he was the guy down from Dublin, come to tell them how they do it in the big city. He had no idea that he had hit the wrong mark and carried on regardless. It was only years later that one of his colleagues reminded him what he had said and the effect it had had on those who heard him. They simply dismissed him as not worth knowing, and they were probably right. Never be rude or insensitive in front of people you don't know – it will be long remembered.

If it is at all possible, conveying an interest in what someone says or does is one way to practically guarantee a positive response to you. Projecting that interest to the other person often requires an effort and a genuine attempt to listen to them. The genuineness will be picked up and responded to, thus saving many potentially embarrassing situations from getting worse. I have seen fanatical golfers converse with determined environmentalists, car mechanics talk with professors, hairdressers chatting to anybody, and all on the basis of simple, interested questions and genuine attentiveness. After all, even accountants find their own jobs interesting, strange as it seems to the rest of us.

It would be great to be able to entertain and educate a disparate bunch of social strangers with sparkling conversation and dry wit. It would be lovely if we could all be like Oscar Wilde, making funny comments and witty analogies, being conversationally brilliant and becoming socially invaluable. Unfortunately few of us are that brilliant socially and few of us have those social graces and talents that give us such an enviable reputation. But we can learn, and we can improve our ways with effort. It requires a certain verbal ability but also, and more important, a self-confidence that is not easily come by. That confidence can only come with practice, and the best way to gain practice is in little ways.

Every time we approach a stranger at a party and a conversation is initiated, a little pebble is removed from the defensive wall around us. It makes approaching and conversing with every other person just that little bit easier. There is no alternative to building that social confidence than trying and trying again, learning social and conversational nuances along the way. Learning from mistakes we make is also vital, and the only way we can do that is by checking on ourselves afterwards and seeing what we did wrong. Making a social diary of day-to-day contacts and how we did socially in each of those contacts is an excellent way of monitoring our own social progress. By learning from our mistakes, we cut down on those little irritants that others might react to. We should focus on positive social achievements and write them down each night, for example 'Chatted to new colleague for ten minutes today.' This increases our confidence in ourselves and makes the next occasion easier and better. It is not a quick process – it takes months and even years to achieve – but the results are as tangible as the weather and longer lasting. It is inevitable that there will be dents in our confidence along the way, from rejection or rudeness, but the thrust of learning at every opportunity means that we will be able to put them in context and not overemphasise them.

If we admire someone's social style, we should look at what they do and follow their example. For example, I remember noting the social grace of a colleague, who managed to be both popular and not overbearing in small social groups. I noticed her ability to keep everyone in a group aware of her and also not to take over the group by blustering and talking too much. It was afterwards I noticed that every time she joined a group socially she would say 'Hello' to everybody personally, while looking directly at them. She would then ask something or mention some personal item of interest to each person around her directly, not just generally to the group. I didn't realise until later that she had a technique. At the time I, like everybody else, just thought her charming. It was when I thought, 'How does she do that?', that I realised just what she did to make herself so gracious. I learned from her that the best way to learn to be gracious and charming is to observe and copy those around us whom we think are socially impressive.

Rudeness

A difficult concept to appreciate when suffering either rejection or rudeness is that it more often reflects the other person and not us. When someone is rude to us, the likelihood is that they are rude to others as well, and if we are hypersensitive to others' opinions we sometimes lose the ability to observe them and judge them properly. The correct attitude to take is, 'That's their problem, not mine,' and move on. If we contributed to their attitude by what we said or did, then we will know it by checking ourselves afterwards. But if we didn't cause their attitude, it is important for us to be able to say 'not me' and try again with somebody else, or in some other situation. The point about being self-aware socially is not only to judge ourselves and improve ourselves, but also to eventually judge others and to ignore them if they are wrong.

A university lecturer came into class one day, and gave a dreadful lecture. He was late, he came in looking unusually well-dressed, and he was rather brusque in his manner. The class responded by talking and laughing among ourselves and he responded by getting irritated at the class. He shouted at us and ordered us to shut up. He was booed and hissed during the lecture and he eventually stormed out. The class laughed at his departing back and thought little of their response to him. Later on, we found out that his wife had died two days previously, and yet he still thought enough of his responsibility to the class to turn up and give his lecture. The class was mortified at our own rudeness and sent him a note of apology for our behaviour. It simply never occurred to any of us that something had happened to him to explain his different appearance and behaviour. Mobs of immature students are different from individuals, but the principles of understanding other people and trying to look at things from their point of view are common to all human interaction. If we find ourselves being the victims of inexplicable irritability or rudeness, we have to accept that it is probably their fault and not ours. Endless self-defeating self-interrogations that produce no explanation for social rejection only end up undermining the successes we achieve at other times. The purpose of questioning ourselves is to learn, not to wallow in the mud.

Margaret Thatcher was one of the most powerful women in the world towards the end of the last century. She was elected three times to the position of prime minister of the UK, and stayed in power for eleven continuous years. Whatever about the rights and wrongs of her politics, her personality is written large across the pages of history. Yet, when she was elected leader of the Tory party as a relative unknown, she had a very poor public manner, and little social grace or media appeal. In order to win her first election, she had to convince a large number of people that she was worthy of being in power. She had no problem with self-confidence, but she came across publicly as boorish and hectoring. (This was mainly because she actually was boorish and hectoring.) She had the wisdom to see that something was wrong, and hired a public relations firm to help her image.

Saatchi and Saatchi moulded a new 'public persona' for her. She stoked up her image with smart tailored suits, carried a neat handbag with her wherever she went, and toned down her voice into a 'smooth and charming' instrument. She stopped talking down to people and made noises about being a housewife in charge of the household budget. In short, by effecting a change in how she looked and how she sounded, she managed to become Prime Minister – and did it twice more. She herself remained the same, but how she appeared to the general public was different, and that's how she succeeded. We all don't have to like Mrs Thatcher, nor do we have to emulate her, but we certainly can learn from her.

Other People

In trying to convey an image and give an impression to someone else, it is important to give consideration to another aspect – the other person. Do we like the person we're talking to? Are we attracted to or impressed by them? Do we really want them in particular to notice or be impressed by us? The answer to those questions is often 'No', and because we are often not even aware of that fact we don't even analyse why. If we are genuinely interested in people, especially those we are talking to, it is a lot easier to convey it to them, and it is a lot easier for them to pick up the good 'vibe' because it is genuine. If, conversely, we aren't really interested in those around us, and only relate to them in terms of how they attempt to relate to us, they will pick up that disinterested vibe and drift away. If we are so caught up in ourselves that we do not have, let alone project, any interest in others, how in all honesty can we expect them to show any interest in us? Think over any large group of people you have known well, for example your class in school. Who did you get on with and who liked you the most? The people you liked, simply. The converse is also true. The people who didn't like you were probably those you didn't like.

We play a larger part in our common social relationships than we give ourselves credit for. We are not so much victims of circumstance as arbiters of our own fortune. It is quite possible – and even easy – to turn an acquaintance into a friend by simply paying small attentions and showing genuine interest in that person. If we continually go out of our way to enthusiastically greet them and demonstrate our regard for them, almost everybody will respond to us with some degree of affection. It's actually very simple, and the reason we don't do it more has as much to do with our lack of genuine interest in others, our own mental lethargy – we're not really prepared to invest the time and energy in it – as it has to do with our 'inability' to get on with people. That perspective doesn't often appear to us when we're having bouts of self-doubt, but it is a large component of the truth.

Effort

If we are having recurrent cycles of negative self-image, it is quite easy for us to convey that unconsciously or consciously to other people. There is a part of us that feels so unworthy that we feel we have to bring others to the same low opinion of ourselves that we have. We may feel perversely that we are hard done by when we find out that others have a low opinion of us, but often we have done our utmost to bring that opinion about. It is almost as if we defy others to like us in spite of what we are doing or saying to them. Unfortunately this often means that they end up almost as annoyed with us as we are with ourselves – they pick up that negative vibe around us. Indeed, one of the best ways of knowing how someone else is feeling is by assessing yourself after being in their company – if you start off feeling cheerful and relaxed and end up feeling tense and irritable, that's probably exactly how they feel.

If we want to be lifted out of a negative, self-doubting cycle, we can do it by projecting the opposite to others. Although it may require a supreme effort, putting a major effort into projecting self-confidence can conversely lift us out of that negative cycle. If, instead of a self-deprecatory vibe, we can project a positive interest in and zest for others, that will lift them up, make them feel a little better, and in turn lift us. The cycle can be reversed by outside people and influences and, if we can encourage it, we end up benefiting from it even more.

One summer, many years ago, I was working on Long Island in a restaurant to get some college money. My friends had gone home, and I was alone and rather lonely. I wasn't getting on very well in the job and I felt rather insecure about it. I decided to go to mass at a local Catholic church one Sunday to pray for, among other things, myself, as I felt so isolated. I slunk into the church and sat at the back away from the altar. The mass proceeded uneventfully, as far as the 'Our Father' towards the end.

Now I was used to the normal Irish way of standing up, reciting the prayer into the prayer sheet and not looking at anyone else. But this was an American-style celebration and it was rather different. Everyone grasped the hand of those to the left and right of them, and began to sing the prayer. I wasn't very impressed with this until a large, bespectacled, middle-aged man beside me offered me his hand. It appeared to me to be a genuine offer of support or friendship, because he wasn't afraid to look me in the eye when offering his hand, yet he wasn't in the least bumptious or pushy. It was just offer of connection, simply made. I did take his hand and surprised myself by joining in the singing. Gradually, over the next few minutes, I felt the warmth of the congregation around me and it lifted me out of myself. There was no shame in this rather open display; it was actually sincere. At the end I smiled to my companion, and he smiled back. That's all. I don't really believe it was a religious experience; I believe I was touched by the warmth of the people around me, and it helped break my cycle of negative thoughts.

We have the power to influence and uplift those around us, if we really want to and if we really try. The trick is to project it outwards, as that congregation did by stretching out their hands and raising their voices. It was good.

Layer 2: Our Self-Image

The second layer of personality is a more complex entity –
our 'self-image' and how we regard ourselves. Our image of
ourselves is neither how we really are, nor how we appear
to others. The truth, especially the truth about ourselves, can
be desperately hard to realise and face up to. Avoiding the
truth, both consciously and unconsciously, is what we are
busily engaged in doing a lot of the time.

If we look at ourselves, we want to appear less negative
and more like our ideal self than we actually are. We are thus
constantly deceiving ourselves, for we all have negative characteristics and we are not the same as our ideal self. The way
we deal with these discrepancies is the defining characteristic of ourselves. How we obliterate and distort both internal
and external reality becomes the pattern of our behaviour
and our thinking – in other words, our personality.

That pattern of thinking is defined by our 'personal
survival kit', the set of defence mechanisms originally
defined by Sigmund Freud, and his greatest contribution to
psychiatry. We develop, over years of internal and external
interaction, a pattern of dealing with reality that is peculiar
to ourselves – nobody else has the same personality as we
do. It could be argued that nobody else has the same experiences as we do, and that our personality is shaped by our
experiences. But it is not purely these experiences but, more
important, how we deal with these experiences that shapes
us the most. Our fundamental urge when faced by life's chal-
lenges and problems is to survive, and the pattern of our
'survival kit' is the defining characteristic of our personality.

Our survival kit consists of any number of defence mechanisms, and their use in everyday life is one of the basic tenets
of psychiatry. The number of them varies, according to who
we read, but the characteristic they all share is that a great
truth, reality or emotion is taken and the emotional energy

from it placed elsewhere in the psyche. These mechanisms may be conscious as well as unconscious, and the distinction between conscious and unconscious becomes hazy when dealing with them. There are some basic mechanisms:

- *Denial* – some truth is rejected by the mind and the energy is invested in shoring up that rejection.

- *Repression* – the upsetting emotion is forced back down into the unconscious, but leaves some upsetting traces in the conscious world.

- *Projection* – the blame or responsibility for something is pushed out from ourselves on to another person and the energy is invested in blaming or hating the other person.

- *Sublimation* – the energy of some emotion is transferred into a more wholesome and acceptable pursuit or an alternative, perhaps artistic, method of expression.

- *Reaction formation* – we deny reality by placing our energy in exactly the opposite direction from the reality we can't face.

- *Intellectualisation* – the emotion invested by a person who generally uses their mind rather than their body in their daily lives, in verbiage and discussion rather than facing the emotion itself.

- *Regression* – we cope with a new situation we find difficult by behaving and thinking as we did at an earlier age.

The list of possible defence mechanisms is larger, but as the list becomes longer, so each mechanism becomes not a distinct mechanism in itself, but a variation upon common themes. The commonest theme is avoidance – avoidance of truth, avoidance of emotion and avoidance of reality – and investment of that energy in shoring up a more personally palatable view of external or internal reality.

The defence mechanisms in our survival kit are used all the time, all day, in little ways and big. We are all hypocrites, especially those of us who try to be nice and friendly and try to get people to like us. We avoid truths and confrontations with little lies and obfuscations that aid diplomacy and avoid external conflict. And this may become a way of life. We often lose track of whether we are being honest and truthful to ourselves, and others, in the small things as well as the big ones. After all, in a social sense, letting it all out and telling everybody exactly what we think of them head-on is a sure-fire way to universal dislike and rejection and it isn't worth the pain for the small emotional gain in being 'honest'. The same thing applies to totally and truly facing ourselves: it may be too painful or too difficult, and so it is easier in everyday life to employ our survival kit to get by. Thus in everyday life the defence mechanisms are good and useful. They drive us in useful directions, help us avoid things we can't face, and generally help us put a good front on things.

However, when those defence mechanisms get too big they end up being the problem and not the solution. When a survival kit changes from a useful adjunct to daily life into a problem in itself, then we must each explore our personal defence mechanisms and come to understand our personal make-up. We may not be the best judge of our own defence mechanisms, quite simply because if they were 'designed' to avoid reality and they are doing their job, of course we won't be able to see them at work. Other people, especially those personally close to us or those trained to observe, such as psychiatrists or therapists, can see these mechanisms at work and the problems they cause, but we are often blind to ourselves and the workings of our own survival kits.

When I was at school, I had a friend with a club foot. He was a charming chap, humorous and intelligent and about as well-adjusted as anyone. During his teenage years, however, he developed a fascination with war, fighting and especially with Adolf Hitler. He immersed himself in the details of Hitler's rise from obscurity, his personality, his armies, the dates and details of all the battles of the Second World War, and why they were won or lost. He would talk at length about Hitler's plans and his philosophy – the belief in racial supremacy and the need to subjugate the inferior races. Most of all, he admired Hitler's strength and his refusal to tolerate any personal weakness. It didn't take a psychological genius to figure out where the obsession with Hitler and his strength came from – it came from my friend's club foot. Identifying with an all-powerful figure meant he didn't have to face the reality of his own 'weakness'. While the rest of us identified with and dreamed of becoming pop stars and footballers, he identified with and dreamed of becoming an all-powerful figure who didn't worry about the little weaknesses and problems we all have. To me it was very clear, but to him they were two totally different things: there was no connection between his battle to accept or reject his physical limitations and his absolute admiration for one man who proclaimed a race free of imperfections and all other humanising traits. I don't know what happened to my friend in later life – I just hope he doesn't still have a swastika emblazoned on his T-shirts.

While we might label that particular defence mechanism a 'reaction formation', it exemplifies the purpose of the defence mechanism – taking a negative or distressing emotion, and turning the force of that emotion, either consciously or unconsciously, in another psychological direction, one that is more palatable to ourselves.

Beyond Defence Mechanisms

When we are talking or thinking about some subject close to us, and we hit a 'truth', we know it. There is an emotional resonance with our core that gently explodes inside us. 'That's it!' we say, 'I've got it!' It may be hard to put words on it, but in trying to do so we may be able to put rational understanding on what is essentially an emotional and personal experience. By exploring these accounts and these 'truths' we can learn more about ourselves than by any other process. A great hint as to where those 'truths' lie is given to us by our defence mechanisms. The emotional areas that trigger the greatest anger at others, that produce the most intense immersion in work, that produce great intensity and rigidity of thought, are those areas where our emotional 'truths' probably lie.

There is a profound 'eureka' sensation on reaching a core truth, and a great emotional release on expressing it in words. Taking that emotion, telling it to someone else for the first time, helps release the part of energy that our defence mechanisms had bound it up in. The first time we explore the experience in words is the time when we are telling that truth most accurately. It is the crystallising of the experience into words that helps free us from the experience. The next time, we often repeat the words, but miss out the revelatory explosive aspect of the first time – the emotional resonance has gone or is at least diminished. When we watch someone reveal a 'truth' on *Oprah*, it isn't the genuine emotional truth we are watching but the 'truth' that is parroted and paraded for viewers' entertainment. What may initially have been an emotional truth becomes a parody of the truth and maybe a form of denial in itself. If we say it loud enough and often enough, we might convince ourselves that we are telling the reality of the situation, but we are probably not.

Who we tell our truth to, particularly the first time, can be vital. If the words are important to the person listening and evoke genuine emotion in them, it helps us resonate their emotion with ours. In the film *Born on the Fourth of July*, Tom Cruise's soldier character returns from Vietnam wounded and eventually crippled. He tries to maintain his belief in the righteousness of the American cause by going on parade in his wheelchair, wearing his uniform, but he begins to unravel when making a speech about duty and honour. He has a sort of mental breakdown and rejects the whole system for which he fought and gave up his future. He begins his mental rehabilitation, not by leaving the army or sleeping with a prostitute in Mexico (which he does), but by confessing to the mother and wife of the man he had shot in error that he was responsible for their loved one's death. It was that experience of facing up to the truth of his own actions, it was the expression of what he had done to the people that mattered, that made it possible for him to put the past behind him and start life anew. From then on, he could begin to purge the ghosts from his experience. He could live his denial no longer.

The truth, our truth, like the defence mechanisms that surround it, is a personal truth. No one has the same experiences, the same make-up or the same reactions, so coming to terms with ourselves has to be a personal process, not a collective one. The solution to the dilemma we have when we face ourselves cannot be handed to us on a plate by some quaint philosophy or some cult cure. There is indeed a great spiritual truth to be discovered in religion; but immersing ourselves in religion or philosophy to the exclusion of our own persona is not the solution to our personal difficulties. Many cults and quacks offer the illusion of certainty and parade before their believers the answers to all questions. This quick fix is made possible by adapting and moulding the believers' way of thinking to the point of excluding individual reasoning and personal development. That way offers temporary solutions only, avoids real personal issues, and actually inhibits us in the long term. The basic problem is that quick fixes are just too easy, too pat, and involve no personal thinking. It is very easy, when going through a troubled patch, to get swamped by a powerful voice or intense persuasive philosophy. Don't fall so fast. The improved self-image we get by immersing ourselves in someone else's idea of what we are and what we should be leads us to initial happiness and then increasingly bitter disillusionment as we realise the limitations of what we have wallowed in.

The scandal of Bhagwan Shree Rajneesh is a perfect example of this. He was a cult leader who built a city in the wilds of Oregon and fooled thousands of people into giving up their time and money to come to live with him in the wilderness. While his followers built his city, he drove around in a Rolls-Royce and made occasional speeches and pseudo-religious statements. He developed increasingly bizarre habits and began to profess silence as his preferred method of teaching. He confessed to his personal bodyguard of ten years, 'Enlightenment? I haven't got a clue about enlightenment', but he kept on 'teaching' his followers anyway. He eventually fled from the USA before he could be arrested for fraud, abandoning his followers as if they had done nothing for him. He was refused entry into many countries before returning to his native India. Although many followed him, he left a sense of disillusionment behind him. It is a lesson to us that we must make our personal journeys in a questioning manner, questioning both ourselves and others.

Layer 3: Our Inner Being

The third layer of our personality is the deepest and most important part. It is our real self, our core and our fundamental being. It is our truth, and our emotional centre. It is often what our defence mechanisms try to hide from our own conscious view. Our core influences our life direction as well as our surface being or public persona. Our inner core is often closer to our public persona than we would like to admit. Those traits seen clearly by others in our superficial appearance often reflect what goes on deep down, even though we may not be aware of it ourselves. After all, that is what our second layer, our self-image, is all about: hiding little bits of unpalatable external and internal reality from ourselves. Such classic tricks as Freudian slips – words that come without being thought through – and behavioural parapraxes – mistakes or omissions we make inadvertently in our behaviour – are just surface manifestations of our deeper selves at work. For example, I recall a friend at a party looking at the people in the room and commenting about one of the girls there who was rumoured to be 'generous to others' with both her mind and her body, 'Ah, there's Julia, she is a tart of gold, I mean heart of gold.' He could not help his unconscious opinion of the person coming through.

The old proverb that actions speak louder than words is manifest in a million ways. I once visited a psychiatrist in Canada and joined him in therapy with a couple who were having difficulty in their relationships with their children. Each partner in the couple had been married and divorced previously and each brought a child into the marriage. The stepfather of the woman's little boy had been imposing a severe disciplinary regime on him for a number of months for no apparent reason. She was reacting badly and threatening to walk out on her second husband as she had walked out on her first. He was having a hard time in the therapy sessions explaining why he was punishing her son so hard for trivial things. He started missing the sessions or coming late to them, but always had a perfect excuse for each time he was unable to attend. It was obvious to both the therapist and the wife that he was avoiding the issues but he persisted in saying he wanted to come to therapy to sort these issues out. Yet he kept on missing sessions.

Eventually he was confronted with his avoidance of the problems and he vehemently denied doing what it was obvious he was doing. Like all of us, he believed that he knew what controlled his actions, and unconscious avoidance of the issues that related to his stepson wasn't part of it. Decisions we make, choices we make, people we like or dislike instantly and yet can't understand why, are all hints of our innermost thoughts. We can learn about ourselves via our emotions and our defence mechanisms, but they are not in themselves our full selves.

Our core personality can contain many negative as well as positive aims and drives. The early psychoanalysts talked about the 'life instinct' and the 'death instinct', the life instinct representing the positive drives and goals in life and the death instinct representing the negative instincts and components of our inner being. If we really are gay, for example, and we find it impossible to admit to anyone – including ourselves – there is good reason for defence mechanisms to go into overdrive. If we deeply hurt a friend or lover through our selfish wants, we may need to obscure the real reasons for our acts and we may not want to see the damage we have done to them, and so our defence mechanisms may shield ourselves from it.

As well as containing our noble aspirations and intentions, our core contains all our lusts and aggressions, desires and dislikes. There is no right or wrong to that part of us, there is only the reality of personal truth. Hiding that truth, especially the negative components of that truth, from ourselves and not becoming aware of what we truly are is a guaranteed way to discontent, because it means that we disregard a whole part of ourselves.

Conversely, entirely indulging every little whim and want doesn't produce 'wholeness', it produces selfishness. When Hamlet plots to kill Claudius, who has killed Hamlet's father, the king of Denmark, he doesn't just go ahead and do it, he thinks about it, prays to God for guidance, and then goes ahead and kills him anyway. It is very important to become aware that deep down we have negative and unattractive wants and desires, but we don't have to indulge them in order to control them. Simply becoming aware of them is half the battle against them. The solution is to become aware of our truths, both positive and negative, and then decide which ones to indulge and which to hold back on.

Our core personality is not a fixed entity. It can change and develop over time. We are none of us the same as we were twenty years ago; our wants and desires are different, our aspirations and our sorrows are different and our experience is different. If we do well in a psychological sense, our fundamental characteristics – our core and our truths – develop with us, and we evolve into mature, happy people. We all have underdeveloped areas and traits within us, from a talent for impersonating others to an ability to care and nurture, and we can develop these fundamental areas to the full by exploring and indulging them. We all also have gaps and things we cannot do, for example paint a portrait or become a dynamic leader. There is no doubt that we are as varied in our fundamental characteristics as we are in our surface ones – we do not have one common great big centre that we all share and we all relate to. Neither is there a common shared ideal person that we all really want to become. We are all truly individuals and we are all fundamentally different.

Because we are so different in ourselves, there can be no real rules set out as to what we can or cannot do, what we can or cannot explore, or what we should or should not accomplish. There are no rules – we make them for ourselves. A lot of people never explore what it is they want, or attempt to explore or develop their own talents and abilities that aren't immediately visible. We don't know unless we try them out and see what we have inside us. Winston Churchill became British prime minister when he was in his sixties, and wasn't afraid to develop his leadership skills even at that age. There is no shame in trying something and failing – this can be positively rewarding in itself. But there is often regret at not trying at all, generally in later life when we no longer have the opportunity or the enthusiasm. Our abilities and talents are as much a part of us as our emotions, and they deserve as much exploration. We create the space for ourselves by finding out what it is we want, the desire for change comes from not being fully content with exactly how we are. We deal more fully with the developing possibilities of life and how to choose a direction and goals in Chapter 13.

Because we change fundamentally in our inner selves as we grow older, we have to change externally, and throughout our personality, in order to become or remain contented.

As we change slowly over the years, so we must renew our efforts to stay in touch with our own 'core', because that part of us may be evolving towards somewhere else away from the place we presently inhabit. We can thus never give up our attempts to see through ourselves and get behind our own defence mechanisms and explore our emotions, because the minute we do, we begin to lose touch, and drift away almost imperceptibly from the contented balance we sought to achieve or have already achieved.

The layers of our personality provide a useful function: they enable us to live with ourselves and the outside world. When any part of us escapes the dynamic balance between our component parts and becomes excessively large or even the dominant part of us, we lose the balance, and we lose our personal contentment. Our personality is an active communicating enterprise, with its various parts constantly to-ing and fro-ing. The key to development of our total personality is that thing that cuts across all the parts and layers – self-awareness!

The U-Turn: Self-Mastering Techniques

The object of these exercises is to gain insight into our own personality structure and how we use it to cope with the world. This exercise is not an attempt to change our structure but to comprehend it, and gain understanding into how we cope with internal and external stress.

1. Take a pen and a few sheets of paper and go to a quiet place to concentrate for a while. At the top of the first page write down the heading, 'My Personality Structure'.

2. On the first page, beneath the heading write down a description of how you appear to others. List the ten words that others would use to describe you and write them down in a column. If this is difficult, think of the last time you met and had a conversation with a relative stranger, and think of the impression you left them with on that specific occasion. Write down the five best characteristics you left them with and also the five most negative characteristics.

3. On the second page, look at the list of defence mechanisms listed earlier in this chapter and write them down in the order you use them most frequently. If you have difficulty with that, think of the last time someone felt very irritated or angry with you, and examine the way you reacted to that negativity. Examine each of the defence mechanisms in turn and see if it applied to you.

4. On the third page, list your five most positive and five most negative core traits. Think of your best and your worst characteristics and don't be generous to yourself. Make sure you think not of what impression you give to others or want to give to others, but of what you feel your true personality is like, warts and all.

5. Now compare the first page with the third. There should be a difference between the two sets of lists. If the lists are broadly similar, look at the defence mechanisms you listed on the second page, and see if any of them might explain the differences between your superficial characteristics and your true inner core.

One of the most difficult things about dealing with the outside world is finding the right way to communicate with it. If we are to complete a U-turn in our lives we have to find a way to increase our skills in expressing what is inside in the way we want to. This is what we deal with in the next chapter.

10

Talking and Communication

> Learning how to communicate well is as vital as learning how to breathe

The world is a very loud place, abuzz with the noise of machines, cars, music and, above all, with talk. People are constantly communicating with one another, chattering and making conversation in a never-ending cacophony of words and voices. We communicate about business, hobbies, plans, gossip, worries and pleasure, and we devote a large part of our days to doing it. We cannot enter an office, a restaurant, a pub without hearing the dull and the brilliant, the witless and the wise holding forth on the topics of the day. We cannot turn on the radio without hearing politicians selling themselves with self-generated controversies, DJs playing phone call jokes and talking about Hollywood, and callers telling us about everything from Wall Street dealers to babies. The internet is full of blogs and opinion pieces, and YouTube is filled with personal commentaries about everything under the sun. Social networks such as Facebook and Twitter are built upon the individual word and personal communication. It is a world of words and a world of expression. Talking is how things get done and it's how people get to know each other. There is a whole TV industry of talk shows, in which people do exactly that – talk. We live in a world in which the mute and the silent remain just that, while the world gets on frantically with its own wordiness. In the universe of sound, nobody listens to the silent.

When people are talking to one another, there is more to it than just sounds, words and sentences. There is communication going on, and that is so much more than just talking. Everybody carries with them a personal and emotional background that manifests itself in everything they say and do. Everybody has a reasoning and a message, a desire or an intention behind the words they use. The messages behind the words vary according to the setting. In a political setting, the intent 'I'm going to stab this guy in the back' may be presented in the words, 'Let's see where my new plan leaves Bill's old plan'; in a casual setting, the intent 'I'm bored and I want to be entertained' can emerge as the words, 'Where did you go on holiday?'; in a salesperson's work setting, the intent 'I'm going to get this man to buy the policy and I'm going to get the 20 per cent commission' can emerge as, 'Let me tell you what you need from a modern insurance plan'; and parental concern, 'I wonder if Jason is really on drugs and he's not telling me', may be expressed as 'You're looking pale, dear.'

We all have things going on in our minds that are inevitably reflected in the words we use and the way we use them. Our motivations may not be clearly visible through the maze of verbiage and we may even consciously design our conversation to avoid revealing our intentions. Talking can be used to obscure just as much as it can be used to reveal; it can become a barrier instead of a gateway. But we can use talk to communicate our ideas and feelings to others, and when it is used masterfully, we can use talk to make minds up, to reverse firm decisions and to change people's lives.

Individuality

Our superficial pattern of conversation is as much a part of ourselves as our nose. No two people see or talk about the weather in exactly the same way and in exactly the same words. Our individuality bounds through, even if it is only in the inflexion of our speech or the length of our silences. Our social conversational ability, small talk ability and style, is part of our self-presentation – it is the basis on which people form an impression of us. Along with our looks and grooming, our chatter tells people what we are like and allows people to slot us into various categories: attractive or unattractive; interesting or not interesting; worth listening to or not worth listening to.

One of the first basic rules of talking and of communicating is to listen to the other person. When I was studying psychiatry as a medical student, I was part of a group being given psychology tests by a tutor. One of these tests involved splitting the group of twelve of us into groups of three, and then each of us was given a pen and paper. We were asked to look at each of the groups of three people and define those personal characteristics that separated two of the three from the other one in the group. We listed all the characteristics for each group and then we were all asked to call out not the names of the people we isolated but simply the characteristics we had judged them by. The descriptions produced by the group were fascinating not for their diversity but for their similarity. We found that we judged each other on a similar set of characteristics – appearance, grooming, friendliness, confidence, humour and attractiveness. The other interesting thing was that the words called out by each individual reflected not the people being judged but the judges themselves. When a shy person judged others, they thought shyness an important category. When a humorous individual judged others, they thought a sense of humour an important characteristic to include, and so on. From this exercise I learned that we judge others by a limited set of characteristics and that we judge others by comparison with ourselves. So if our superficial chatter is individual, our ways of looking at and judging others are also individual.

How can we apply this information? How can it be of use to us? Well, if we want to make an impression on others, we already know we have to impress them with our appearance, our friendliness and our confidence. We must also pay attention to their nuances and their preferences. Being aware of them rather than of ourselves gives us a better chance of making a positive impression on them, since they will be judging us by their own characteristics. A large section of the armoury we have in self-presentation is our social chatter. Nobody ever teaches us how to talk to people. We have to do it for ourselves, and we have to learn the rules as we go along. Below are some of the rules.

What to Say

There are a few different ways of tackling the feeling of having nothing to say. The most basic way is finding out whether we have no thoughts on something or if we simply don't have any words on something. Have we no thoughts? The answer to that is, 'Of course we do; we are thinking things all the time.' We all have a thought-filled background commentary on what is going on around us. We are constantly having a private conversation with ourselves. Most of the time we are not even aware of what we are thinking. When a pimply teenager is serving us a hamburger in a fast food joint, we are probably looking at the spots on his chin and wondering why they are the same colour as the hamburger sauce. When a police siren goes off and a squad car zooms past on the wrong side of the road, we find ourselves thinking, 'Oh, some young cop who thinks they're on TV.' When we hear a train clack-clacking across an ancient track in the distance, we find ourselves slipping into the rhythm and humming a pop tune in our minds.

Our background thoughts may be at odds with what we are saying or doing, but they are there nonetheless. The level of awareness of our background thoughts is different for different people, and different for each person at different times. The important thing is that it is present.

Therefore it is not thoughts that are lacking when it comes to conversation, but forming these thoughts into words and then expressing them. We inadvertently inhibit our natural thought flow by excessive self-consciousness and self-awareness on the one hand, and an excessive desire to say something, anything, on the other. We desperately want to say something and this desperation feeds our own self-consciousness. We can also, of course, be simply reserved or lazy in conversation and we dry up because we don't want to bother to talk to someone. This is often picked up by the other person and can lead to embarrassment and even dislike. We owe it to ourselves at least to make an effort, for lack of effort in social circumstances is at best an insult to others and an injustice to ourselves.

Thinking the Thoughts

If we wish to improve ourselves socially, the first task we must undertake is to free up the barrier between brain and mouth. We have to learn to tune in to our thoughts, organise them coherently and then express them. The easiest component of this is actually tuning into what goes on inside, this time not necessarily in an emotional sense but in a simple verbal one.

As an exercise, see what runs through your head when you look at a shoelace. 'Not much,' you might reply, 'it's just a shoelace.' But in fact lots of things run through our heads about it that we notice but don't generally note. Its length, for example, its colour, its thickness, its texture and its quality. We may notice if the ends are tipped in plastic, or if the ends are frayed, and if the lace is full length or cut short. It may have a knot in it or it may be creased into angles where it curves around eye holes in the shoe. It may be the short type designed for sneakers, with thick multi-coloured threads, or it may be a thin plain type designed for gents' brogues, or it may be thick, rough and plain, like the ones used in hiking boots.

In short, there is a whole world in a shoelace (a mild exaggeration here) and we think a multitude of thoughts quickly and imperceptibly when looking at it. If we were asked to speak to a crowd of people about shoelaces, we would probably feel we had nothing to say except, 'This is a shoelace.' Yet we have noted all these shoelace characteristics, and if we were aware of our thoughts we could talk about it for at least a few minutes. The essential trick is first of all to realise that the thoughts are actually there, and, second, to translate these thoughts into words.

Forming the Words

This second ability is much more difficult. If it is not in our genes (i.e. if our mothers weren't able to melt telephones with their ability to talk for hours) or acquired over the years in an ad hoc fashion, it must be acquired by sheer hard work and effort. As with any other skill, we acquire it by learning from those who are good at it. We should listen to other people's conversation and see how they express ideas, and we should listen especially to those people we find interesting. It may eventually dawn on us that most people do not have a wonderful expressive poetic mind bursting with new ideas and wonderful phrases. In fact most people tend to repeat opinions or thoughts heard elsewhere, or express one original idea or thought in a few different ways. If we ever have conversations with a number of different people after a big football match, for example, we often find the opinions of a TV expert rehashed and served up as original conversation. Very few people have Oscar Wilde's ability to think original thoughts and say wonderful things in an entertaining way. He was famed as the best talker of his time and held forth at the dinner tables of royalty and the aristocracy of British society. He made several trips to Paris, and on one of these trips he was guest of honour at a dinner party, at which he talked about poetry and history, French culture and politics, in a seamless weave, as though he had written a PhD thesis. 'Several of his guests wept,' says his biographer Richard Ellmann, 'to think that words could achieve such splendour.' He was the world's most famous conversational genius, and his genius has never been replicated.

Practising

There's no shame in practising a conversation piece before putting it on public display, nor is it shameful to consider what topics we should talk about and what we have to say about them before we use them. Some people are so good at entertaining guests and friends with stories and anecdotes that they must have been planned beforehand.

In fact it is an essential conversational skill to have something to say to help break the ice at the beginning of a chat. If we can regale our companions with an amusing or just averagely interesting anecdote, detailing something that happened to us or to someone we know, this often prompts a response to some of the things mentioned in the story. If we can then reply with something that picks up some aspect of their story, we've got a conversation going. The trick is concentrating on what is said to us and then tuning in to the thoughts that run around our minds that were prompted by the conversation, latching on to one thought or story that is relevant and then thinking consciously of what we're going to say in reply, before we say it.

Consideration

It is extremely important to run our background thoughts past our conscious minds before expressing them, because that is how we prevent ourselves from saying something dreadful and embarrassing. I was once sitting down to lunch in a cafeteria with a colleague when a blind man sat down at the table with his guide dog beside him. My friend started a conversation with the blind man and then, after a pause in the conversation, began a story about his old dog. He told about the dog getting old and blind but not realising it, and mentioned its habit, when it heard a car in the distance, of rushing out of the house as far as the garden fence to bark at it. 'One day the dog heard a car coming and ran out the door barking and then ran in to the fence and hurt its nose. The poor thing forgot he had gone blind!' He then looked up and saw the expression on the blind man's face and realised that he had made a dreadful social error. He just hadn't thought before he spoke.

A lack of consideration for others when we make conversation is extremely common and can cause a considerable amount of pain to them. I have a clear recollection of admitting into a general hospital a 45-year-old man with a severe chest pain. He was brought straight to the coronary care unit, and was hooked on to cardiograph machines and various other machines that beeped at regular intervals. He was a jovial and blustery man and he professed little concern for his own condition. He managed to mask a quite natural fear and worry about himself, joking and chatting throughout his time in the unit. Fortunately he hadn't suffered a heart attack, but he had had a warning bout of angina, which was worrying enough in itself, but not life-threatening. When he was told this two days later his relief was instantaneous and it was visible; he sank back into the pillows and let out a tremendous sigh. I asked him if he had been worried about his heart, and scared that he had had a heart attack. 'Well, I was a bit worried about it at first,' he replied, 'but it just got worse after my mother visited me.' I recalled seeing a fussy elderly lady beside him some time after he was admitted. 'She just sat there and told me all about our old neighbours who got heart attacks and died. She thought she was being kind but I just felt sick listening to her. It was the last thing I wanted to hear.'

Such stories are extremely common in hospitals, where people – for want of something to say – say something wrong and cause more suffering for the patients. Tact in these circumstances, and in most others, is a matter of thinking before we speak, especially if we are going to relate something vaguely acerbic or gossipy.

What About the Other Person?

A wonderful technique to help superficial conversational ability is to concentrate not on what we are going to say and whether we are going to be appropriate and entertaining, but to concentrate on the other person in the conversation. We should ask ourselves, 'What would they like us to say to them?' If we can free our minds of ourselves, our own worries and thoughts, and focus our consciousness on the person we are talking with, we can really tune into that person. For example, if we spend time in the company of an irritable person, and they are behaving in an annoying and irritating way, we pick up those vibes in numerous ways and become fractious and irritable ourselves. Even the effort of trying to cope with the other person's irritability makes us annoyed. If, on the other hand, we are with someone who is friendly and bubbling over with *joie de vivre*, we have to be very depressed and despairing not to be infected, and end up in almost as good a mood as our companion.

Thus moods and mental states are communicable, like colds or herpes. The communication processes are numerous, subtle and quite powerful, essentially when we pick up others' vibes. If, instead of being passive recipients of other people's vibes, we actively concentrate on listening carefully and paying attention to someone else's conversation, they will pick this up and will be encouraged. In the same way as it is so offensive to be ignored and passed over in conversation, it is conversely very flattering and encouraging to be genuinely listened to and appreciated in a conversation. It is impossible to mistake the warm and welcoming attention of someone prepared to put effort and concentration into a conversation as anything but sincere and genuine. It cannot be faked. The secret is to be more interested in the other person than in making a good impression on them. If we actually have that interest or acquire it by concentrating on it, we end up actually creating a better impression of ourselves than if we were just trying to impress.

I remember an occasion when I was involved in a group therapy session as a facilitator. I played very little part in the discussion and, because the group members knew me quite well, they let their guard down and started discussing various therapists among themselves. I was rather surprised at the sharpness with which each therapist's personal conversational and therapy style was dissected. Not only were the group members able to gauge the degree of competence of each therapist, they were able to clearly pick out who was really paying attention to them and who really cared, and who did not. The opinions expressed accurately mirrored my own opinion of the therapists involved, but I was very impressed with the strength of the emotions expressed – either for or against each therapist – based not on the therapist's skill or experience but on their genuineness. Burnt-out or lazy therapists were bitterly criticised and warm ones strongly praised. A therapist's genuine effort to help was the most prized quality that was discussed. The principle burned itself into me. Not only in a therapeutic situation, but also in a social one, the most prized social characteristic is a genuine interest in the other person, and people know when their conversational partner is caring and interested, and – more important – when they are not.

Public Speaking

It is a wonderful thing to behold a genuine orator in full flight. Barack Obama can sway a crowd when he wants to with his soaring rhetoric and beautiful words. What he says is almost irrelevant – it is thrilling and moving just to hear him say it. It is impossible not to be impressed by a dynamic and erudite personality projecting themselves through their words into the hearts and minds of those listening to them. We can be swayed into believing what they believe, into thinking what they think and into doing what they want us to do, simply by the breathtaking mesmerism of their words and voices.

Adolf Hitler kept a whole nation in sway for twelve truly dreadful years with his powerful personality, his appeal to the 'nobler' aspects of his people, and his awesome prowess as a speaker. Most of the time he was spouting nationalistic gibberish, dressed up to sound like a coherent philosophy, but the content was essentially just rabble-rousing repetition. He consolidated his grip on political power with a grip on the hearts of the German nation through this ability. Was he born an orator? Not at all. Did he acquire his gifts through his family? Hardly! Then how did he do it? He simply practised in front of a mirror until he got it right. He knew what he wanted to do and he watched how he did it until he perfected it. Every tone and every gesture was perfected before his speeches and then he put on a performance for his audience. And what a performance. Even seventy-plus years later, and with the hindsight of history revealing the true malignancy of his mind, he can still amaze us on old newsreels with his awesome powers. And if he could do it, with all his perverseness and his problems, why shouldn't we, who are infinitely more worthy human beings compared to him?

Standing up and addressing a crowd is not the same as holding a conversation with another human being, but the talents are related. The ability to speak before others simply requires two things – preparation and guts. The secret is in the preparation: knowing what we want to say, choosing ways in which to say it, and practising saying those words out loud in front of a mirror or our trustworthy friends.

The guts to actually do it is often best acquired by being in a position where we have to do it and can't get out of it. There is nothing like *having* to do something to force us to actually *do* it. Any speaker or performer who is honest will say they get 'butterflies' before standing up to speak in front of others. But they also talk equally truthfully about losing that fear when they become engrossed in their performance, when they almost forget who they are addressing and concentrate on simply communicating to them. The railway tracks through the performance are the actual words and, if they are rehearsed so that we are familiar with them, they are not a problem once we get over the initial hurdle of actually starting. The rest is plain sailing. And what an impressive power it is to have over people, to be able to educate them, change their opinion and even inspire them through our words and our performance. The confidence it gives us is more than enough to justify the angst and effort that goes on beforehand, and it can give us a belief in ourselves that transcends the mere act of giving a speech. The victory to savour is the confirmation of our ability – however limited we feel it is – in the shining eyes and rapt attention of our audience, and if we are lucky, in the congratulatory words later. The next time we are called on to make a speech, we can fall back on our previous experience, no matter how small a triumph, and use the memory of it to stop ourselves refusing the request.

The usefulness of actually making a speech goes beyond mere ego-feeding and self-indulgence. Practising speech-making makes it easier to hold up our part of a conversation and say something that someone will want to listen to. If a group of people listened to us when we were saying some-thing reasoned and practised, it gives us some small belief that our opinions may have some validity and that they are worth expressing in conversation. That confidence in our own worthiness frees us up to some extent from our natural self-consciousness, and it actually helps clear up that foggy barrier between brain and mouth. When we believe we have some-thing worthwhile to say, even if it is simply our opinion about a TV game show, confidence makes it much easier to formu-late that opinion and express it. The same spiral that inhibits us when we feel shy and unworthy, preventing us from saying what we think because we are so caught up we lose track of our thoughts, can actually work in reverse. We can manage to express our thoughts and then encourage ourselves to tune in and express ourselves further through belief in their worth. One thing we are guaranteed, they will certainly be better than Adolf's – he wasn't shy of expressing himself!

Humour

A sense of humour is one of the most precious assets to have in a social context. Of course it is a very individual charac-teristic, and 'one person's humour is another's pain', but an ability to see things in a slightly odd and quirky way can help grease the wheels of conversation, and can also help us to appreciate this quirk in others. A serious analysis of what constitutes a sense of humour seems like a contradiction in terms, but it is not as ridiculous as it sounds. Umberto Eco based his best-selling novel *The Name of the Rose* on the quest for Plato's lost second book – *The Book of Laughter* – if it ever existed. It is a well-worn cliché that behind every clown's face lies a soul of misery, but it is probably no more than a cliché – it is not likely to be true.

Getting a laugh from someone socially is one of the ways of making someone like you and helping you become accepted and self-confident. Laughter is both personal and universal, in that we all claim to have an individual sense of humour, yet we almost all laugh at the same things.

The easiest way to get a person to laugh is to tell a joke, and the only way to learn a joke is to listen to one, and concentrate on remembering it, even rehearsing it in private and then producing it in public (preferably with a different bunch of people!). It's as simple as that and it always goes down well, even if it's a bad one, i.e. no one laughs at the way we tell it. A good rule is not to tell a dirty joke unless you know the taste of the people listening – the appreciation gained from one person may be more than balanced by the antagonism earned from someone who's unimpressed by blue one-liners. Telling jokes is not a particularly intellectual or taxing pastime, but it is remarkably effective at breaking barriers and making someone else take notice and even appreciate us. I don't think Graham Norton would count himself as the most intelligent human in the world, but he is probably one of the most popular, thanks to his ability to tell jokes. The trick is to use the ability to tell jokes as a social entrée and confidence-booster, not to depend on it as an entire social repertoire.

People who tell jokes often have a good sense of humour – not because they are the same thing but because they both indicate an interest in the lighter side of life. Having a sense of humour that others appreciate, however, is a much more sophisticated and worthy characteristic than simply an ability to tell jokes. It essentially entails an ability not only to look at life or objects or events in an off-key manner, but to make that manner appealing and humorous. It is so easy to look at things a little skew-wise but inappropriately or offensively, so that the direction is well-intentioned but the remark or story lands upside down. There must be enough truth in a story to make it sound realistic and appropriate, and yet enough novelty and quirkiness in it to make it funny. For example, you could describe a stupid person by saying, 'He's really stupid.' That's a very ordinary way of expressing yourself. If you said, 'He's got a hole in his head', that's quite an interesting way of saying what you think. But to say, 'He's got a hole in his head the size of Dalkey Island' is not necessarily hilarious but is certainly more humorous. The point is to take what should be an ordinary comment and then examine it for ways of making it more interesting.

The first step is to look for a slightly unusual way of looking at an ordinary situation. The second step involves taking that unusual way of looking at things and then exaggerating it. The humour for the listener lies in the leap from incomprehension to comprehension following the path indicated by the speaker. There must be some distance to be travelled down the road because if the comparison is too obvious and the analogy too close, there is no leap of comprehension and no humorous dawning of understanding. 'He is a stupid person with a hole in his head' simply isn't funny because it is obvious.

For a perfect example of humour, watch Dara Ó Briain's comedy performances or read his book *Tickling the English*. He manages to take relatively ordinary situations and interests, his relationship with his fiancée (now his wife), his thoughts about science, where a member of the audience comes from and their occupation, and make that relationship or situation gloriously funny with a quirky expression and exaggerated phraseology. We can incorporate the same style of personal observation and amusing choice of words by the best method known to humanity: practice.

Sarcasm

Directing humour and wit against another person is a very dangerous game, and there is a very definite tightrope that you risk falling off when attempting it. It is very easy to be too harsh in our criticism of others and quite easy to raise a laugh at someone else's expense. We all have quite visible character quirks and faults that even the most indifferent of observers can spot, and it doesn't take a genius to explore, point out or exaggerate those faults to get a laugh. The way it is done, however, determines the reaction of the person being 'attacked'. It is quite possible to humorously dissect a person in front of others and not cause offence but it is an art form akin to origami – extremely delicate and difficult to perfect. People have very different 'touchiness' levels and if the dissector picks on a sensitive soul, he can make an enemy for life. How many of us genuinely forgive someone who makes a fool of us in front of others, while we keep a frozen smile on our faces? Most of us can remember remarks made about us many years later, even though they may have been funny to the other listeners.

As an example, here's something that happened in an English class at my school many years ago. The class was discussing William Wordsworth's poem about Tintern Abbey. The title of the poem is actually 'Lines written a few miles above Tintern Abbey', and my friend innocently asked, 'What does he actually mean, "a few miles above Tintern Abbey"?' The teacher witheringly replied, 'What do you think he means? Do you think he was skydiving or something?' The rest of the class cracked up laughing but my friend went bright red and sat down. He told me afterwards that he felt utterly humiliated and found it hard to forget the implication in the teacher's reply that he was being incredibly stupid. While I felt that the remark had the saving grace of being at least a bit funny, my friend could not see it in the same way at all.

A much safer way to use sarcastic or pointed observations on life is to direct them against ourselves, when the only person we can offend is ourselves. Just think – if those comments are difficult to direct at ourselves because they are so pointed, how much harder would another person find it to tolerate them? 'I must be very stupid to forget this was Christmas' sounds much more wholesome than, 'You must be very stupid to forget this was Christmas', because all the people listening can laugh at it. Nobody is affected, and indeed our personal standing is improved by our ability to laugh at ourselves. It is not often easy to do it because our pride says we deserve better than getting laughed at. But in fact we are getting laughed with, not laughed at, and we are appreciated for both our wit and sense of humour and also our self-deprecating humility.

Former President Bill Clinton, for all his faults, has the ability to direct wit against himself and create an image of being above the situation he describes. When he was in the middle of the Whitewater scandal, which concerned whether he had made shady land dealings while he was Governor of Arkansas, he attended a conference for TV and media personnel, and among the attendees were some journalists who had been attacking him strongly about the scandal. He made a speech in which he remarked, 'Any of you who think I am glad to be here should ask me if I want to buy some land in northern Arkansas.' There's a lot to be said for self-directed sarcasm – you hurt nobody. (Mind you, Clinton went on to hurt quite a few people in a later scandal with the intern Monica Lewinsky, and even his self-deprecating wit was unable to help him then.)

Another point to remember is that the person who succeeds in making a name through sarcastic and fiery comments about others ends up being more feared than revered, as people ask themselves the inevitable, 'What does he or she think of me?' If we think that the person is particularly malicious and full of invective, we do not appreciate the associated feeling that they might speak or even think of us in the same way. If the comments or humour reflect a person's chip on their shoulder and their exaggerated sense of inferiority, the comments come across as malicious rather than humorous, as put-downs rather than one-liners.

I used to work in a McDonald's fast food restaurant to pay my college fees. My favourite person there was one of the managers, a Sri Lankan immigrant. He was a genuine, friendly, hardworking and funny guy who made working in a fairly awful place pleasurable. Another manager, an Australian, used to tease him about being 'black' and used to gaily recite the latest racist jokes to his face, much to everybody's, including the Sri Lankan's, amusement. Or so it seemed. I never joined in because it simply made me uncomfortable. Soon after, the Sri Lankan left to work at a local vegetable shop. He met me some time later and surprised me with his interest in and knowledge about me, who had after all been only one of scores of workers under him. 'You know,' he said, 'there's a lot of racism about, even in Ireland, and you've just got to work twice as hard to get past all the prejudice.' No matter how much he pretended to laugh at his fellow manager's 'jokes', he wasn't as impervious to insult as he had initially appeared.

Being Interesting

If it is impossible to be humorous, if there are simply no funny bones in our bodies, and if our wit is simply doggerel, the next best thing we can be is interesting. It's not that difficult to be interesting but, like everything, if we're not born with it we can have a good shot at it by effort and perseverance. Interesting is not the same as ridiculous, or attention-grabbing – any fool can turn up to a social function wearing a revolving bow tie and a silly hat, but if he is unable to back up his attention-seeking garb with something to say, he will simply be branded as stupid and ignorant. But being interesting rather than just being visible is simply an exercise in understanding what other peoples' minds are attracted to. They are and we are attracted to novelty, variety and freshness – the spice of life and the thing that makes us get up in the morning.

So if it is possible to be novel, varied and fresh in our conversation and ideas, we will have a wonderful social attractiveness about us that others will pick up. While 'there's nothing new under the sun', making novel ideas is essentially the process of taking old ideas and turning them around or expressing variations on them. For example, saying in conversation that 'George Bush had no right to invade Iraq' is neither new nor exciting and you would be unlikely to encounter much challenge or encourage a debate. But to start a conversation by saying, 'You know, President Bush had a good few reasons to invade Iraq' would get at least a response and provoke some thought in those around you. The object of the exercise is not to throw out a bold blanket statement, but to have one or two points to back it up so that it can be seen to have at least a toehold in common sense. To go too far in an 'interesting' direction, for example 'Bush was completely right to invade Iraq and kill thousands of Iraqis too' can be a ridiculous exercise, which invites only derision and ends up producing not a true debate but just derogatory contradiction. The purpose of the conversational gambit – to provide some entertainment and to enhance our audience's (even if it's only one person) respect for us – would be totally lost in the ensuing verbal fray.

From when I was at college, I recall a particularly boring, wet November morning when I sat down in the general common room. A classmate sat down close by and picked up the newspaper. I greeted him and started a conversation with him about how I had always wanted to go to Trinity College (the rival college) rather than our own. I then threw in a couple of mildly prejudiced opinions for my reasoning, and let him reply. He felt honour bound to defend our own establishment and did so with some animation. We were joined by first one, then two, then four more classmates, and all began making contributions to the discussion. Soon there were about a dozen or so people talking enthusiastically about the various merits and demerits of our education. At the end of half an hour we had to adjourn for a lecture, but it had changed the tone of the morning, and it had passed the time very entertainingly. The point I learned from it – and I hadn't planned to start such a debate – is that it takes very little to 'be interesting'. The first thing is to have an idea that is off-centre enough to grab attention but not so much that it's completely outside the ballpark. The second is to put that idea across with enough verve and enthusiasm to hold others' attention. It is still a useful lesson.

People like the US radio show hosts Rush Limbaugh and Howard Stern are obviously not being sociable when they say incendiary and deliberately provocative things on their shows. And they are very successful at what they do – they provoke people into a response by going too far with their comments on sex or politics – and that's how they make their money. But if they carried on like that in their private lives, saying too much too loudly, there would be a different reaction. There is a fine line to be trodden between being interestingly different in our ideas and being downright boorish or ignorant. People will not necessarily tell us to our face that they find us intolerant or highly opinionated, they simply will not invite us back. Thus there is an art in finding the right way of being interesting in what we have to say, and being over the top in the way we say it.

Non-Verbal Communication

Part of our social armoury should be awareness of others – not just of the way they look but of the way they act. Communication occurs at different levels, and it occurs in different ways as well. 'Body language' is the phrase used to describe a whole range of non-verbal communication that passes between humans. The individual components of body language communication are legion, but the overall effect is unified. If someone is interested in us in conversation we notice their eyes keeping in contact with ours for longer than normal, we notice that they move closer to us. They may touch our arms or hand to make a point; they may face us if standing or turn towards us if sitting. They smile at us, they stop looking around at others, and their voice becomes more animated and enthusiastic when addressing us. Similarly, if they are not interested in us, they move away, look around, smile only momentarily, their voice flattens, and they turn away and may cross their legs away from us. The individual components of their body language can be divided up and microscopically examined. A knowledge of these details may make us slightly more socially aware, but it can also give us apoplexy every time our girlfriend crosses her legs in the 'wrong' direction or our boyfriend makes eye contact with another woman. The main thing about non-verbal communication is that it gives us a 'vibe' about how much interest someone has in us – no more, no less. Whether or not we are aware of the components, we will pick up a vibe, positive or negative, if it is there. All we have to do, essentially, is become aware of the other people and their responses to us.

In *The Bonfire of the Vanities*, author Tom Wolfe describes his bond-selling 'Master of the Universe' hero going to an uptown New York socialites' party. He is accosted at the door by the hostess, his arm is taken into hers, and she leads him away from the door towards the reception area. For about thirty seconds, he is treated to the best in verbal and non-verbal 'good vibes' a person can get and is then dumped for someone else who is then given the same treatment. This behaviour is social learning çarried to an extreme, where it is used to cover up lack of interest (she really didn't give a damn about him) rather than to convey genuine interest. It is debatable whether that degree of social learning is a boon to humankind – sincerity would probably be of more use.

Levels of Communication

Communication, at least the talking component of it, goes on at a number of different levels. It is possible to split talking, and especially communication, into as many levels as there are people, but essentially there are three different levels of communication.

Level 1: Oral Communication

The first level, which I call 'oral communication', includes superficial social chatter. I have already discussed this at length in this chapter, and its importance as the axle grease of life cannot be overstated. It is this level at which we live most of our lives and conduct most of our communication. Without the ability to master this level of communication, we will be deficient and frightened of simple superficial communication. It is worth learning well.

Level 2: Emotional Communication

The second level is important in a different way and for a different reason. This level of communication I call 'emotional communication'. When we go beyond social chatter into purposeful communication, we are talking at this second, deeper level. This type of communication is for an emotional purpose and a personal purpose, and it is closer to our real selves than our Level 1 type of communication, our social chatter.

When we talk to one another about purpose, emotions, upsets and joy, we are aiming to do more than just pass the time. There is a deeper motivation. It may be sheer ego, telling us to show others what wonderful thoughts we have or what marvellous things we have done. It may be simple work information – we want to complete a task and also show the boss how hard we are working. It may be to obtain relief from some intolerable situation that makes us unburden our worries on to anybody from the bus driver to the neighbours. It may be to seek advice from a friend about how to handle a relationship that is going awry. It may be anxiety about our job that makes us buttonhole a neighbour for an hour to tell him how to do his garden properly. Most of the purposeful conversations we have are important not just because we want something informative from them but because we gain some small emotional comfort at the end of them, and we feel better in ourselves. It may only be a small bit, but the feeling that someone else is aware of our troubles partially relieves us of them. We may not be fully aware of all the reasons that we feel the need to converse with someone, but it generally isn't too difficult to tell.

I was involved in a road accident at about eight o'clock one morning. I was returning from a weekend working trip, and I had stopped at a traffic light beside a massive earthmover which was being given a police escort. As the giant machine began to turn to the right, its tail end swung around, hit the back of my car and began to drag it into the middle of the junction. I had the dreadful feeling of the car moving without my being in charge of it. My car and I were deposited in the middle of the junction and the earthmover slowly moved on. I was shattered but alive. I jumped out of the car and – very illogically – ran screaming up the street after the earthmover. A very helpful lady stopped and gave me a lift to catch up with the monster and flag it and the police escort down. It took about fifteen minutes and I was not in a good mental shape when we finally succeeded. I talked to the police and the driver, who weren't interested in my story but came back to the scene of the accident and took down details. My car was crushed at the back and on the driver's side but was just about driveable. I drove the seventy miles home, and took the day off work.

Over the next few days I was unbelievably talkative to just about everyone I met. I talked to anyone about anything. I just couldn't stop. It took about a week for me to calm down properly, and it was only when I looked at my hands and saw that they were shaking constantly that I realised that what I was doing was talking to get the shock out of my system. Once I realised this, my talking diminished in intensity – though I was still willing to tell my story to anyone who would listen. This is a good example of communication at the emotional level. I was talking to relieve the shock of the accident, even if the topic of conversation was totally unrelated to the accident.

People's 'purposeful' conversation always comes from their own personal angle. I've never heard a husband giving out about his income tax in order to relieve his wife's feelings (or vice versa), but I've heard plenty doing it to relieve their own. When we do someone the favour of listening to them when they have something personally important to say, we generally realise that they are doing it for themselves and not for us. We are not being enlightened; in fact we are being used. Allowing someone to do that to us is one of the most generous things we can do for them.

When we are asked in these circumstances, 'What would you do if ...?' it is quite obvious that we are being asked, 'What should *I* do when ...?' People seldom ask emotional questions or have emotional needs that are unrelated to themselves. You are doing that person a favour when you answer that question or allow them to talk to you about their problems. But the corollary is that when we have been 'dumped on' in this fashion, we are often genuinely appreciated because we have indulged someone's ego, and shown enough care about them to take the time to listen. And the converse of this is that when we feel the need to 'dump on' someone we in turn realise just how important a listening ear is, how much we appreciate it, and also how rare a true listener is. Psychologists and psychiatrists are mainly paid listeners, and most honest ones will agree.

One elderly lady used to come to see me at a hospital clinic. She had a long-term psychiatric illness and lived alone, but was well looked after at the daycare centre she attended, and she also had a good social worker. She used to come to see me every few months or so, and I would spend about fifteen minutes chatting to her about her medication, the day centre and any other problems that were on her mind. I didn't think I was doing very much until her social worker approached me after one of her visits and said that she had wanted to tell me how much she appreciated my kindness and thoughtfulness during her visits to me. I replied that I really didn't think I had done that much; I just listened politely to her for a while. 'Don't underestimate the importance of those visits to her,' he said. 'She spends weeks looking forward to them, and talks about them for a long time afterwards. They are absolutely vital to her and your attitude helps her a lot.' It is very easy to dismiss the value of a listening ear, but it can be a powerful support to others.

Level 3: Core Communication

The deepest level of communication we can have is when we open up our core to someone else. This is in one sense an extension of the second level of communication, the emotional level, but this time it is our true self and inner being that is being exposed, not just the bits we want to reveal. About the only time we can let our defences go enough to communicate at this level is when we are with someone we can totally trust, be it a friend, lover, psychiatrist or therapist. Gently probing our own feelings and defences can reveal great truths or depths that we were not aware of. Indeed a psychiatrist friend of mine described the deep intensity of psychoanalysis as exploring the same emotional territory all the time but at a deeper level on each occasion. Figuring out those inner truths for ourselves is important, but expressing them to another person in words releases them from deep inside us. We are at once educated and freed. This type of communication is the deepest and most therapeutic communication possible. It heals us by exposing us without threat. We are made more whole by doing it.

In the movie *The Prince of Tides* Barbra Streisand plays a New York psychiatrist who becomes involved with the brother (Nick Nolte) of a very dysfunctional and suicidal female patient. As the story of their relationship unfolds it becomes clear that the patient's problems relate to her upbringing in South Carolina. The psychiatrist explores the patient's history and asks Nick Nolte's character for help in piecing the background together. Eventually, in the movie's seminal moment, the brother tells of an incident that took place thirty years before. Three prisoners escaped from the nearby maximum security prison and knocked at the door of their family home. They burst in and immediately attacked and assaulted the people in the household – the mother and her three children, two boys and a girl. The mother and her daughter were raped. One of the boys went out, got the family shotgun and shot the three intruders. The family then conspired to keep the whole incident quiet, and all four cleaned up the house and buried the prisoners before their father returned. They told no one. It was the pressure of the trauma of the incident itself, and the denial of it to the world, that led to the patient's suicide attempts. As Nick Nolte's character tells the story it becomes clear that he is describing what happened to everybody else in the story but not himself. Eventually he confesses that he too was raped by one of the prisoners, while his brother went out and got the shotgun. As he tells of this moment of dreadful emotional and physical pain, he bursts into tears, and you can see the burden he had been carrying for all those years without talking to anyone. It is very difficult to describe the cathartic effect of the release of so much pent-up and denied suffering. This is a moment of true 'core communication', and when we are capable of communicating in this way, we can enrich our lives for ever. It is a very healing thing.

More than one person has told me that finding a way to express a great hurt or a great worry or a great truth was the turning point in their lives. An alcoholic telling the truth for the first time to an AA group, confessing his alcoholism, is one of the finest uses of language possible. It is truly meaningful core communication.

Communication and talking happen in many different ways and at many different levels. No two people express themselves in the same way and our speech always reflects our individuality. We owe it to ourselves to develop the social techniques of superficial communication as well as to use the healing powers of deep communication. No one is a rock or an island, and the way to end isolation of any sort is to learn the rules of communication and then to practise them.

The U-Turn: Mastering Communication

1. Practise making a speech in front of a mirror. Pick a topic and spend at least an hour thinking of things to include in the speech and choosing how to say them. Think clearly about the four or five main points that you are going to make in the speech. Then order those five points in the most logical and persuasive way. Next, write out those points and expand each of them a little. Keep your imaginary audience in mind – aim neither too high nor too low – and make sure that the points would be interesting to someone in that audience. Finally, deliver your speech out loud and practise it in front of the mirror until you are happy with it.

2. Practise making conversation by picking a topic from the newspaper that you know nothing about and then giving yourself two minutes to talk about it without thinking about it beforehand. It is important not just to think about what you would say but to actually say it out loud.

3. Listen in to other people's conversations. Note a number of things about those conversations. Note the individual style of the conversationalist, what words and phrases they use most often, and the degree of repetition and the degree of dominance of each partner during the conversation. Note also the body language and posture of people during the conversation, and decide what each individual's body language is saying about their level of interest in the conversation. At the end of the conversation, or as you're listening to it, play it back in your mind and see if you could improve on the conversation by (a) being more responsive and considerate to the conversation partner; (b) making more interesting or stimulating points; (c) making some humorous crack or statement during your imaginary conversation. (Replay the conversation to yourself!)

4. Think over the conversations you have had in the last week and decide what levels of communication they are at. A

good rule of thumb is that four out of every five conversations should be at Level 1 (oral communication); and one of every five should be at Level 2 (emotional communication), but this should be spread between you listening to others' emotional communication and having others listen to your emotional communication. We are lucky if we have a Level 3 communication (core communication) every few months, and even then it is the quality and not the quantity that counts. If we are not having any core communication at all, we should actively seek some, either through friends or professionals. It is vital for constant self-development.

5. Go out and meet strangers and new people with whom you can practise your new-found conversational skills. This is the hardest part. It is no use having perfected the art of being entertaining and humorous all by yourself. It takes courage to get out and take advantage of the multiple opportunities to meet people that are there for the asking. Courage means facing what you fear, and if you fear meeting and making conversation with new people, it will take courage to do so. That courage comes from believing that you can change yourself, and this is one step on the long road of the U-turn.

Talking is one of the essences of communication, and communication is one of the essences of sharing. In the next chapter we deal with the ultimate in sharing: finding and developing a relationship, and understanding the nature of that relationship to bring us further along our personal U-turn.

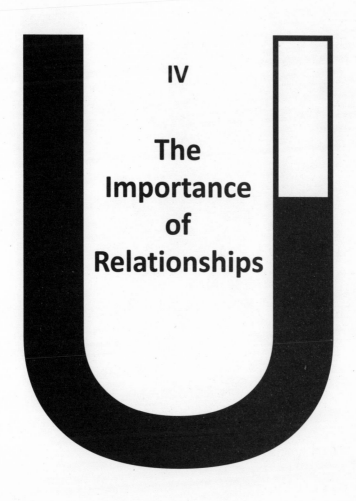

IV

The
Importance
of
Relationships

11

Relationships and Intent

> We can find contentment without love, but we need to love to be truly happy; and what we fundamentally want from a relationship often determines its outcome

There is an inbuilt desire in humanity to share. Somewhere deep in our genes there is a need to be with another, usually a member of the opposite sex, to spend our lives with someone else. It is different from, but closely allied to, sexual desire. Discovering this is part of the process of maturation, and it is easy to see when growing up that those who grow up more quickly and mature earlier tend to get into long-term relationships earlier. It is one of the emotional tasks we set for ourselves, and a vast amount of our self-esteem and self-worth is wrapped up in achieving a successful long-term relationship. Long-term love is the easiest path to happiness, and the route almost all of us want to travel on. When we haven't got a relationship, we tend to be obsessed with achieving one, and when we have one, we tend both to appreciate it and not appreciate it at the same time. Good, lasting relationships are hard to come by, as anyone with any romantic history will tell you, and they are often difficult to maintain, but the rewards greatly outweigh the difficulties. However, when things go bad and a relationship turns sour, life can turn into a miserable prison cell sort of existence. The important thing to know is that what determines how a relationship will turn out, and thus which way life will go, is as much a matter of will as of luck.

It is no secret that in the USA more second marriages fail than first marriages, even with a 45 per cent failure rate for first marriages. The point to be taken from this alarming statistic is that despite the 'learning' experience of one failed marriage, the same people go on to make the same mistakes in the second marriage as the first. They don't learn from the first experience, or perhaps they don't learn enough. One basic lesson that should be learned is that desire is not enough – will is required too.

Desire

Relationships, all relationships, start off with desire: if not sexual desire, then at least a desire to have a relationship. There must be a positive intent on both sides for anything to happen at all. From the first glance on the dance floor, or the first glance at the internet dating profile, to the stroll down the aisle, there must be a want for someone else in order to find that someone else. There must be a hole in our lives for someone to fill it.

The ways of meeting the opposite sex are as numerous as the day is long, and the ways of approaching them as varied. Sufficient desire and sufficient need should be enough to do the necessary and break the ice. What attracts one person to another is a mixture of looks, presentation, conversation, style, status and a host of smaller details which are tremendously individually variable.

In fact, the whole process of finding another person with whom we are interested in forming a relationship is fraught with individuality and idiosyncrasy. There is no golden rule that automatically says we can or cannot form a lasting relationship with someone of a different race, background, height, personality or star sign. Every person is unique, and what attracts him or her to another person is unique to that individual and the relationship formed is also unique. But through the maze of individuality a few hints about some of the rules that govern attraction emerge.

Attraction

To say that opposites attract is to reiterate a well-worn cliché. But that does not deny its undoubted veracity. James Joyce believed that you should look for the deficiencies of the husband in the attributes of the wife. Love isn't far from admiration and we all admire what we haven't got. We often have gaps in ourselves – whether in learning, in beauty, intelligence or status – and the next best thing to acquiring those attributes is to acquire somebody who does have them. There have been numerous marriages, affairs and matches between opposites – beauty queens and politicians, sinners and saints, bimbos and bishops – and something has to bring them together. That something is the very powerful attraction of an opposite type of person.

The other point to be made is that 'similars' also attract. People who are alike in temperament, ambition, looks, status and aims also find themselves attracted to one another. People look for confirmation of themselves and their personalities and habits, and what better confirmation and confidence-boost exercise can there be than finding a perfect reciprocal match for ourselves? To find someone who thinks, looks and acts like ourselves is a tremendous self-validation: I'm right to be like who I am. The recognition and reinforcement of our personal qualities by seeing them in the other person often leads to mutual satisfaction and progress of the relationship. If that sounds rather boring, just think how interesting we find ourselves and thus how interesting we must find someone who resembles us.

These apparently incompatible rules, or half rules, are not absolute. No two people are exactly opposite in everything, and no two people are exact matches, however many similarities they have. The 'types' of relationship which people have shade from the extremes of opposites attracting each other into the grey areas of somewhat similar and somewhat dissimilar people finding each other attractive. We all have components that others tolerate because they like the other bits of us. No couple of people get on completely well, and if they claim they do they are lying or at least deceiving themselves. Nobody is perfect and therefore nobody can perfectly accommodate another human into their lives. Just what it is that makes us want to accommodate another human to this extent is impossible to pinpoint but equally impossible to avoid.

Progress

When we are trying to establish a relationship and we have got past the point of at least communicating with each other, and giving out and receiving all the subtle signals that mean 'I'm attracted', we have to face various obstacles and problems on the way to progress. The main problems are the rate and the depth of that progress. To go too far too fast, both physically and emotionally, is a recipe for disaster (with some notably impressive exceptions). To go too slowly – emotionally, whatever about physically – is to go nowhere. Like sharks, relationships have to keep moving or they die. Relationships have to pass through a number of layers to fully progress and mature, and the entrance to each of these layers is a turning point in the relationship. These points are the places where a relationship can founder, despite the goodwill of both parties in the relationship.

Step 1: Courtship

The first stage in a relationship is the one established in the first few weeks or meetings. This is when the basic unique rules and characteristics of the relationship are set out and the stage at which the initial spark between the couple is either enhanced or quenched. The rules that may govern the relationship for years – the power balance, the degree of politeness to the other, or who tends to do what in various situations – are often set at a time when the focus of each member of the couple is on trying to impress the other and trying to judge the relationship. This is the stage at which basic personality and social characteristics are evaluated and judged as good or bad. There is a buzz about people in this stage as they try to put their best foot forward and show off all their positive personal qualities.

A lot of couples go very fast physically and end up sleeping together without knowing their full depth of commitment to each other. Quite simply, those who are sexually experienced tend to go faster physically than those who aren't. Also, the sexually experienced tend to value sex less, and tend to regard sex as being less important than the relationship itself. Alternatively, if they have been burned too often and feel unable to make any commitment, they might feel sex is a good substitute for a relationship. Those couples or individuals who are less sexually experienced place a much higher value on sex as an emotional and relationship yardstick and, consequently, the physical relationship doesn't go as far as fast. There is a tremendous relationship-enhancing value in sex, but this tends to diminish the more sexually experienced a person becomes. The main problem about going 'too far too fast' is that it tends to leave the relationship itself lagging behind, and it may actually never catch up.

Two friends of mine, Jack and Pam, met at a wedding. Both were in their late twenties, and both had been 'burned' in various relationships in the past. They hit it off immediately, and were very attracted to each other. Both were exceptionally sociable people, and they were soon on the social scene together, being seen at all the right places and with the right crowd. They started sleeping together after their second date, and it was tremendous fun. When they were out together, they looked lovingly into each other's eyes and all conversation was directed to their 'darling' or 'sweetheart'. However, each of them brought an amount of emotional baggage with them that they never got to explore before falling into bed. Thus they each felt that the relationship was further on than it actually was. They began depending on the other to give more support to themselves than they were capable of. Pam began to complain that he dumped too much of his work anxiety on her, and Jack began to feel that he was a substitute for one or other of her former boyfriends. They started in each other's arms and beds and were eventually at each other's throats. The split was difficult and acrimonious and both felt used and underappreciated.

This is not an unfamiliar story, and basically stems from going too far too fast, and letting the desire dictate the relationship rather than being just a part of the relationship. The tragedy is that they could still be together and happy if they had got to know each other before beginning to make such emotional demands on each other.

Physical intimacy, and especially broaching the different stages, from kissing to making love, is the fundamental fuel that drives the sexes together. To place too much emphasis on it is to leave the real relationship lagging. To ignore it is to leave aside the most tangible part of the relationship, and probably destroy it in the long term. There is no correct way to handle desire and lust, but it is wrong that it should go either further or less far than the relationship. There should be a mutual progression of the physical and emotional, thus allowing the two aspects to enhance the whole.

There is no absolutely right way of handling sex in a relationship, but there are plenty of wrong ways, all involving either too much or too little emphasis on it. If one person in a couple decides that they want to sleep together, and the other decides that they don't want to, it can also lead to friction in the relationship, with the whole relationship a tug of war on the subject of sex. What is interesting is that a lot of couples don't really talk about it except in simple terms of 'shall we or shan't we?' Sex is only a part of a relationship and if it is the only part, the relationship will eventually fail. It is a well-worn cliché to say that 'men want sex and women want love'. But, speaking as a man, that is only what we think we want – it is not necessarily what we need.

After the first short period of a relationship, people make up their minds whether or not there is something worth pursuing. The initial excitement evaporates to some degree and we are better able to judge the person we are out with as a whole; their likes and dislikes, their temperament and habits, their degree of attraction to us, our attraction to them, and mutual suitability. It is here that most relationships end, and probably for the best too. Instinct is vital, and if the 'zing' isn't there, it probably won't ever be and it's no use flogging a dead horse. The tragedy is that relationships and attractions in them may be powerfully one sided and no matter what we do, we can't make someone genuinely interested in us if they aren't. It is far better to try, fail and then move on than it is to stay and try and fail and try and fail again. The truth about attraction and infatuation is that it is not the same as love, it just feels that way at the time. It is genuinely possible to move on after a relationship that is dreadfully one-sided and look for the real thing elsewhere. It's a sad but basic rule.

Infatuation and Love

'Infatuation' is the slightly derisory term given to the idea of inappropriate affection, usually described in an adolescent who is 'too young to know better'. Infatuation isn't just a phase, though, it is a very intense variation of love, and most of us who made it through adolescence relatively intact will be able to recall some period in which we existed in a turmoil of love mainly characterised by the intensity of the emotion and the unavailability of the partner. It is not by any means unique to adolescence, but the unique combination of personal insecurity coupled with a naive, exaggerated belief in the ideal human being during adolescence makes us more prone to being bowled over than we are in later life. Infatuation is an absolute killer, because if the freely given affection isn't reciprocated, it leads to the most dreadful feelings of desolation. If our whole being is immeasurably wrapped up in someone else who isn't interested, there can be traumatic personal results.

Barry was a 21-year-old student I met in hospital one day. A handsome, big athlete and an intelligent young man, he had taken an overdose the previous night and then come into the hospital in a panic. When he was eighteen he had been going out with a girl, but they had lasted just a few months together. Although she was two years younger than him, he was the one devastated by the break-up. He couldn't get her out of his mind and he kept hanging around various places she would go and people she knew just in the hope of glimpsing her and maybe even snatching a brief conversation with her. Eventually he decided to get away from her, and he emigrated for two years. He settled in France, and found a job and met a lovely French girl who became his girlfriend. He gradually settled, forgot the first girl, and became happy again. He then decided to come back to Ireland and soon after he came back he saw his old girlfriend again and found himself falling in love all over again. She didn't want to know him, and in a torrent of despair and helplessness, he swallowed a load of tablets. He simply felt he couldn't get over her, and he couldn't handle it anymore. He recovered from the episode physically, but emotionally he still felt half an inch tall.

The only cure for a dreadful infatuation like that is to get away from the other person, and to create distance. If we continually see them, hear about them or talk to them, they cannot fade from consciousness and the emotional recovery that happens naturally after separation and loss isn't allowed to take place. The urge to find the other or at least find out about them is often overwhelming, but having access to them ensures the perpetuation of our misery. The strength of feeling involved can be tremendously powerful, verging on the psychotic. Time, without interference, is literally the only cure, and hitting hope on the head the only way to survive the experience.

Step 2: Intimacy

The next stage in a relationship is much more variable in length, nature, intensity and intimacy. The two people involved gradually spend more time together, expectations of commitment are laid down and people become more concerned for the other as a person, not just as a fun maker for themselves. Trust is given over to the other and there is more revelation of the true person, without the same need to act or 'impress' the other. As the relationship deepens, the capacity for being hurt also increases, as we leave ourselves more emotionally open. The growing certainty of affection and mutual trust encourages the further laying down of bonds of genuine love. Consideration for the other is a vital quality, and lack of appreciation of the sacrifices someone is making, or the depth of revelation someone is plumbing, can lead to tactlessness and serious offence.

Head and heart tend to go along at slightly different paces, and there are often explosions when someone realises they are in deeper than they thought or when they don't realise the implications of an intimate relationship for their whole life. Ideally two people develop a relationship at the same pace, but usually at some point or other they are at different levels from one another.

The important thing is to let the other person progress at their own pace. Making excessive demands on the other that they don't feel ready to offer, be it time, physical intimacy or emotional commitment, is a recipe for disaster. Demands produce resentment, and resentment can produce dreadful consequences, often at a later date. The ability to allow the other person freedom to go at their own pace is a self-sacrificing ability that is ultimately selfish, because it is the most successful way of handling a relationship. In the film *When Harry Met Sally* the relationship between long-time close friends played by Billy Crystal and Meg Ryan takes a nosedive when they go to bed. She is delighted, and he is scared witless, unable to face the prospect of a deeper relationship. In true Hollywood style, the relationship eventually succeeds, but not before the couple go through a bad patch brought on by their different pacing. Not all couples are as lucky.

During the stage of true intimacy in a relationship, there is an emotional dropping of the guard, and a courageous self-revelation in just about all areas. This is where the bad as well as the good sides of the couple are revealed, and, as one writer put it, the 'farting in bed' stage is reached. We never truly know someone until we are aware of their unattractive as well as their attractive features. We never really know someone until we see them lose their temper, act like a selfish pig, or be rude to shop assistants. It is not possible to be truly intimate with an idealised person – we can only be truly close to a complete human being, warts and all. If we spend our time looking for a perfect person, we will never find them – they simply don't exist. My experience is that the least experienced people in relationships demand more from their partners in terms of matching an unattainable ideal than more experienced people. The real test of this stage of a relationship is whether we can stand the shattering of the ideal image we have of our partner and go forward from there to a realistic and yet still highly positive view of them.

Of all the movies dealing with relationships, one of the most touching is *Eternal Sunshine of the Spotless Mind*. It deals with a relationship between a couple played by Jim Carrey and Kate Winslet. When the relationship goes sour, each of them undergoes a procedure that erases the other person from their memory, but it is only through the process of loss that they discover what they had to begin with. It is a crazy and surreal movie, with each of the couple undergoing the memory procedure at different points, but it manages to convey the determination of the couple to have a relationship despite knowing the faults and limitations of the other. Towards the end of the movie, both characters hear a tape recording of comments they made about each other when their relationship was going sour, but despite that awareness, they commit to each other and take another chance on the relationship. That aspiration is what we need to bring to a relationship – awareness and commitment.

Step 3: Commitment

The next stage in a relationship could be described as a progression rather than a new stage. It is the final commitment to spending a life together. For most people it involves getting engaged and then getting married. More and more couples nowadays are deciding not to marry but simply to live together, and eventually this will be seen by society as being equivalent to marriage. For some people the decision to marry is a logical step forward and is as simply taken as the first kiss. For others, it is a more dramatic step, with many lifelong implications, and it is the most important decision they take in their lives. I suspect the latter is the predominant view, despite frequent declarations by couples that the main reason for marriage was that 'it just seemed like the next step', and that it was as easy as cutting the cake. We owe it to ourselves and to our partners to consider marriage in the cold light of day and not in the fiery heat of passion. There are no guarantees in life, but thinking through consequences is one way of preventing some of the most obvious pitfalls. Nobody else can or should take the decision to marry for us. Bowing to pressure because of pregnancy or poverty or someone else's opinion is a recipe for disaster in the long term. The decision should also be mutual; nobody should marry for someone else's sake. Marriage is a matter of will as well as emotion, and it takes both components to make a true marriage. If one component or the other is lacking, it may make no difference in the short term, but it makes all the difference in the long run.

Helen, a recently married thirty-year-old teacher, told me the story of her romance with her husband. She had met him three years previously and they had started going out soon afterwards. He was a graphic designer and she fell in love with him and his artistic temperament, his style and his talent. They were married, with great joy, after seeing each other for eighteen months. Five days into their honeymoon, she woke up in Florence, looked across at her husband's sleeping figure and got an awful sense of fear and panic. 'Oh God, what have I done?' she thought, 'I hardly know him.' Her husband woke up, looked at her and instantly knew what was going on. He put his arms around her, smiled and said, 'I was waiting for this; it was bound to happen.' He knew what she didn't – that she had never sat down and coolly faced the reality of what she was doing and where the relationship was going. She was swept along by her heart right up to the wedding, but her mind didn't catch up with her until five days into the marriage. They faced the problem together, and she got through it, but she never forgot the sense of fear that hit her that morning. Her marriage is now relaxed and content, and she blames that panic on herself for not being aware of what was going on.

The approach to commitment in a relationship can be a make-or-break factor in the relationship. Frances was an attractive young woman who had married early, only to find it didn't work out as planned, and her marriage ended in divorce when she was twenty-eight. She spent the next few years drifting from relationship to relationship and was decidedly promiscuous for a few years. She eventually met a handsome Italian who was kind and loving and a lot of fun. She went out with him for four years and then they moved in together. It was only after she suggested they get married and he proposed to her that the trouble in their relationship began. He began avoiding physical contact, he cut her off emotionally and eventually he hit her. She finally ordered him out and, years later, when trying to piece together the reasons for his strange behaviour, she came to the conclusion that he felt unable to commit to the relationship. He loved Frances and he wanted to be with her, but he couldn't face the prospect of giving up his 'freedom' and thus destroyed their relationship in the process.

Not all relationships have to get to the formal commitment stage in order to survive in the long term, but if there is a permanent reluctance on one or other of the partners side, it is often a sign that the relationship will run into trouble at some stage.

Step 4: Maintenance

This last stage of a relationship – the marriage or long-term commitment stage – is (hopefully) the longest one. All the rules of sharing, intimacy, courtesy and consideration that applied during the other stages apply to the married state, with the added premise that there must be constant mutual effort and renewal to preserve the quality of the relationship. It is impossible to live with someone for a long time and not take them for granted to some degree. One of the tricks is to notice it ourselves and try to fight against it. Little things mean a lot, especially over a long time, and little offences can multiply in significance. A reliance on the little bit of paper to solve the problems in a relationship wears the paper away over time. Good intentions are not enough – they must be made manifest to each other.

Mark and Frances had been married for six years. To all intents and purposes they were very content and didn't have more than a few rows over the years. One morning Mark woke up, looked across at his wife and suddenly it occurred to him that he hadn't bought her flowers in some time. 'How long is it since I last gave you a bunch of roses?' he asked, with a quizzical smile on his lips. 'Three years, two months and seventeen days,' she snapped back. He bought her some flowers later that morning.

The art of maintaining a hard-won relationship is an individual one. It is also an art, which – unlike most arts – is one that is learned rather than one we are naturally endowed with. A good marriage is founded on the rocks of previous relationships, and the lessons thus learned cannot be too highly valued. Not all the lessons learned will be negative ones, but there are a lot of 'don'ts' associated with a good relationship that involve a tremendous understanding of the nature of relationships, and the nature of the emotions that help make good relationships flourish. We will deal with the maintenance of long-term relationships more fully in the next chapter.

Intent

The intent we have going into a relationship determines the attitude we have to it and generally determines our contribution to the relationship's outcome, in the short or long term. We are not all shining angels, with honourable intent written across our stiff upper lips and the starched epaulettes of our scouts' uniforms. We're a mangy lot, us humans, and we bring to our relationships all the messed-up components of our psyche that we bring to every other aspect of our lives.

We all have secret desires. For the males of this world these generally consist of jumping on a nubile young woman, doing unmentionable sexual things to her and running away before romantic or domestic consequences ensue. But this is by no means the intent we men bring to a relationship. Our wants are not necessarily our needs in this context. It is no secret that divorced men fare worse than divorced women in just about every way, despite divorces being caused more often by men than by women. The appeal of sexual desire without responsibility is by no means confined to the male community – a glance through *Cosmopolitan* or any other 'glamorous' women's magazine will confirm that.

Both men and women bring to our relationships the desire to feed our egos, to lord it over those around us, to indulge ourselves at others' expense and, moreover, to give ourselves whatever was lacking in our previous relationships and often our upbringing as well – a tall order for one other person to provide, even if we were able to communicate it. Half the baggage we bring with us is hidden from our own eyes, so we couldn't communicate it even if we had the courage to. In this context it is amazing that so many people actually settle into comfortable and relatively stable relationships that can last a lifetime. The thrust of internal wants and desires is balanced with those of our partners and we arrive at a happy equilibrium. At least that's what is supposed to happen.

Peter and Margaret were one of the most interesting couples I know. They were opposites, but extremely well matched. He was artistic and homely, and she was scientific and mathematical. They eschewed the idea of marriage as passé, but lived together in some splendour in the company of a large Afghan hound. However, once or twice Peter looked beyond their relationship to find some romantic excitement and on one occasion Margaret found out about it. Being more rigid than him, she walked out, leaving him hurt and devastated. He recovered quickly, however, and went on to live with another woman, a scientist, a year later. 'I must never have been fully committed to Margaret,' he observed later. 'Otherwise I wouldn't have gone after anyone else, would I?' While this is a poor excuse for infidelity he did have a point: he mustn't have been intent on preserving the relationship – if he had been he probably wouldn't have been unfaithful.

We have to carefully judge our partner's intent in a relationship in order to prevent our own hurt and pain later on. Even more so, our *own* intent in a relationship should be carefully judged, so that we don't end up hurting others and deluding ourselves.

Motivation is the vital factor that takes a relationship past the initial attraction through the different stages and through our married life. If our motivation is completely lost at some stage, or if it was never there in the first place, the relationship itself is lost. If all we want from a relationship is sex, the self-esteem from having a relationship of some sort, or simply a desire for company, we should at least be aware of this motivation, even if our partner isn't. It is very easy to fool ourselves into believing we really want more than we do, and very easy to fool the other person too. Feigning affection where none exists is a cruel and heartless thing to do to someone, but there's hardly a person alive who hasn't done it at one stage or another. If we are aware of what we are doing we have some chance of stopping ourselves going too far, physically or emotionally. If we refuse to see what we are doing, we have every chance of fooling the other person too and ending up stuck in a situation we don't want to be in, or having to make a break, which can cause severe damage to another. More relationships break up than make up, and it is possible to drift along in the wrong direction for a long time. Oscar Wilde got it right when he said, in *The Ballad of Reading Gaol*:

Yet each man kills the thing he loves …

The coward does it with a kiss,

The brave man with a sword.

We owe it to our partners to be brave rather than cowardly and we owe it to ourselves to know our own intent.

As the years go by, relationships change with them. As circumstances change, so does the way we view each other. If children arrive, they fundamentally alter the nature of the relationship between a couple. It becomes easy to neglect the renewal of a partnership that is required to keep the 'shark' alive. New habits become old, considerations become expectations, and stagnation becomes the death knell of affection. There is no one golden rule to follow to keep a relationship alive, but the one guarantee for failure is to lose the intent and the motivation that keeps it going. The next chapter deals with the balance of forces in a relationship and what keeps it going through the 'slings and arrows of outrageous fortune'.

Intent in this circumstance is a 'will' factor, not an 'emotional' factor. When we marry or commit ourselves to someone, the heart may provide the motivation but the head must provide the intent. There is a wilful border to be crossed and a conscious decision to be made at the time of commitment to one another, and there is a wilful renewal of commitment through the years at times of stress and conflict to be made in order to continue that commitment. There is a vast difference between having an argument about your girl-friend flirting with an ex-boyfriend, and then walking out; and having an argument about it but staying anyway. The argument will blow over, but the intent stays on longer. As the poet said, 'The intent is the cement.'

In the next chapter we deal with various components of long-term relationships and the U-turn rules and exercises that can help maintain them – and turn them around when they are going in the wrong direction.

12

Relationships and Power

> Understanding the importance of power in a relationship can save it from destruction

Politicians are a different breed. In general they are egocentric, power-obsessed, often superficial and of limited vision. Having met of a few of them, I have consistently felt the question welling within me, 'How can such a set of people, with such a limited perspective, go so far in society, and why do we let them?' Why we let them go so far is generally because nobody else is prepared to do the job – that is one answer. The reason they go so far as individuals is because they are one of the most dedicated types of people you can meet. They are dedicated to their own obsessions, to the exclusion of almost everything else. Wives or husbands get 'postponed until later', while the potential presidents put in the hours at meetings and gatherings of people around the country. They crave power like an addict their heroin. They are prepared to lie, cheat and backstab in order to gain or maintain power. You only have to look at the life of Richard Nixon to see what the breed does at its extreme. He lied, cheated, bribed and burgled his way into the history books, destroying lives and careers in his lust for power. He himself said that the only important thing is to win, and he lived by that statement. He described politics as a virus, and if he had a political virus it was the political equivalent of Aids. Politicians would be terribly easy to despise if there wasn't a little bit of them in us all.

Power

In every relationship there is an underlying power struggle between the loving partners. Underneath all the cooing and cuddling, the loving and the doving, lie two pit bull terriers ready to tear the heart out of the other to gain superiority. If this analogy seems a bit strong, it is simply to emphasise the point that the power battle is an intrinsic part of any worthwhile relationship, and pretending it doesn't exist is simply sticking our heads in the sand.

In most relationships the power brokering is done relatively early on, and the various individual roles in the relationship are determined at the same time. In some relationships, the question of a power balance is never addressed, the balance is thus never achieved, and a constant bickering and jockeying for superiority ensues.

Frank and Patricia were married in their late twenties. They both had a strong personality and had a lot of discussions before their marriage about who would do what when they married. After they did marry and had their first child, Patricia gave up her job in a delicatessen and worked full time at home. She became increasingly resentful of her husband's position 'over' her and began to complain – about money, about decision-making and about any time he spent away from home. He didn't want to change his bachelor habits and felt that he did enough for the marriage by bringing in the money, and so they began to argue. And argue. Eventually the bickering extended into almost every area of life and they would have a five minute 'to-do' over what TV channel to watch. But they still loved one another: they couldn't live with each other, and they couldn't live without each another. Their lives were made unhappy by constant jockeying for position in the partnership, and they didn't even know why they were doing it. They eventually found a way to compromise on major issues, but they maintain a fractured and half loving/half argumentative relationship that rumbles on.

Sex Roles

What determines power in a relationship? The first thing that determines it is sex – not the sex we do, but the sex we are. Until recent times, sex roles were stereotyped and power was divided into pre-set roles: women made their place in the home, and men brought home the bacon. The fact that numerous courageous and independent women, such as Eleanor Roosevelt and Countess Markievicz, were prepared to break out of their gender roles and make their own lives, made little impact on the lives of the vast majority of women.

Since the 1960s, however, the sex roles have become more indistinct, and thus the areas for conflict between the sexes in any one relationship have increased. Women are rightly prepared to battle for their position in the workplace and are not prepared to simply accept the role their mothers had. There can be a vast difference in opinion between men and women about what each of the sexes is capable of doing and, more important, what each expects to do. To achieve a working relationship between a man and a woman there is a capability and an expectation that must be faced and matched. There is a midway point between the expectations of each partner that each couple must work out for themselves.

Men traditionally had the upper hand in a relationship, and women traditionally learned the subtle art of manipulation in order to get their own way. Along with the breakdown of sex roles, a breakdown of the power according to these roles is also occurring, both in general and in individual relationships. As you go up the social scale, gender roles become less definite, and women essentially more powerful and liberated. As you go down the social scale, there appears little room for a more modern view of female power. Money, or more particularly the lack of it, reinforces role stereotyping and unequal division of power. Men have an ingrained tradition of superiority in a relationship that is reinforced by the power over money. In a situation (which has become much more common in the current recession) where the man is unemployed or ill, and the woman becomes the bread-winner, there is often a slow but definite change in the power struggle, with the man either fading in the face of a frontal assault, or else going down kicking. The superiority of the male in the power battle is as much a consequence of money and tradition as it is of his male hormones and aggressiveness.

The Power of Love

The second thing that gives power in the struggle between the sexes is affection. In his autobiography, *Home Before Night*, the late playwright Hugh Leonard said that in every relationship there is a lover and a loved, and then he went on to describe the relationship between his Da, the lover, and his Ma, the loved. His 'Da', about whom he wrote a Tony Award-winning play, was a shy and cantankerous man who spent his life working as a gardener for a local grand family. His mother had been a 'catch' in her day, and the only way 'Da' could ever hope to win her hand in marriage was to ask her father, which he did. She eventually agreed to his proposal, and settled into domesticity, knowing that she would have the upper hand in any potential disputes. She used it sparingly and affectionately, but she always had the upper hand, because she was the loved and he was the lover. On one occasion she bumped into a former boyfriend and went home to announce this fact to her husband, and her son, the author. She also announced that she was going to visit him for tea the next week. Her husband exploded, storming around the house, ranting and raving, cursing the old boyfriend, and throwing tea cups at the wall. She shouted back at him, saying she would do what she damned well wanted and he wasn't going to stop her. The young boy looked on amazed and astonished, never having seen his father lose his temper at his mother before. The father stormed out of the house, and the mother stopped fussing after him. Hugh Leonard stared over at her and was surprised to see tears welling in her eyes, 'Ah, the jealous old bags' she said, and she never went to tea with her old beau. She didn't really need to – she had asserted her authority, had confirmed his love for her, and that was what she ultimately wanted.

In any relationship, the power to walk away is the ultimate power, and the person who is prepared to use it, or who actually does it, has the upper hand in the relationship, no matter what the circumstances. The risk in doing it is that the relationship may, quite naturally, founder as a result. In most relationships, it is the 'loved' who has the emotional strength to threaten or to carry out the threat of desertion and who carries the day in any power struggle. The 'lover' generally hasn't got the guts to walk out because he or she values the 'loved' too highly to play poker with the relationship. If the 'loved' is worth their salt, they will instinctively know the degree of the 'lover's' devotion and know they can win any major battle. Such is the strength of love that any power accrued to the partner by reason of sex, money or status is wiped out by love. There is simply no contest.

A patient of mine described his first serious relationship to me. He was about twenty, reasonably confident and moderately attractive. She was younger, beautiful, vivacious and charming. She ran rings round him, telling him she loved him one week and breaking off the relationship the next.

He spent a year of his life in alternating periods of despair and ecstasy, according to her moods and whims. Finally he could stand it no more and he drove over to her house one day and without giving any warning or chance of explanation he broke off the relationship. She was floored and asked for time to reconsider the whole thing, but he was adamant and walked out. 'I won,' he said. 'I beat her at her own game and I kept my sanity. All I lost was her.' It's a chance that we all have to take when exercising the power of veto over the relationship, and the chance is that we may lose the relationship. He had taken back the power, but lost the relationship.

Dependence

The relationships we develop and the behaviour we develop in them are extensions of ourselves. All the problems and deficiencies, all the strengths and positive aspects of our personalities are brought to bear on a deep long-term relationship. If we find ourselves immersed in a relationship, or more particularly a marriage, in which we feel dependent, unloved and unable to express, let alone assert, ourselves, we have to shoulder a lot of the responsibility ourselves. We may find ourselves in a situation where the relationship appears to be quite sound – no power struggle, no bickering and with every outward appearance of a happy normality. But the preservation of the relationship may involve surrendering to the other all responsibility and authority, to the extent of self-abasement and what feels like self-extinction. The dominant half, who is generally but not always the male, may not even be a particularly aggressive, bullying variety of the species (even though God knows there are enough of those around). If the 'weaker' half of the partnership refuses to fight their corner on anything, if they give up trying to assert themselves and they continually back off 'for the sake of the marriage', they walk themselves into a personal and marital cul-de-sac. Preservation of a marriage or relationship that isn't worth preserving is not a worthwhile ambition in life. Developing the personal strength to deal with the situation for better or worse is a much worthier ambition, and the initial stage is to carefully apportion blame for the situation.

Blaming someone else for our own situation is a universal trick among humankind. It is often the only way we feel we can cope with a given set of negative circumstances – 'It's not my fault, it's theirs!' We all use our defence mechanisms on a daily basis, and projecting our inadequacies on to the other person in a relationship is common even in the best of partnerships. Projection can lift an emotional burden and make it somewhat easier to bear. It doesn't, however, tend to give us the motivation to change our circumstances, or even get a handle on them. By projecting the responsibility for our dependence on another on to that person, we allow ourselves the luxury of blamelessness. Ultimately, however, we have to face up to ownership of our own faults. We all have the ability to be controllers and not victims. If we refuse to point the finger at ourselves for our own dependence, we then become responsible not only for its existence, but also for its continuation as well.

Lydia, a 35-year-old Canadian housewife, was a member of a therapeutic support group. She was attractive but had 'let herself go' after her marriage to a shoe shop manager. She was a doormat and offered control of her life to anyone who would take it, as she said herself later. She had a pleasant, kind husband who, however, took her for granted, ordered her about the place and wouldn't help out with the kids or in the house. She had dreadful trouble with an abusive babysitter who let her boyfriend in to smoke joints when she was supposed to be looking after Lydia's daughter. Lydia found it dreadfully difficult to even consider firing the babysitter. Her life consisted of lurching from crisis to crisis, fuelled by her inability to grasp her existence between her hands and hold on to it. Gradually over weeks in the group, she began to see her problem as being her own and not her husband's or her babysitter's. With tremendous support from the group, she gradually overcame her fear of others and her dependence on them and began to take charge. She left the group soon after she fired the babysitter, and after reporting that her husband had stopped leaving his socks all over the bedroom when she firmly asked him not to. She was batting for herself now. The change was long and tortuous and involved major changes in self-perception, from seeing herself as the victim of circumstances and of other people, to taking responsibility for her own situation as it stood, and ultimately changing it.

Truth

There are many dangers inherent in a long-term relationship like marriage, and being aware of them is one way of not falling into their clutches. Truth is a delicate entity, and a very subjective one. No two people see things in exactly the same way. Telling the truth to our partners is a vital component of a successful marriage, but so is being 'economical with the truth'. We do not need to criticise them, to deflate them, to let them know exactly what we think of their painting ability or how they look first thing in the morning, unless there is some positive point to doing this. If we feel that revealing certain feelings or events would be detrimental to that relationship, we should think carefully before laying bare our souls. As long as the intent for the good of the partnership is true, this shouldn't be a problem, but a considerable benefit. If, however, the purpose of not telling the truth is to deceive the partner (for example about multiple, ongoing infidelities), we are obviously not being truthful to the good intent of the relationship, and not telling the truth is avoiding the reality of our own soured motivation.

Judging whether we tell something major to our partner or whether we omit to tell something major to our partner should involve very intense self-questioning. We must constantly judge our own motivation for doing or not doing something and we must be sure that we are genuinely acting for the good of the relationship before we actually do it.

Francis and Siobhan had been going out for a few months. She was a legal secretary and he was an attorney in another office. He moved jobs to another town and they continued to see each other, albeit less frequently. Eventually things got a bit difficult, and they met to sort things out. She accused him of being indifferent. Stung, he blurted out that he had difficulty with her being what he considered a social status lower than his. She was devastated, as she had never regarded their relationship as anything other than a partnership between equals. Not surprisingly, they broke up a month later. Despite trying to get back together some time later, they never quite got over his remark. How much wiser he would have been to keep his mouth shut and get over his perspective problem alone. If he had been true to the good intent of the relationship and not the 'truth' as he saw it, they might still be together now.

Self-Indulgence

Once we cross a certain wilful or emotional negative barrier in a relationship, it is very hard to get back to the other side. We can be very annoyed with our partner at various times and that is impossible to prevent, no matter how good our intent. What we do with that annoyed emotion is vital to the wellbeing of the relationship. If we grasp that emotion and walk out in high dudgeon, we are indulging ourselves and are basically enjoying lording it self-righteously over our other half. But the price to be paid is the insidious resentment and even downright furious reprisal engendered in the partner. To paraphrase Isaac Newton's third law of motion: to every emotional action there is a massive and unequal emotional reaction against it. We have a voluntary, willed decision to take regarding how to use the anger we feel at our partner, and petulantly hitting out at the relationship is a recipe for disaster. If, however, we take that anger, throw it up in the air a bit, and don't walk out, we save ourselves a mass of trouble later. The important thing to decide is whether we are more committed to our anger than we are to our partner. If we are more committed to our self-indulgent anger, then we will suffer the consequences, in the long run if not in the short run. If we are more committed to the relationship we can still be angry about whatever the perceived wrong is, but we can prevent it getting to the relationship-threatening stage.

My friend Mark told me he was furious at his fiancée one night for not telling him about an important man in her past. They had been partners for quite some time and he hadn't kept secrets from her and he felt she shouldn't have kept any from him. He dragged the story about this other man from her, and was furious with her for having said nothing during their relationship thus far. He let her know he was angry at not having been told, but he stayed the evening and didn't storm out on her, to let her know that his commitment to her was greater than his commitment to his anger. It blew over and he sent her flowers the next day to say he was sorry for losing his temper. They are now happily married, but the outcome could have been very different. It is moments like those that shape the future of a relationship.

Negative Emotions

Inside us all are various nasty, negative emotions which aren't particularly pleasant to recognise. We are all occasionally jealous, vengeful, bitter and hateful. We are not angels, we are humans – and even saints lose their temper sometimes. What is just as important as recognising these unattractive components of our psyche is deciding what we should do with them and where we should direct them. More often than not we direct these nasty bits on to our nearest and dearest, and end up taking out our frustrations on them rather than on the real target, or the real origin of them. It is a very common habit and a very unrecognised one, and it causes untold marital misery. Coming home after a hard day in the office, when the boss ate us for lunch, the secretary was sick and we had to answer all our own calls, and the car had a flat tyre on the way home, and then getting into the house and finding an excuse to blow up at our partner is a recipe for long-term disaster.

More insidious, and less easy to detect in ourselves, is our ability to take our own deep-seated deficiencies and push the blame for them on to our partners instead of facing up to them and taking responsibility for them ourselves. It is very common for us not to see ourselves, but to judge our partners with our own insecurities in mind, and blame them at the slightest excuse. For example, I have seen many alcoholics being very aggressive about their partner's drinking as a way of distancing themselves from facing up to their own drinking; and in some families with a teenage daughter suffering from anorexia, the intense focus by the couple on their daughter's anorexia may obscure problems and deficiencies in their own relationship, which may have led to their daughter's anorexia in the first place.

The converse is also true. If we can redirect and displace all the negative aspects of our emotional being on to a figure of hate or contempt, we can improve our core relationship. In this way the emotional need we have to find some outlet for what Carl Jung called the 'Thanatos' or 'death instinct' – the destructive side of ourselves – can be satisfied without doing any harm to our marriage or central relationship.

Peter was a medical colleague of mine who was having mild difficulties with his wife of many years, despite having a basically sound marriage based on a solid friendship. He found her just a little bit clingy and dependent, and it irked him. He began to stay on late in the office and find excuses not to rush home in the evening. Soon afterwards he employed an assistant who proved to be particularly troublesome and incompetent. He found himself increasingly irritated by his assistant, and began to develop a thorough dislike for her. Conversely he found his relationship with his wife more relaxing and enjoyable and he could share his growing frustration with his employee. By the time he got around to firing the assistant, his marriage was blossoming again, and he wondered how he could ever have doubted the wisdom of marrying such a beautiful and charming woman. There was nothing basically wrong with his marriage, he just needed an outlet for his negative emotions, and the solution was to direct them elsewhere.

Consideration

Constantly picking at touchy areas is a sure-fire way of creating resentment. We can indulge ourselves in picking on our partner's weak points, exhibiting them, finding some irksome habits and pointing them out, and generally goose-stepping into quicksand. We often don't realise we are doing it, and we don't realise that we are trying to make a power statement and win points on some great scoreboard in the sky. Its a risky strategy and one that is guaranteed to manufacture more resentment than it is worth.

A middle-aged alcoholic once described to me the wonderful ability he had to let his wife down and make her feel small, just when she was recovering from his previous bout of drinking. He would promise his wife, an avid theatre-goer, that he would love to go to see such and such a play, he'd go and buy the tickets and generally build up her expectations. Half an hour before they were due to leave, he would suddenly cry off, claiming he was sick, wasn't up to it, or some other lame excuse. He would then tell her to go on her own, knowing she probably wouldn't go, or wouldn't enjoy it if she did. He basically decided that she should be punished for his wrong-doing; he ignorantly projected his guilt on her and made her suffer. It wasn't a very successful marital strategy. He indulged this habit once too often, and is now indulging alone.

Betrayal

Marriage, and the relationship in it, is a living thing. Like all living things, it can die, leaving only an outer shell remaining with nothing going on inside. The surest way to kill a marriage or long-term relationship is to sin against it. If we stab it in the back, it almost certainly won't survive, and if it does it will be damaged beyond repair. The surest way to kill it is to sleep with someone outside it. That act of betrayal affronts the marriage in a number of ways.

The first is the wilful act of crossing the line beyond which we know we are doing harm to the marriage. No matter how willing the third person, no matter how casual the fling, no matter how quick it's over, there is nobody alive who isn't aware of the potential consequences of what they are doing, and that they are risking the marriage for a 'quickie'.

The second way it destroys a marriage is the reaction of the wronged party when he or she finds out or even begins to suspect. The enormous devastation felt, the peeling back of the years of the relationship and of love, the massive disappointment and loss of admiration for the loved one, and the deepest of hurt that is felt is practically beyond repair. Anyone who says they don't mind if their partner sleeps around is simply lying – to themselves and to everyone else.

It is impossible not to mind unless there is no affection left anyway, and thus the marriage is already dead.

The third aspect is the diminution in respect the adulterer feels for the wife or husband. Because we are too proud to accept guilt properly, we translate it into excuses to ourselves as to why we wronged him or her. Because we are unwilling to face up to what we have done, we push the blame off ourselves and towards our partner. We may find it in ourselves to forgive those who wrong us, but we can never forgive those we have wronged.

Bob Hope, the wonderful comedian, had numerous affairs with various aspiring actresses over the years, and was what can only be described as a chronic adulterer. He had been married to the same woman for fifty years, and she either didn't know what was going on or simply pretended not to know. An example like this might make some people think that you can have your marital cake and eat it. She, however, is the exception. Women now don't have to put up with that kind of behaviour, and with separation and divorce agreements often giving each partner a 50 per cent share of the spoils, there is less economic pressure on a woman to tolerate this kind of behaviour. Unfortunately a divorce rate of 45 per cent in some countries, such as the USA and the UK, says otherwise. Currently in Ireland the separation/divorce rate is around 10 per cent, so maybe we are doing something right as a nation. A lot of people play away from home and, indeed, some get away with it. But a lot of marriages pay the price in the long run for short-term fun.

No amount of liberal thinking, bohemianism, intellectual sophistication, or artistic indulgence can free us from our emotions, and our emotions say 'adultery equals betrayal'. I have worked in medicine for some years: I've seen a lot of disease and death, and I've seen some of the desperate misery wrought by serious psychiatric disorders. But nothing prepared me for the devastating intensity of the pain felt by two perfectly sound rational intelligent human beings pulling each other's lives, and their children's lives, apart after infidelity and betrayal. I recall one couple, an attractive married couple in their late thirties, with two lovely children. The husband had had an affair with someone at work, and the 'wronged' party, a strong-minded woman, simply could not bring herself to believe what her husband had done. He was an architect, a polite and gentle man who didn't know how to handle the dreadful abuse his wife hurled at him. He also didn't know if he loved her now, though he had loved her before he started the two-year affair with his assistant. Their two children, aged eleven and eight, were simply disregarded by both parties, despite protestations on both sides that they were the main priority, and they were used like golf balls to be whacked around by their increasingly bitter and intransigent parents.

Most of us will have had friends or relations who are essentially decent people, but who end up in a very bitter situation because of divorce. In the movie *The War of the Roses*, Kathleen Turner and Michael Douglas end up destroying everything around them, including their beautiful house, in their battle with each other. The only thing that mattered to each of them was to defeat and destroy the other. There was no low that either side would not sink to in order to get one over on the other. The intensity of their original love was mirrored in the intensity of their anger at its demise. Although in the movie no adultery was involved, each partner might as well have slept with the entire population of Boston for the level of betrayal felt by both parties. There seems no way out of a situation like that beyond the destruction of the relationship. As Richard Nixon should have said, 'It's not worth it.'

Reciprocity

There is a great tendency in human beings to ascribe to our other half what we ourselves are thinking. We expect them to feel as loving and affectionate as we do, when we do. We also ascribe to them feelings of distance and ambivalence at the same time as we feel them. It is a mixture of genuine belief in the exact reciprocal nature of emotions coupled with a hope that their feelings mirror our own at the same time as our own. When we feel independent and strong, we don't really feel the need for a whining, puppy dog lover, dependent and clingy, stuck at our side – we want a firm and resilient partner. But when we feel unloved and insecure and would relish the comfort of a close and warm confidant, we don't want them telling us to get our act together and stop feeling so miserable. We want and even expect them to match us feeling for feeling, and intensity for intensity.

Nevertheless, it is impossible for any couple, however well in tune they are with each other, to exactly match the timing of emotions. Expecting this to happen can lead to awful accusations of the partner not understanding the sufferer, and – worse still – not trying to. As it is impossible to be totally in sync, the most that we can ask for is for tolerance and effort: tolerance for the unexpected blast of positive or negative emotions that might come our way; and an effort to understand the causes and origins of them. We should do our partners the justice of always viewing them as independent people, and of viewing the alliance between partners as a mooring and not a rock. The constant renewed appreciation of the other is the secret of keeping the relationship alive over years. Without it, we run the risk of complacency and then risk drifting away without realising it. When Chris de Burgh sings in his song 'Lady in Red', 'I hardly know this beauty by my side', he means that he has just woken up once again to the attractions of his wife.

A young woman told me about her divorce. She turned to her lawyer after drawing up her divorce agreement and said, 'You don't go into marriage thinking this is going to happen, you know.' Nobody expects their relationship to fail. Nobody (unless they are marrying purely for convenience) makes vows in the hope of breaking them.

There are all sorts of reasons why people break up. If a relationship fails because, for example, he is too dominant or drinks too much and she is too dependent and feels too powerless to do anything about it, breaking up isn't a failure but a recognition of reality. The relationship has already died on the bed of his indifference and her unwillingness to fight. In this case, splitting up may be the only chance the relationship has of actually renewing itself, with the split precipitating a review of personal positions, especially in the drinking or aggressive offender. If one half of a partnership spends his or her life feeding and supporting the rotten habits of the other half, he or she has to take some responsibility for the consequences, easier as it is to simply blame the other person and not face up to those responsibilities. Altruism, helping our fellow man and giving rather than taking, are all very admirable traits, but not when they occur at the expense of courage.

A Different Perspective

An objective view is a wonderful perspective to get on a relationship. If the love is all tangled up, the relationship appears to be going nowhere and each partner is blaming the other for not putting the relationship first, putting it all down in front of a neutral and objective eye can help us to see the wood from the trees. It is the least the relationship deserves, if either side considers it worthwhile. It may prevent that awful crossing of the line in the sand when one or other begins to fight against the relationship rather than fight for it.

A neutral person may be able to focus the attention on specific character or behavioural flaws that do greater damage than either partner believes. Every antagonism, like every affection, is based on specific reasons or incidents, and is not just an overall feeling. Like a football match, the outcome isn't certain until the final whistle blows, and how much effort we put into the game often determines the 'score'. If there is a risk of the relationship going seriously awry, getting a counsellor or doctor to help both sides focus on the good and bad things about it is not only useful, it is vital. If marriage splits up even after counselling, it is more likely to happen for the right reasons, and not for reasons that were redeemable.

A middle-aged motel chambermaid once told me her rather troubled marital history. She had two daughters by two different fathers, a South African circus performer and an American salesman, and had had been briefly married to each of them. She said the real love of her life was the teenage boyfriend she had had when she was growing up in Liverpool. He proposed to her when she was nineteen, but she was too restless and wanted to go away and see the world: so she did. One failed marriage, one daughter and seven years later, she returned to Liverpool to take him up on his offer. She appeared on his doorstep after not being in contact for the seven years and gave him three days to make up his mind about her. By the fourth day he had decided to give it a go, but by then she had gone off on her travels again. She heard later that he was willing to try again, but by then she was married for the second time. She always regretted it, and regretted not giving him time to come round. An attitude like that may be the recipe for an interesting and adventurous life, but it's also the recipe for a Mickey Rooney marital history. It may be fun in the short term but it's hardly conducive to happiness in the long run.

So the final and vital message about troubled ups and downs in a relationship is 'Give it time.' Never let it be said that a relationship broke up because either party didn't give it enough time to work out: that can be the source of much later regret.

U-Turn Relationship Rules

1. Put yourself in the other person's shoes and then communicate what you want to say.

2. Be open and honest. Don't hide the truth from your partner or from yourself.

3. Never insult your partner – not to their face and especially never in front of others.

4. Always fight your battles away from the public eye. Washing your dirty linen in public only increases the humiliation felt by both sides.

5. Make a thoughtful gesture to your partner every day. This might be a phone call, a present or simply a kiss – just do something nice every day.

6. Always ask, 'What do you think?' and wait for a reply before offering a solution.

7. Never walk out or walk away from a problem or argument. If you're having an argument, stay and resolve it: don't walk out on the situation just to make a point. Never threaten the relationship just to win a battle – it will be the costliest win in the long run.

8. Never pick a fight with your partner because of what happened at work or elsewhere in your life. Make sure that if you are irritated with them it is because of what they did or did not do and not because of what your boss said that morning.

9. Always give your partner the final veto over any decision. Make it both the unwritten and the stated rule of the

relationship that if the other person wants something badly enough, they get it. If both of you make that rule, you simply state your case and the person with the biggest want wins. If the partnership proceeds along the lines of both sides conceding to the other, both of you win in the long run.

10. Never blame the other person for your own failings and your own feelings.

11. Try to speak gently when communicating with the other person. Anger is the hardest emotion to forget.

12. You can flirt with other people if you want; you can ogle them to your eyes' content; you can chat them up until your throat is dry – but never, ever sleep with anyone else if you want your partnership to survive. Sex lasts a minute, love lasts a lifetime; so make your choice. Salvador Dali may have lived with and loved his astoundingly unfaithful wife Gala until her death – but remember that he was quite probably mad.

The U-Turn: Mastering Your Relationship

1. *Communication.* Each partner makes a list of their own five most irritating characteristics as they feel would be perceived by their partner. Hand the finished list to your partner and compare each list with the partner's opinion.

2. *Opposite role play.* Taking the characteristic at the top of partner A's list, partner B takes the role of partner A in a debate about how to resolve the argument. Partner B has to argue Partner A's view of the situation.

3. *Good and bad points.* Each partner lists the five worst points about themselves, and the five best points about their partner. The list is then exchanged and discussed for accuracy.

4. *Being nice to each other.* Each partner has to do something nice for their partner once a day for a week. It has to be

something thoughtful and kind, and not part of the daily routine. Suggestions could be: a phone call to make sure that everything is going well; a surprise gift such as a box of chocolates or a book; or a surprise trip to a movie or a show. The next week it is the other partner's turn at being extra nice.

5. *Expectations in household tasks.* Each partner makes a list of tasks they expect they should do and that their partner does in household duty terms. The lists are exchanged and discussed and a compromise worked out.

6. *Why did we fall in love?* Each partner lists the reasons why they fell in love with the other partner. The important thing is to recall the original feelings of attraction and not the subsequent change in that opinion over the years. The list is then handed over to the other person.

Finally ...

If all is not working and it is impossible to get out of the relationship rut you are in, seek professional help from a qualified psychiatrist, psychologist or marital therapist. The better the qualification the less likely you are to run into a potentially damaging therapist with their own agenda, but unfortunately that is always a risk, especially with unqualified therapists.

V

The Reason
for It All

13

Joel and Purpose

Finding a real purpose in life is a journey, not a destination

So where does it all end? What is the purpose, why are
we here, and all that? Is there more to the whole shebang
than simply coping with day-to-day life? Is there a greater
purpose in life than battling to keep control of ourselves? Is it
our greatest ambition to simply make it from cradle to grave
without major embarrassment? Are we simply chasing our
tails, eking out an existence determined by other people's
rules? Are our lives determined by fate, not choice, and do
we spend them muffled in straitjackets of somebody else's
design? Are we powerless over ourselves? Even when we
have the freedom to take control, are we too uncertain and
confused to find our direction?

The answer to all the above is a resounding yes, and, er,
no. We are not entirely in charge of our lives, but neither
are we entirely the victims of fate. A chance meeting with
a wonderful woman or man may change the course of the
rest of our lives, but only if we put in the effort to make the
most of the meeting. 'Overnight' success usually takes years
to build, together with the determination to make full use
of opportunities that drop by. We are only victims in the

sense that we cannot take charge of every aspect of existence and expect it to come out as we want. But dreadful, horrible things like the deaths of close friends and family members, physical and mental illness, financial difficulties and poverty do also happen to us, and if we are to have any chance of getting by, let alone being actually in charge, we must cope with them.

Trauma

When something truly awful happens to us, it can take us a lifetime to recover from it. Our lives are shaped to a dreadful extent by rotten things occurring, and it is in truth the ability to deal with the adversity rather than the adversity itself that determines the overall outcome. If Whoopi Goldberg could escape from the housing projects she grew up in to become a famous and successful comedienne and actress, then it is possible to overcome any adversity in life if we try hard enough and get the technique right.

Acceptance of a great and traumatic event in our lives requires a two-stage battle. The first stage is to come to terms with it, and the second is to get on with life in spite of it. The two stages require two totally different personal approaches.

Coming to Terms

Jane was a 22-year-old French student whom I met because she had recurrent bouts of self-destructive behaviour including cutting her wrists with razor blades, and swallowing handfuls of tablets and getting rushed into hospital. The whole precipitating factor behind this behaviour was the fact that she had been raped at the age of seventeen when walking home from school. She was so frightened and upset that she told no one for years, and apparently coped well enough externally, getting her high school graduation and then starting at university. She always avoided the particular area where she had been attacked, until one night when she was strolling home with a boyfriend they passed the exact spot, and repressed memories flooded into her mind. She ran away from her surprised boyfriend and ended up in hospital later that night, having swallowed a large number of pills. She survived to enter into a nightmare existence of recurrent memories and recurrent suicide attempts.

She eventually told her doctor about her original experience, and the dreadful effect it had had on her. With that she was able to relive and partially get rid of the hidden and pent-up emotions she had about the rape, and go through a process of coming to terms with it. It was a long and arduous process and there were setbacks, but eventually she was able to deal with it. However, the coping – or should I say non-coping – mechanisms she had learned during that intense period of suffering also had to be unlearned. She had to rediscover a purpose in life, and learn not to cope with all her various life stresses with self-destructive behaviour. That was a much more difficult and, indeed, a much more long-term task.

So coming to terms with a dreadful happening or an upsetting event is only half the battle. Readjusting the life priorities that have been knocked out of kilter, re-establishing personal values, breaking habits learned during the bad patch, and setting new goals form the other half of the battle, and this generally takes much longer to do.

Getting 'stuck' in the first stage, wallowing in denial and repression, and failing to come to terms with the intense emotions surrounding the trauma, is a major problem. In psychiatry a 'grief' reaction can be 'complicated' by protracted denial; that is, by an emotional refusal to accept the reality of a loss, even if the intellectual part of our minds has accepted it. How to emotionally accept something we don't want to have to face is one of the great stumbling blocks of psychiatry and, indeed, of humanity. Eventually we have to wallow in what we fear, be it a death or a personal trauma. We have to think about it, we have to talk about it and we have to cry about it. We have to explore our emotions, and even define them and go through them one by one. We can do this in the company of others, especially if they are going through a similar difficulty, or we can do it with one other person, preferably someone we trust and who is willing to give their time and effort to help us, or we can do it alone. What we are forced to face up to is the dreadful pain and suffering surrounding the original experience. It is our inability or lack of desire to face the pain that is the hub of the problem. By wallowing in it, we eventually free ourselves from it. It is by no means pleasant, but it is the only route to success.

Rebirth

The second stage of recovery from trauma is the long-drawn-out, more protracted stage. It is the stage involving rebuilding ourselves out of the emotional wreckage. It is the piecing together of the various strands of our personality and capabilities and forging something new out of them. The object of the exercise should be not just to put the trauma behind us, but to learn something about ourselves, and use that knowledge to build more balanced, considered and purposeful lives. This may sound pompous, but it actually comes down to practicalities, putting a bit of effort into things, and getting on with it. It isn't, however, simply a matter of getting back into doing what we've always done; it involves reassessing our old ways and habits, judging them in a critical and personal way and then getting back into them when we understand a little better our reasons for doing them. If we fail to journey out of the traumatic experience, we cannot renew and reorient our lives. Not only does our emotion become focused and fixed on the trauma, but that fixation becomes an end in itself and, indeed, almost a way of life. Our existence circles the trauma, and either partially facing it or, more commonly, making incredible efforts not to face it becomes the major part of our mental life. Not only is that very unproductive, it is also deeply hopeless.

Carrie, a girl I treated, had one of the most horrendous stories of personal trauma I have encountered. She was living in one of the war zones in Northern Ireland and became friendly with a guy from the 'other side'. She was warned by two of her 'own' people that if she continued to see her friend, he would be shot dead. She was frightened by that threat and kept away from him. One day she spotted her friend in the street and raised her hand to wave to him. At that precise instant, he was shot in the head and he fell to the ground, dead, not ten feet from her. She ran away, screaming. Two days later she was warned by one of the two gunmen who had shot him that if she told anyone about the warnings she had been given, or that they were the guilty parties, her brother would be shot. They then gave her a detailed account of her brother's movements, so she knew they were serious. She emigrated to live with other members of her family in another country in order to escape the situation. She felt overwhelmed on all fronts. She felt guilty that she hadn't warned her friend about the threats against him. She felt guilty that she was responsible for his death. She couldn't get out of her head that sight of him being shot precisely when she was waving to him. Finally, she felt frightened that if she revealed the identities of the gunmen to anyone, her brother would die, and she would be responsible for the deaths of two people she loved. She was traumatised and trapped and overwhelmed on all sides.

Not surprisingly, she was unable to get over this series of appalling traumas and found herself reliving her friend's death again and again in her dreams and also during the day. She also found it terribly difficult to do anything in any area of her life, to such an extent that she stayed at home and stared out of the window all day. The only way to deal with such a dreadful situation was with little steps, trying to get Carrie to take control of her life in simple, easy stages. And this did work, to a degree and over a long period of time. Carrie is still living with her family, but she is attending a workshop and feeling less depressed about her life.

Rebuilding a life after a crisis is like building a life before a crisis, except this time it is faced with more wisdom and insight. Short-term goals – looking forward to the next beer, the next cigarette or the next – you know – tend to be placed in context, and longer-term ambitions rather than short-term goals tend to emerge. We tend to see and value life in its entirety rather than for its individual components. It is a perspective that those who have had a brush with death – either when someone close to them has died suddenly or when they have come close to death themselves – develop, if they manage to get anything out of such dreadful experiences.

Positive emotions, such as simple joy and fun, don't affect us as much as negative emotions. While memory is always tainted by mood, negative traumatic memories are etched more deeply than lighter, brighter ones. One of my own childhood memories is of playing on a rusty old ship in a car park beside the sea. My parents called me a few times and I just went on playing because I was enjoying myself. To my horror I then saw the car driving off, parents, family and all. I was horrified, and I burst into tears and ran across the car park after the departing car. I can still remember the feeling of desolation and abandonment at being 'left behind'. Fortunately the car stopped after about fifty yards, and I got into the back both relieved and furious, and battered the back of my father's neck with my two little fists while the rest of the family laughed at me. While the feeling soon left me and I forgot all about it and enjoyed the rest of the holiday, I remember the feeling of aloneness hitting me for probably the first time in my life. The incredible horror of being 'abandoned' still reverberates down the years. A friend of mine can recall being put into hospital at the age of fifteen months for an appendix operation, and screaming the place down for three days until he went home. And these are only minor traumas, tiny relative to the major stresses and upsets we all go through. Examples of personal trauma that affect life profoundly are so numerous that we need not list them here.

Aiming simply for fun in life seems not to satisfy a life's effort or a life's ambition. The pursuit of fleeting pleasures doesn't make you happy in the long run. Short-term gains attained by short-term plans inevitably lead to long-term frustration and dissatisfaction. The constitution of the United States embodies the pursuit of happiness as one of the goals of the human spirit, but this seems trite and shallow compared to deeper, sadder emotions, and isn't as embedded in the consciousness as other more intense emotions. To manage to make a worthwhile life for ourselves we have to define explicitly just what we want from life in the long term, and this is closely tied to just what sort of person we really are.

Decisions

There are times in life when we have to take important, even momentous, decisions that will change the direction of our life. Some are obvious – 'Is this the person I'm going to marry?' or 'Is this the right career for me?' – others are less obvious but equally important – 'I refuse to take this any more' or 'I want to do something different with my life.' We all have to face taking these decisions, and the reasons we choose one path or another are as important as the path we actually choose.

These decisions should be made according to where we are, emotionally and developmentally, at the time, and should be made in the context of the inner person as well as external forces. The parameters of a decision are defined by external circumstances, but we should not make decisions totally reactively – that only leads to poor decisions that we quickly come to regret. It is very easy to tread the path that is taken by the majority, simply because we don't have to think about it, and there is a great feeling of safety in numbers. It is very easy to succumb to outside pressures or outside voices at a time of great indecision and panic, but resisting the temptation to go with the flow will pay off in the long run.

When making a big decision we should always ask ourselves two questions: 'What shall I do?' and 'Why am I doing it?' To respond 'It seemed like a good idea at the time' to an inevitable 'Why did you do it?' twenty years after you married the wrong person isn't really adequate. We owe it to ourselves to know the reason we do things even if they end up being mistakes. If we can turn around twenty years later and say 'It was definitely the best idea at the time', the decision is easier to live with, because at least we had considered the options before committing ourselves. If we can't say that we actually considered the options, we are fools, and the definition of a fool is to be wise too late.

One of the most tragic people I have had to deal with was a 45-year-old bank official. He was married with three young children, and had inherited a large house from his uncle. He also inherited his uncle's debts and had to sell the house to settle them. However hard he tried, he was unable to get the house off his hands and he felt increasingly under pressure to pay off the debts. The day he got back from a week's holiday down the country, he found a demand for €30,000 on his hall floor. The next day he drove to work, said hello to his secretary, put his briefcase on the desk and threw himself out of the fifth-storey window. He survived, ended up in hospital with severe head and spinal injuries and took six months to recover. He was left with paralysis down one side of his body, speech difficulty and, not surprisingly, adjustment difficulties. 'I didn't think,' he said. 'I don't know what came over me, but I just went out and did it. I didn't decide; I just did it.' On top of it all he described how four years earlier his father had died, he had got married and lost his job – all within a six-week period. He had suffered tremendously during that time, yet he had coped and hadn't tried to kill himself or do anything drastic. To say that he and his family are worse off now after his 'accident' is an understatement. Perhaps the worst part of his situation was that he had to come to terms with the fact that he was completely responsible for what had happened, and he hadn't anybody to blame but himself. I felt awful that the only thing I could offer this extremely nice guy was my sympathy and my sincerity. There was nothing anyone could do to ease the burden that a snap decision had laid on his shoulders for the rest of his life.

When we are faced with different options, and are uncertain about which to take, it's a good idea to broaden the horizon of the decision. Talking with superiors, relations or friends helps clarify the processes that are going on in the back of the mind. Writing down the advantages and disadvantages of each option can give a remarkably clear insight into aspects of the decision that aren't immediately apparent. If the worst comes to the worst, tossing a coin can show us what we want to do by forcing us to go with or against the result. We quickly find out if we didn't really want to take option B when that's what the coin chooses, so we then go and take option A. We don't have to go with what the coin says, we go with what it makes us think we want to do. It's a little mind trick that often works.

Sometimes the decisions we take and the direction we move in are not visible to us when we are actually making those decisions and choosing that direction. Often it is only in retrospect that we can see the way our mind was working, and what we were trying to do. 'Oh, I must have wanted to get out of that relationship, because in retrospect I engineered it to fail, even though I wasn't aware of it at the time'; 'I must have wanted out of that job, because I spent most of my time plotting against the boss and avoiding doing any work.' With a little more effort, and a little more insight, we could figure out what we really want to do, and try and do it directly, not indirectly; but that isn't always possible at the time. So a part of what we should be doing in engineering a U-turn is evaluating the underlying reason we do the things that we do. There is very little in our lives that is without purpose, even if that purpose is hidden from ourselves.

Indecision

One of the biggest problems about making decisions is indecision. The inability to make a decision can be one of the most difficult characteristics to get over. The indecision itself can be very traumatic and can cause suffering far beyond the significance of the decision itself. It is often far better personally for us to make a decision, whether it's the right or wrong one, rather than to wallow in an agony of dithering. Any time (beyond basic thinking time) spent going from one option to another in our minds greatly undermines the decision we take and our confidence in that decision. We are better off picking one option and going with it until it proves correct or incorrect than spending an age wondering. People call great leaders decisive people, and the ability to take decisions is often more highly regarded than the correctness of the decision. Decisiveness breeds respect and builds our confidence, and it is not an amazingly unobtainable objective.

The Power of Positive Thinking

A lot of this book has so far focused on negative emotions and difficult situations, and how to overcome them. It is indeed a difficult task to turn negative emotions around and use them for our own good. But if our minds have almost unlimited power to hurt and diminish our lives, it follows that our minds have equal and unlimited power to develop us and enrich our lives. There is no doubt that negative emotions register deep within us, and they seem to make a longer and deeper impression than positive ones. We can all recall upsetting events from our childhood, ranging from momentary abandonment by our parents in a shop or car park to genuine trauma or loss, illness or grief, but we are often hard pressed to recall the (hopefully) majority of the time, when we were well treated or, indeed, happy. It is an unfortunate truth that negative emotions register a lot more deeply than positive ones, and leave a deeper track in our psyche. That can lead us to think that negative forces are more powerful in our lives; but if we choose it, the opposite is true.

Seeing a hypnotist at work on stage can be an awesome experience. The most normal people can do the strangest things under the 'power' of the hypnotist. I've seen people imitate washing machines and giving birth, seen them believe that everyone in the room was naked, seen them react as if they were in love with the person next to them on stage. There is virtually no limit to what the human mind is capable of doing, simply under the power of deep relaxation and suggestion by the hypnotist. I have seen sceptical doctors have needles pass painlessly through their skin, and the resultant wound not bleed, simply by the power of suggestion. Why can't we use the tremendous power of our minds in our own favour, instead of just coping with life? Why can't we unleash those unconscious powers that lurk under the surface, and make them work for us, instead of seemingly against us? Why are we so limited in what we can apparently do?

The most important part of performing a U-turn in our lives is figuring out the direction we want our lives to turn to. The most effective way of unleashing our dormant unconscious power is working out a direction in which to invest it. If others can influence our lives negatively, we owe it to ourselves to influence ourselves positively. If we have been subjected to powerful upsetting emotions and have achieved an understanding of them, it is time to put our emotional power to good use. If we want to align the different layers of our personality into a unitary force, we must give ourselves a sense of purpose.

It is not possible to perform a U-turn quickly. While it may take a few weeks or months to work through a particular trauma, or get over a particularly unnerving event, turning your life around is a long-term effort. Self-understanding takes months, even years, and making careful, balanced decisions and getting them to bear fruit can take many more years. It's too easy to say that no worthwhile life journey is ever complete, and it is of course true. But I have seen many, many people work through an episode of depression or anxiety, get over it, learn from it, and make positive fulfilling changes in their lives over the period of a year. It is not an unreasonable period to hope for positive things to take place after a series of negative ones. The key of course is processing the emotional upset, learning from it, and then working out what to do with that knowledge. The key is to turn a cul-de-sac into a U-turn. The last component, the final part of the journey, is to figure out where to go!

Aims

When making decisions that may affect us for a very long time, we must have some idea about where we want those decisions to take us.

Aiming for the happiness that comes from personal satisfaction and genuine contentment, and not simply attaining the latest in a series of little pleasures, is a deep and worthwhile ambition. How that is faced in practical terms is a very individual and often lifelong exploration. Dylan Thomas began a short story once, '… some years before I knew I was happy …', which says to me that he only realised how happy he was in retrospect. There is more to contentment than just the absence of unhappiness, though after a life of unpleasant and bitter experiences we may settle for just that. But after time passes and we suffer less and less from the poignancy of sad memories, we often search for more in life, and are left supplicant, waiting and unanswered. We search for meaning and contentment, and we don't find what it is we need.

Ways of Fulfilment

Love of Another

Where we find purpose and contentment is something that we must explore and decide for ourselves. Humanity at large seems to divide itself into a few different categories when facing this task, but the first group probably contains just about the lot of us. This is the group that longs to find hope and satisfaction through love for another person. A life of happiness or a lifetime of despair hangs on finding the right person and keeping them. If it is not the be-all and end-all of existence, it is pretty close to it. Love can settle down the most wild, desperate and hopeless of lives, and its absence can harden and embitter the sweetest of souls.

History abounds with the stories of what people will do and suffer for love, from Antony and Cleopatra to Edward VIII and Mrs Simpson. To ascribe it all to pure lust and sexual energy doesn't do justice to the complexity of the emotion. Love is difficult to define or even describe, and it is often clearer in its effects than its definition. To be in love is a lot more than an ego massage from someone close at hand – though that is part of it. To have somebody accept us totally, even though they are aware of all our deficiencies and uncertainties, gives us a reason to exist that no degree of fame or fortune could. That affirmation and acceptance satisfies and fills holes in our personalities we never knew existed. A poor self-image can be abolished almost overnight, and the effects on self-regard can last years longer than the love itself. Similarly, when so much is invested in the opinion and esteem of another, a cutting remark, a slip of the tongue or a hint of disapproval can wound the recipient far greater than if it came from any other source. As the saying goes, 'Sex lasts for a moment, but love lasts a lifetime.' If we get it right, and especially if we get the right person, we have the potential to give meaning and fulfilment to our lives, throughout the course of our lives. The prominent British historian A. J. P. Taylor said that 'The secret of a good marriage is finding the right woman', and he should know – it took him three marriages to find the right woman. The price we have to pay is the pain that we go through on losing that love, whether through death, desertion or the natural end of the relationship. The depth of the pain reflects the depth of the love that went before it, and the pain is inescapable if that love was real.

Within Ourselves

The second way of finding meaning and fulfilment lies not in the love of another human, but within ourselves. It is quite possible to come to terms with life, the universe and everything by fully coming to terms with our true selves. It is quite possible to become self-contained and self-content through a process of suffering, introspection and learning. In fact this could be described as the ultimate direction in life, quite simply because we would be truly independent, needing no person or God to make us whole. By learning to understand and accept all our vagaries and inconsistencies, all our good and – especially – all our bad points, all our talents and our deficiencies, and to see ourselves fully as we are, warts and all, and then by using that knowledge to develop and become closer to our ideal self, we could become content. Reinhold Niebuhr, the twentieth-century American theologian, prayed for the wisdom to know the difference between what he could and could not change, and in that wisdom lies happiness.

At the end of this chapter there is a series of exercises to help you trace a path through the discovery of just what sort of person you are, what it is you want to become in life and how to get there. This is the ultimate U-turn, where you U-turn your life around, not just away from the direction you don't want to go, but towards the direction you do.

In a book about the top deathbed regrets that a palliative care nurse found among her many patients over the years, Bronnie Ware reported that the top one was: 'I wish I'd had the courage to live a life true to myself, not the life others expected of me.' So many of us do things according to the expectations of those around us – our parents, our partners, our friends and colleagues – that it is only at death, when the possibility of doing things differently is removed, that we can see what we might have been. This involves a very clear-headed assessment of ourselves, our strengths and our desires, and a clear assessment of where we wanted to go in life. Of course we are often so busy with day-to-day living that we fail to see where we are going.

A forty-year-old salesman who came to my clinic had recently tried very determinedly to kill himself. He had tried three different methods over a forty-eight-hour period, soon after his fortieth birthday. He felt so disgusted at how his life had turned out by that milestone that he saw no alternative to ending his life. Fortunately, with appropriate support and care, he began to change his mind, and began to explore ways of changing his outlook, his perspective and, most important, his choices. Traumatic as his experience was, it was better to have gone through this distress, and then try to change his life into something more like what he really wanted, than to make the same realisation on his deathbed at the age of eighty. Some of the U-turn exercises at the end of this chapter are designed to explore those realisations and choices.

Love of God and Spiritual Meaning

An alternative or even complementary way of finding fulfilment is finding a spiritual meaning in life. This is altogether a more complex and taxing question than even the vagaries of the love of another human. At its best it is as simple and pure as a child; at its most difficult it is more complex and confusing than the theory of relativity. A person can arrive at faith through their upbringing, as most of humanity does; through trying to understand suffering, as the Buddha did; through simple blinding conversion, as Saul did on the road to Damascus; through the contemplation of nature and of humanity, as Carl Jung did; or simply through searching for meaning in a random and chaotic world. The love of God can give meaning and fulfilment to anyone, and help them go through and come to terms with great suffering and hardship. An increasing number of people look for a purpose in life outside organised religion, and look within themselves for that personal purpose. It is very difficult for a person with faith to explain it to someone with none, and it is also very difficult to acquire if it is not somewhere in our upbringing.

Probably the biggest motivation to look for the meaning and fulfilment of life outside the ordinary life all around us is the inevitability of death, and especially the awareness of our own death. Only by coming to terms with our own death can we hope to round off our life in a proper and full way. Ageing, and the death of a parent or a loved one, brings the reality of death a lot closer to us, and forces us to ask questions we would prefer to leave unanswered. There are many arguments about the existence of God, and to date his existence has been impossible to prove or disprove except in the minds of believers – or non-believers. The reality of God is a personal and emotional reality, not a rational one, and thus it is a very individual reality. We may be strongly influenced as to the existence of God by those around us and the faith or lack of faith of those we become close to, but this matter is very much an individual choice, and an individual journey.

I met Frank when he was recovering from a lifetime of self-abuse and destruction. He was raised in a quiet rural town and was reasonably happy as a child. His father began to drink when he was laid off from the local factory, and life began to get worse. Eventually Frank left home to seek out life in a big city and to escape the torture of his father's angry outbursts and violent drunkenness. He got a series of low-paying jobs and then began to drink and experiment with drugs. He got hooked quickly on heroin and cocaine and sank into the junkie's lifestyle of stealing and incarceration, overdoses and detoxes, deprivation and degradation. He was eventually put in prison for a period of two years, and on release he went into a rehab/halfway house. There he met a counsellor who was a born-again Christian and who encouraged his clients to find a way out of their lifestyle through God. Frank tried and failed, and then tried a second time. This time something happened and, by the time I met him, Frank had managed to keep off narcotics for months. He was now trying hard to reform his life, was attending meetings of Narcotics Anonymous, and was working at a restaurant. He had found God and thanked him for the changes that had taken place in his life. And indeed he was sincere: he wasn't trying to pretend that there was nothing wrong in his life, not trying to shove his faith down everyone else's throat; he was just trying to get by with his new life and his new faith. The changes that he had made in his life were extraordinary and it was an impressive demonstration of the power, for him, of the love of God.

There are many ways to find God or at least a personal spirituality, and some of the pathways are through organised religion. Many of the pathways are through individual spiritual searches, through reading about others' spiritual journeys, through meditation or, indeed, through religious practice. There are as many ways of finding a spiritual meaning to life as there are individuals on earth. However, there is no spiritual journey that happens by itself, without intent or without effort. A search for meaning involves engaging in that search, not simply waiting for it to land in our lap by happenstance. It is unlikely that we will find a complete answer to all the mysteries of life before we die, but we owe it to ourselves to keep trying. In the famous song, Bono said, 'I still haven't found what I'm looking for', and unless he is lying, he is not going to call the next album 'Finally got there!' In the quest for meaning, life is truly a journey and not a destination, and we owe it to ourselves to keep trying to find our own eternal truth. Laziness is not an option: this is far too important.

The 95 Per Cent of Life

Part of the secret of persisting and finding purpose in life is to keep going at the little things in life. If the 5 per cent of life – the big decisions and events that change the course of our personal destiny – were to last even 5 per cent of the time, it would be exceptionally long. The 95 per cent of life, the normal everyday trivia, from watching soap operas to watering the flowers, from walking the dog to brewing the morning coffee, is what occupies us well over 95 per cent of the time. Little tasks, little problems, small chats and small plans take up far more of our time and energy than major things like natural disasters and global warming. To wallow in the habitual, the banal, is not a negation of existence, but a confirmation of life. There is no shame in regarding the mundanity of everyday existence as important: it is in fact far more important to each of us than being famous or rich – which is only the problem of the few.

Watching mentally handicapped people is a real education. Each performs his or her role and tasks according to ability and temperament. Getting a moderately handicapped young boy to use a fork instead of a spoon, or seeing a mildly handicapped girl take a bus into town on her own, puts our own busyness and self-importance into perspective. What right do we have to claim superiority over them, when they are as cantankerous and as loving, as selfish and yet as open and generous as all the rest of humanity? Just because their intellectual ability is less than ours, we find it difficult to ascribe the range of personality and emotions to them that we have, and – as anybody who works with handicapped people will tell us – that they have too. Their lives are no less fulfilled for not having astonishing mathematical skills or billionaire-sized bank accounts. Human relationships flourish and die, friendships bloom and wither, and life goes on day by day. Even though they are often denied one whole area of potentially great fulfilment – a loving sexual relationship – this does not prevent genuine happiness or contentment. And most of their lives, like most of our lives, is just day-to-day plod.

Small Steps

When we are recovering from a great mental or physical trauma, it is far better to start with small tasks, work at them until they are mastered, and only then move on to bigger things, master them, and then finally move back into the full occupation or tasks we had before the upset. By taking small, well-defined steps that are achievable and concrete – like getting a moderately handicapped boy to use a fork, like an agoraphobic walking to the local shop, like a bereaved person getting back to going to the morning coffee break, like a depressed person finding the energy to get up in the morning – we can begin to rebuild our shattered self-confidence and our dissipated self-belief. By trying too hard to recover too fast, by going too far too fast, we lose our confidence and we get lost. By going at a pace we can handle – one task done, completed and satisfyingly put behind us, and then on to the next one – we give ourselves a platform from which to tackle the next step. The slow meticulous achievement of small things gives us back our backbone. To have those achievements noticed and praised by others is an added bonus, but it is our own appreciation of our achievements that is the vital thing. An old Chinese proverb says, 'The journey of a thousand miles begins with the first step', and it is no different for us.

A medical student colleague of mine was studying for his medical exams at the end of his first year. He had to cover three subjects: anatomy, biochemistry and physiology. I met him in the corridor outside the library two days before the anatomy exam, when I was all hot and bothered and thinking I knew nothing and that I would certainly fail. He announced that he had that very morning completed his programme of study for the anatomy exam and that he had now nothing further to do before the exam. I was not gratified to hear this news as I had certainly not completed my study for the exam and felt I would be very lucky to revise everything in time. Well, we all sat the exam, and a few weeks later we gathered to hear the results. I had passed, with a good result, and felt pleased that my hard work paid off. My friend, who had completed all his study much better that I had before the exam, didn't pass, and had to repeat the exam to continue in medical school. I commiserated with him about the result, but never told him my secret thoughts about what had happened. I resolved never to let the same thing happen to me, never to think that I had learned everything and there was nothing left to learn. I learned most of all that we can never know enough, we can never feel we have it all sussed, because that is the time we let something major slip by.

We are always learning in life, and no one has all the answers. If anybody says they do, it is because they have a limited vision and not because they actually know it all.

Great Purpose

I once visited Dachau concentration camp near Munich. The town itself is a pleasant country town at the terminus of one of the city's tramways, but the concentration camp is very difficult to describe. The compound itself is rather unimpressive and rather small, with planks on the ground delineating the places where the huts stood. The accompanying film and permanent exhibition begin to communicate the degree of horror and human depravity that existed there seventy years ago. The pictures, the grim lists of people who died, the description of the workings of the furnaces on an average day in 1938, the occasional individual stories that bring the enormity of the whole monstrosity down to humanly tangible things, begin to impinge on you and gradually a numb horror pervades your mind. It's impossible not to be deeply affected. The movie *Schindler's List* tells the same story, the story of the Holocaust, the wilful evil intent to destroy an entire section of the human race. It is a horror beyond belief and so most of us choose not to think about it all that often.

I remember hearing a description of those who survived the appalling conditions, the mental and physical torture, and the dreadful gas chambers themselves. The ones who survived were the ones who had some great purpose in life; who had a wife or lover or children on the outside to whom they wanted desperately to return; who had a great faith, who believed strongly that God would pull them through; or who had enormous personal strength, who would endure anything to survive. Perhaps a great purpose, great enough to get through hell itself, can be found in all of us and around us, and if we can find that purpose for ourselves, we have truly found that meaning of life.

Ambitions

The aims and ambitions we set ourselves in life change as life goes on. Goals become long rather than short term and ambitions should become more emotional than financial. Our goalposts keep moving, and as we become content in one area of life, we dismiss it somewhat, take it for granted and move on to something we feel we lack. Knowledge of what it is to be without something in life tends to make us appreciate it and value it. This was borne home to me when I visited a very happy, contented couple with a wonderful marriage, a lovely new house, good jobs, rounded personalities and excellent health. The man of the house was incredibly struck by a newspaper story of a twelve-year-old boy who, after the death of a rich relation, had become a millionaire in his own right. He talked frequently about the benefits that would come to the child because of his riches. This boy also had an emotionally stunted personality and no friends, but all my friend could see was his millions – and all I could see were my friend's riches in every other area. We all want what we haven't got, and my friend really didn't see the wonderful things he already had.

Setting down our goals and ambitions on a piece of paper is a great way of concentrating our mind and energy on what we want from life and where we want to go. At the end of this chapter I list ways of organising your ambitions and dreams to facilitate clarity and purpose in your aims in life. It isn't enough to say vaguely, 'I'd like things to be better in every way'; it is vital to state clearly that *these* are your dreams and ambitions in particular areas and *these* are your goals in the same areas and *this* is how you are going to achieve them. The purpose of this exercise is to make the final journey around the U-turn. It is one thing to get out of the trough, but it is another to start on the ascending limb of happiness, contentment and success.

The essential art of completing the U-turn is detailed self-understanding, and from that detailed self-understanding emerge detailed ideas for self-development. If we want more friends we can write down a list of people we know and want to become friends with and call them up and invite them for dinner. If we want to change jobs, we can write down what we would like to be, and then find out about opportunities and training. It is absolutely possible to do these things – the only barrier stopping us is lack of imagination and confidence. It is remarkably comforting to leave dreams and plans in outer space, where we don't have to deal with them in any tangible way and they are always something to hope for and are yet unobtainable. It is remarkably satisfying to actually call on one of these ideas and attempt to put it into practice. The exhilaration of achieving even the smallest of these plans or ambitions by our own efforts will give us faith in ourselves to try out others.

The simple message is: If you want to get something, figure out a way of doing it and it can be yours. All it takes is the imagination to work out just what it is you want, and that is what the final U-turn exercises help you to do. Once you have completed these, and put the effort into doing them properly, you have started on your way.

There are no easy rules or definite directives that can be given from one human being to another about how to essentially take charge of ourselves and how to change ourselves into our ideal. That it is within our powers is undeniable. That it is difficult in the short term is equally true. That it is a long-term reality is also true – if we choose to do it. Changing ourselves, turning our inward-focused energy outwards, slowly building ourselves into our ideal, is a slow, continuous process. All our instantaneous 'Pauline conversions' in life, the quick fixes that make things better in a second, should be regarded with equal measures of enthusiasm and scepticism. Any worthwhile changes in ourselves are slow and plodding, take place over time and are marked by little victories and achievements. But all worthwhile changes are decided on in an instant – in that instant when we finally say, 'I've had enough', and embark on our own U-turn.

We must learn our lessons from the past, and continue to learn as we go on. We are all formed by our past and never fully escape it – we can only appreciate it better and learn from it. We can decide for ourselves just what it is we want from life according to our own U-turn. We owe it to ourselves to know what it is we want to become and then gently and insistently strive to achieve it. We will probably never actually get there, and the ambitions and aims we have will probably change over the years, but often the journey itself is the real destination. As John Lennon said, 'Life is what happens to you while you're busy making plans.'

We can never hope to understand everything, least of all everything about ourselves. We should constantly check up on ourselves to prevent ourselves sinking into lethargy or conceited complacency. There are seven billion people on the planet and thus seven billion truths, opinions and ways of looking at the world. Therefore, we owe it to ourselves not to invest our ideas and energies in someone else's view of the world. We should have higher ambitions in our one and only life than to pass up control of it to another. That is ultimately very destructive to our own development, as it leads to the erosion of our ability to think and decide for ourselves. But no matter how near to our own personal truth we get, no matter how close to our ideal we become, no matter how much integration and balance we achieve, somehow, as Paul Simon said:

The thought that life could be better
Is woven indelibly into our hearts and our brains.

By undertaking the U-turn, however, we can change the emotional quality of our life from a negative to a positive one.

The U-Turn Exercises

1. Divide life into the four primary areas: Relationship; Career; Spiritual; and Social and Recreation.

2. Make up a 'Dreams and Ambitions' list. Make it complete and specific. Don't settle for a list that is only half thought through and incomplete – make it comprehensive and extensive. Include both your wildest dreams and your strongest ambitions. Your list should cover all the different areas of life (not purely financial dreams).

3. Define your four primary values in life and write them down. Think of values as defining what you do and how you act in your everyday life. If, say, your first value is humility, and your second one is generosity, think very carefully when listing your dreams and ambitions that your primary values in life are compatible with your dreams. There is little point in trying to list ambitions that include becoming a billionaire presidential candidate if your top two values are humility and generosity. Define your values according to what importance you place on the people and things around you. Redefine your ambitions according to those values.

   The values you list may not necessarily be compatible with each other. For example, your list might be: striving to achieve; truthfulness; avoiding humiliation; and loyalty. If you have listed your dreams and ambitions in all four areas of life, go over that list again and see if striving to achieve and avoiding humiliation are compatible when it comes to the dream of becoming a stand-up comic. There is nothing to stop you becoming a stand-up comic, and it would certainly be compatible with striving to achieve, but it is incompatible with the value of avoiding humiliation (which happens to all stand-up comics at some stage). By redefining your dreams and ambitions according to your values, you will best be able to judge those dreams and see if they are compatible with who you really are.

4. Define your goals according to just how you want to bring each of those dreams and ambitions to fruition. Make a one-year, a five-year and a ten-year plan of how you will go about achieving those dreams and ambitions in carefully planned stages. Define how long you think each of those ideas will take to come to fruition. The goals you now define are the markers for your achievements over the years. These goals will change over the years as you adapt and change to circumstances, but the thrust of the goals leading to your ultimate ambitions should remain basically intact.

5. Look at the final product: your U-turn life plan, divided into dreams and ambitions under different headings, and the goals you have made out as markers along the way. This is the ultimate personal plan and it will work because you drew it up according to what you are as a person and what you wish to become and to achieve. This U-turn should be written down and kept somewhere where you can refer to it constantly and adjust it if necessary. This is your personal U-turn, the definition of what you are and what you are going to become. You have made the decision to achieve this. Now all you have to do is put this plan into action.

Oscar Wilde said, among many other memorable things, 'There are only two tragedies in life: one is not getting what one wants, and the other is getting it.' The U-turn you are embarking on – and, indeed, life itself – is not a final destination, it is a journey. We can never be fully satisfied that we have got there or that we have achieved everything we are capable of.

You are probably familiar with the biblical parable of the talents. In this story, a good master gives three servants different amounts of money to use. To one he gives one talent, and the servant goes out and doubles it to make it two talents. The master is pleased and praises the servant for his industry. The second servant is given five talents, and he goes off and doubles it to ten talents. The master praises the servant and rewards him for his efforts. The last servant is given ten talents, but goes and buries them in the ground. He returns to his master with the ten talents and his master is furious with him. He did nothing with his talents, and has nothing to show for his possession of them. We all have different talents, we all have different dreams and ambitions, and we owe it to ourselves to use them to the fullest during our short life spans. John Cleese, the noted philosopher, said that he didn't regret anything he did in life, he only regretted the things he didn't do. That is a philosophy to live by.

We all have the ability within us to go out and do what we want to in life; we all have the ability to U-turn our lives around. All we have to do is go out and do it!

Recommended Books

This list is not exhaustive; it is just a list of prominent titles that many people suffering from various issues covered in this book have found helpful in the past.

Depression
Tony Bates, *Coming Through Depression: A Mindful Approach to Recovery* (Gill & Macmillan, 2012).
David D. Burns, *Feeling Good: The New Mood Therapy* (Harper-Collins, 1999).

Anxiety
Helen Kennealey, *Overcoming Anxiety* (Constable & Robinson, 2009).
Clare Weeks, *Self-Help for Your Nerves: Learn to Relax and Enjoy Life Again by Overcoming Stress and Fear* (Thorsons Publishers, 1995).

Anger
William Davies, *Overcoming Anger and Irritability* (Constable & Robinson, 2009).

Alcohol Misuse
Conor Farren, *Overcoming Alcohol Misuse: A 28-Day Guide* (Orpen Press, 2011).

Self-Esteem
Melanie Fennell, *Overcoming Low Self-Esteem* (Constable & Robinson, 2009).

Projection and Communication
Dale Carnegie, *How to Win Friends and Influence People* (Pocket Books, 1982).

Relationships
John Gray, *Men Are from Mars, Women Are from Venus* (HarperCollins, 1992).

Personal Development
Deepak Chopra, *The Seven Spiritual Laws of Success: A Practical Guide to the Fulfilment of Your Dreams* (Bantam Press, 1996).
Maureen Gaffney, *Flourishing* (Penguin Ireland, 2011).

List of Useful Organisations

AWARE
Depression support
www.aware.ie
72 Lower Leeson Street, Dublin 2
Lo-call: 1890 303 302 (helpline only)
Tel: 01 661 7211

GROW
Mental health awareness
www.grow.ie
GROW National Office, Grow Centre, 11 Liberty Street, Cork
Lo-call: 1890 474 474
Tel: 021 427 7520

Headstrong
National Centre for Youth Mental Health
www.headstrong.ie
16 Westland Square, Pearse Street, Dublin 2
Tel: 01 472 7010
E-mail: info@headstrong.ie

Mental Health Ireland
Mental health awareness
www.mentalhealthireland.ie

Mensana House, 6 Adelaide Street, Dun Laoghaire, Co. Dublin
Tel: 01 284 1166

My Mind
Community-based provider of mental health services
www.mymind.org
1 Chelmsford Road, Ranelagh, Dublin 6
Services: 076 680 1060
Headquarters: 01 443 3961

Pieta House
Centre for the Prevention of Self-Harm or Suicide
www.pieta.ie
Pieta Ballyfermot, Pieta House, Mount La Salle, Ballyfermot Road, Ballyfermot, Dublin 10
Tel: 01 620 0020; 087 690 3236

Pieta Finglas, 47 Mellowes Court, Finglas, Dublin 11
Tel: 01 864 8899

Pieta House, Lucan Road, Lucan, Co. Dublin
Tel: 01 601 0000

Pieta Mid-West, Ardaulin, Mungret, Co. Limerick
Tel: 061 484 444; 061 484 646

Pieta Tallaght, St Thomas's Church, Jobstown, Tallaght, Dublin 24
Tel: 01 601 0000

Reachout
Mental health information for young people
ie.reachout.com

Inspire Ireland Foundation, First Floor, 29–31 South William Street, Dublin 2
Tel: 01 764 5666

Samaritans
Confidential emotional support service
www.samaritans.org
4–5 Usher's Court, 7 Usher's Quay, Dublin 8
Helpline: 1850 609 090
Tel: 01 671 0071

Spunout
Health and advice service for teenagers
www.spunout.ie
Seán MacBride House, Parliament Row, Temple Bar, Dublin 2
Tel: 01 675 3554

Suicide Prevention
Information service for those with thoughts of self-harm or suicide
www.suicideprevention.ie

Index